"*Cosmic Cradle* is a must-read fo[r] of their soul before birth. A penetrating and insightful inquiry into one of the greatest mysteries of existence—where we come from, who we are, why we are here, and why we forget."

—JOAN BORYSENKO, PhD, author of *Seven Paths to God* and
Minding the Body, Mending the Mind

❧

"Modern research into the nature of consciousness is revealing a consistent picture: consciousness is nonlocal or infinite in space and time. It is not confined to the brain, the body, or the present, as many have believed. *Cosmic Cradle* puts a human face on this research. This fascinating book will bring comfort to anyone concerned about our origins and destiny—and who isn't?"

—LARRY DOSSEY, MD, author of *The One Mind,*
Reinventing Medicine, and *Healing Words*

❧

"*Cosmic Cradle* gives me chills of recognition. This book is the truth. And I found it both an affirmation and huge inspiration."

—CHRISTIANE NORTHRUP, MD, author of *The Wisdom of Menopause*
and *Women's Bodies, Women's Wisdom*

❧

"I love the concept of *Cosmic Cradle.* It relates most completely to the unequivocal reality of reincarnation, an essential understanding of life. Pre-birth memories and memories of previous incarnations continue to help us understand our complex Cosmos."

—C. NORMAN SHEALY, MD, PhD, author of *Energy Medicine*

❧

"*Cosmic Cradle* is a stunning achievement, comprehensive in scope, spiritually illuminating! In one stroke the authors have succeeded in lifting out of obscurity a world literature—ignored during the recent era of scientific materialism—representing virtually all cultures and religions from ancient to contemporary times.... This work of encyclopedic proportions is the rare fruit of forty years of passionate and scholarly exploration of human consciousness, the neglected stepchild of twentieth-century psychology. Elizabeth and Neil Carman have thrown open a golden door."

—David B. Chamberlain, PhD, author of *Windows to the Womb: Revealing the Conscious Baby from Conception to Birth* and *The Mind of Your Newborn Baby*

ᙍᙡᙍ

"*Cosmic Cradle* gives us a wider lens through which to view the questions every child asks—where did I come from and how did I get here? *Cosmic Cradle* is fruitful reading for couples planning to have a child, for parents, and family life educators. Thank you Elizabeth and Neil Carman for compiling this tome!"

—Jeannine Parvati Baker, coauthor of *Conscious Conception: Elemental Journey through the Labyrinth of Sexuality* and author of *Hygieia: A Woman's Herbal* and *Prenatal Yoga and Natural Childbirth*

ᙍᙡᙍ

"An extraordinary research work, yielding a quasi-encyclopedic treasury of evidence for the soul's preexistence. *Cosmic Cradle* makes it clear that pre-birth communication has been known and recorded throughout history and across cultures worldwide."

—Elisabeth Hallett, author of *Stories of the Unborn Soul* and *Soul Trek: Meeting Our Children on the Way to Birth*

ᙍᙡᙍ

"Occasionally one comes across an exceptional book. Thus is *Cosmic Cradle*. Spanning the whole of recorded history up to contemporary times, Elizabeth and Neil Carman have collected and then shared with us the lesser-known mysteries surrounding conception, pregnancy, and birth. They have unveiled the soul in all its splendor and glory, and done so with meticulous care and irrefutable scholarship."

—P. M. H. ATWATER, LhD, author of *Children of the New Millennium*
and *The Complete Idiot's Guide to Near-Death Experiences*

"*Cosmic Cradle* points out that the individual must search for the fulfillment of his own truth and depend upon that for his illumination. *Cosmic Cradle* is marvelous, a rare privilege, a tremendous teaching.... It opened new vistas and new horizons. It is a work of illumination. Thank you for the great opportunity to expand my consciousness."

—MURSHIDA VERA JUSTIN CORDA, PhD, founder of New Age Sufi
Schools, author of *Cradle in Heaven* and *Holistic Child Guidance*

"*Cosmic Cradle* offers an extraordinary collection of stories shared by families who experienced pre-birth memories and communication from both the parent's and the baby's points of view. Their portrayals of the incarnation process from spirit to human realms are supported in the book by the timeless understandings nearly every culture has had—that we are conscious spiritual beings coming into human life with purpose and design. We are at a tipping point in Western thought, moving from Newtonian views into a consciousness-based understanding of our core spiritual nature. *Cosmic Cradle* inspires us forward into the new, yet ancient wisdom of that core nature at the beginning of life."

—WENDY ANNE MCCARTY, PhD, RN, author of *Welcoming
Consciousness: Supporting Babies' Wholeness from the Beginning of Life*

"*Cosmic Cradle* is a global mind transformer. Not only is it a masterpiece in how it is written with such clarity, interest, and organization, but the scope of its contents is pointedly destined to change our ideas about life. The evidence is stacked up too high in this book to dismiss its message of the soul's immortality."

—SUSAN HERZBERGER, author of *On Becoming Enlightened*

"*Cosmic Cradle* is an unique book with a soul-inspiring subject matter. This book has the potentiality of awakening consciousness and enriching the human relationships of millions."

—SWAMI DHARMANANDA, director of the International Vishwaguru Meditation and Yoga Institute, Ved Niketan Dham, Rishikesh, India

"I was amazed at the breadth and depth of the information which this book contains. It elevated my understanding of the subject to an entirely new level, and revolutionized my ideas, not only about the consciousness level of the *in-utero* baby but the extent to which mother and child can communicate and interact."

—JOHN W. SLOAT, host of www.beyondreligion.com and author of *A Handbook for Heretics*

COSMIC CRADLE

Spiritual Dimensions of
Life before Birth

Elizabeth Carman and Neil Carman

FOREWORD BY BERNIE S. SIEGEL, MD

North Atlantic Books
Berkeley, California

Published by
North Atlantic Books
P.O. Box 12327
Berkeley, California 94712

Light of Heaven mandala copyright © 2013 by Paul Heussenstamm, www.mandalas.com. Courtesy of the artist.
Cover and book design by Susan Quasha
Printed in the United States of America

Cosmic Cradle: Spiritual Dimensions of Life before Birth is sponsored by the Society for the Study of Native Arts and Sciences, a nonprofit educational corporation whose goals are to develop an educational and cross-cultural perspective linking various scientific, social, and artistic fields; to nurture a holistic view of arts, sciences, humanities, and healing; and to publish and distribute literature on the relationship of mind, body, and nature.

North Atlantic Books' publications are available through most bookstores. For further information, visit our website at www.northatlanticbooks.com or call 800-733-3000.

Library of Congress Cataloging-in-Publication Data
Carman, Elizabeth (Elizabeth M.)
  Cosmic cradle : spiritual dimensions of life before birth / Elizabeth Carman and Neil Carman. — Revised Edition.
       pages cm
  Includes bibliographical references and index.
  ISBN-13: 978-1-58394-552-0
  ISBN-10: 1-58394-552-0
1. Pre-existence. 2. Soul. I. Carman, Neil J. II. Title.
  BD426.C375 2013
  129—dc23
                                        2013002538

1 2 3 4 5 6 7 8 9 UNITED 18 17 16 15 14 13

Printed on recycled paper

Prologue

Stacy: I was feeling nostalgic and said to my four-year-old son Catcher, "It seems like it was just yesterday when you were in my belly." Catcher matter-of-factly replied, "I wasn't in your belly, Mom." I said, "What do you mean, you weren't in my belly?" Catcher said, "I was in Heaven." I said, "What were you doing in Heaven?" Catcher said, "I was waiting for you guys to be ready, silly."

Elsa: A vision of little Soul bubbles floating around in the room appeared to me—like soap bubbles with a pearlescent sheen and having a liquid gold color. There were thousands. The room was filled with them. Each bubble had a faint impression of a beautiful little round cherub face with pink cheeks and golden hair. These Soul cherubim were pulling at my heart with one collective yearning: "What a good mother you would make. Have another baby; have one of us."

Sholem Asch: "Not the power to remember, but its very opposite, the power to forget, is a necessary condition of our existence. If the lore of the transmigration of souls is a true one, then these, between their exchange of bodies, must pass through the sea of forgetfulness. According to the Jewish view, we make the transition under the overlordship of the Angel of Forgetfulness. But it sometimes happens that the Angel of Forgetfulness himself forgets to remove from our memories the records of the former world; and then our senses are haunted by fragmentary recollections of another life."[1]

Contents

Foreword by Bernie S. Siegel, MD

~

THE CONTENTS OF *COSMIC CRADLE* are similar to my personal
and professional life experience. I accept what I experience,
even if I cannot explain it or have not been exposed to it during my medical training. In that way my life is not limited by my
beliefs or what I can accept. During my personal experiences, I have
heard voices speaking to me from the greater consciousness and
their words have always impacted my life in a meaningful way. An
example was hearing a voice ask me, "How did your parents meet?"
This occurred on the day my father was to die and when I asked
my mother in my dad's hospital room, my mother started telling
stories, which started with, "Your father lost a coin toss and had
to take me out." My father died laughing because of that question
from the voice.

I hear messages spoken to me by my dead patients and messages delivered by psychics to me, speaking like the person they
are talking about and sharing their name so there is no doubt of
their authenticity. I have communicated with animals and with my
anesthetized, comatose, and dying patients who responded to my
words. Once a family asked me to see their mother who had been
brain dead for two years, but attorneys would not allow the family
to stop her tube feeding. She died fifteen minutes after I said to her,
"Your love will stay with us and if you need to go, it is alright." I
had an NDE as a four-year-old child choking on a toy I aspirated. I
could see and think when out of my body. I was angry when I didn't
die. I had a past-life experience when a friend who was concerned
about how busy I was, asked me, "Why are you living this life?" I
went into a trance and saw myself with a sword killing people and
their pets. The experience educated me about why I became a physician and have been rescuing people and animals my whole life.

For me, God is intelligent, conscious, loving energy, and we are made of the same stuff. God once explained to me: "You are a satellite dish, a remote control and a television screen." The explanation I received was that there are many channels of consciousness we can tune into and our minds make the decision about which channel we tune into, like a remote control, and our bodies demonstrate which channel we have chosen by our actions, just as the TV screen provides us with images of the program we are watching. I can guarantee that consciousness exists without the body and that we are all impregnated by the collective consciousness, which has preceded us in time. I can also promise you that when it comes time to leave our bodies we will become dreamless, unalive, and perfect again.

As God said, if creation were perfect, it would be a magic trick and not creation. So understand we are here to live and learn, and if we all raise the level of global consciousness, the future for our descendants will be a much happier and peaceful and loving one.

BERNIE S. SIEGEL, MD
April, 2013

Introduction

❧

Amnesia of Our Spiritual Origins

Where did I come from and what am I supposed to
  be doing? I have no idea.
My Soul is from elsewhere, I am sure of that, and I
  intend to end up there.

— Rumi

*Most people report total amnesia of their voyage into this
earthly cradle, and yet a trail of invisible steps retraces
our journey into human form.*

Cosmic Cradle resulted from a string of coincidences that
fell into place in 1989 like footsteps on a hidden path guiding the lead author into a graduate writing program. The
initial sparks for the original *Cosmic Cradle* were interviews conducted in 1989 with women who had blissful pregnancies, including
giving birth with less pain or in a state of ecstasy. These were not
ordinary women. They were a select group of meditating mothers.
Many had participated in long meditation retreats. Due to a lifelong interest in self-actualization, Elizabeth was hooked into deciphering the link between blissful childbirth and higher consciousness. At the same time, scientific support emerged from new brain
studies finding connections between states of consciousness and intelligence and creativity. As research on the mothers unfolded, they
also talked about meeting their unborn children before pregnancy
in dreams and visions, as well as their own memories of life before
conception.

A second coincidence in 1989 served as another inspiration when Elizabeth shared interview material with Neil for a magazine article:

> As I contemplated the mothers' experiences, my body became electrified, vibrating in waves of bliss from head to toe. I felt like I was going to levitate out of my chair. I received an intuitive message: 'Elizabeth, this is more than a magazine article! This is a book or series of books. This is an untold cosmic story about who we are, where we come from, why we are here. Clearly, it is a beautiful, spiritual journey that people need to understand.'

The ultimate inspiration came from the adults and children who shared two types of pre-birth experiences: pre-birth memory and pre-birth communications. Pre-birth memories are defined as natural, spontaneous memories of life before birth: choosing parents and life circumstances, and the journey from the heavenly world to conception, life in the womb, and birth itself. We excluded reports based upon methods like hypnosis, drugs, regression, and psychic readings.

The second set of pre-birth reports involves spontaneous announcing signs or pre-birth communications between a child waiting to be born and parents or relatives. Pre-birth communications are defined as subtle contacts with the unborn via dreams, visions, an inner voice, feeling the unborn child's presence, telepathy, and a host of other announcing signs. These mysterious communications occur before or after conception and establish a new parent-child relationship. Love for a child begins long before birth.

The abilities to remember life before birth and to tune into children seeking birth serve as landmarks on the road to expanded awareness, according to the Father of Yoga and pioneering psychologist Patanjali. Nearly two thousand years ago, the great sage delineated fifty-two human abilities or *siddhis,* including remembering the reason for our birth and discerning subtle, hidden, and remote things beyond the five senses. Sage Patanjali's research reveals that these abilities are nothing new. We are merely rediscovering our innate potential.

We invite you to explore our latest evidence for pre-birth in this revised *Cosmic Cradle*. Our research encompasses interviews with one hundred and fifty individuals from the United States, Canada, England, Australia, India, New Zealand, and the Netherlands as well as cross-cultural cases referenced in books and journals.

Pre-Birth Memories

Why do most people fail to recall the early events in their life such as birth, first breath, first thoughts as a baby, first time they saw their parents, first words, first footsteps, and thousands of other hidden memories? Does an amnesia of human beginnings in this life extend to pre-birth memories? *Cosmic Cradle* suggests it does after finding a rare group of individuals who possess pre-birth memories.

We are explorers who come to Earth as a cosmic spark of consciousness from a higher Source. Our Soul, defined here as our consciousness or immortal essence, seeks experiences in a human body and agrees to a life plan. Once a Soul enters the womb, it helps to spark the growth of the fetus. The Soul adapts to the earthly world by flitting in and out of the womb and may even return to Source. By the time a baby takes its first breath, it has already completed an extensive sojourn.

Once we are born, we become trapped inside a human body and wonder where we have come from. We forget our pre-birth memories. A life-long search is spent trying to remember our cosmic status. How we happen to be born seems as mysterious as the way a caterpillar transforms itself into a chrysalis and finally into a butterfly.

The Soul's journey to find its true nature is the quest of human life:

❈ Who am I? Do I have a Soul? If so, is my Soul immortal?

❈ Why am I here? Does my life have any purpose?

❈ Where do I come from?

❈ How did I get here?

❈ Is there life after death?

❈ Is there a Source, a Higher Power?

Throughout the ages, insights into such questions came from early philosophers of Western Europe such as Socrates (469–399 BCE), who passionately argued at the end of his life: "We have clear evidence that the Soul is immortal."[1] Modern scholars suggest that the Greeks, as glorious as they may have been, most likely acquired their profound knowledge of the Soul's immortality from Vedic India. Legends in Greece, for example, speak of journeys to India made by ancient philosophers who were believed to have traveled widely. "Thales, Pythagoras, Empedocles, Democritus, and Plato were all fabled to have made the journey."[2] Since trading routes long existed between India and Greece along the Silk Road and the sea, these legends are probably more than anecdotes. What the Greeks would have learned in India is that the Soul is imperishable. Krishna, in the Bhagavad-Gita, describes the nature of the Soul: weapons cannot destroy it, water cannot wet it, fire cannot burn it, nor can the wind dry it.

Today, the same eternal message is coming from an unexpected field of inquiry: pre-birth research. Rare people report signs of immortality within their memories and pre-birth communications. Both types of reports open a golden door into the Soul's preexistent state. They serve as harbingers that validate the immortality of the Soul.

Cross-Cultural Parallels

Are pre-birth memories and pre-birth contacts rare in the world?

Elizabeth began interviews with mothers who shared pre-birth memories. One interview led to another via a word-of-mouth process, without any need for advertising. After meeting so many sensitive individuals, we inquired in our initial ten-year investigation: "Have people in other cultures and throughout history reported pre-birth experiences?" The answers were surprising. The more we looked, the more cases appeared. We discovered that pre-birth experiences are not new at all.

Fragments of the Soul's journey have survived throughout recorded history. Based on a limited survey of scholarly books and journals, evidence of pre-birth experiences was found worldwide indicating a universal phenomenon. Greek and Roman cultures alluded to how Souls forget life before birth. Indigenous cultures likewise were familiar with pre-birth experiences. Cross-cultural threads of evidence are mentioned throughout the chapters in Parts One and Two. The five chapters in Part Three contain hundreds of parallels from religion, philosophy, spirituality, mythology, poetry, and anthropology. Pre-birth reports form part of a deep pattern interconnecting cultures and spanning centuries. Table I displays cultures and religions surveyed for *Cosmic Cradle.*

Table 1. Pre-Birth Reports—108 Religions and Cultures

19 RELIGIOUS TRADITIONS			
Buddhism	Hinduism	Manichaeism	Tibetan Buddhism
Christianity	Islam	Shiism	Vedism
Gnosticism	Judaism	Sikhism	Zen Buddhism
Hasidism	Kabbalah	Sufism	Zoroastrianism
Harranism	Latter-day Saints	Taoism	

45 INDIGENOUS NORTH AMERICAN PEOPLES			
Akwa'ala	Great Bear Lake	Maricopa	Pawnee
Algonquin	Hidatsa	Mariposa	Plains Cree
Athabaskan	Hopi	Menominee	Salish
Aztec	Huron	Miwok	Saulteaux
Canadian Dakota	Iowa	Mojave	Seri
Delaware	Iroquois	Montagnais	Shawnee
Cherokee	Kwakiutl	Natchez	Tlingit
Chinook	Lakota	Ojibwe	Wahpeton Dakota
Cocopah	Lenape	Omaha	Winnebago
Dakota Sioux	Lummi	Osage	Yuma
Deg Hit'an	Mandan	Otoe	Zuni
Fox			

19 INDIGENOUS PEOPLES OF AUSTRALIA			
Adnyamathanha	Forrest River	Ngalia	Warlpiri
Arunta	Kimberly	Ngarinjin	Worrorra
Bardi	Mularatara	Nimbalda	Wunambal
Broome District	Murrinh-Patha	Pitjantjatjara	Yolngu
Euahlayi	Nibalda	Tiwi	

7 AFRICAN INDIGENOUS PEOPLES			
Bangwa	Dagara	Igbo	Zulu
Baoulé	Ijaw	Yoruba	

14 ADDITIONAL INDIGENOUS PEOPLES			
Bataks (Sumatra)	Koryaks (Siberia)	Iban (Borneo)	Trobriand
Caribs (Venezuela)	Native Indonesians	Semang (Malay	Islanders (Papua
Finno-Ugric people	Nias (Sumatra)	Peninsula)	New Guinea)
Karen (northern	Khanty (Siberia)	Tapirapé (Brazil)	Tungusic people
Thailand)		Tontemboan	(Siberia)
		(Sulawesi)	

4 ANCIENT CULTURES			
China	Egypt	Greece	Rome

Paradigm Shift

*The mythical tale of storks bringing newborns to their
earthly homes seems to possess more substance than the
materialistic paradigm presupposes.*

The knowledge in these pre-birth reports offers a revolutionary
way of looking at life—a new paradigm—analogous to the way that
quantum physics replaced Newtonian physics. Who we really are
can be better understood if we know where we have come from.
Life on Earth is intertwined with the divine, and why our Souls are
born here fits into that wholeness.

Outdated Pre-Birth Paradigm

Before exploring the new paradigm, let's review the outdated materialistic way of thinking. The four assumptions of this mind-set
presume no Soul exists before conception.

1. The five human senses give us an accurate perception of the
   world. Material science offers a reasonable explanation of
   reality.
2. Memory, awareness, and sensory abilities arrive with the
   development of the brain and a nervous system where memories can be stored.
3. Biological conception is a chance event, marking the first step
   toward creating human life. Parents cannot communicate or
   bond with an unborn child. A newborn is a blank slate to be
   written on by parents and society.
4. Heredity and social environment (nature and nurture) explain
   human life.

In essence, this worldview reduces the mind to solid matter and
eliminates the Soul. Today materialistic thinking still has a dominant
influence in the educational system and media. Typically, people do

not hear reports about life before birth. If they do, chances are that they will be dismissed as anecdotal, without a possible scientific basis. Spiritual experiences are often relegated to the realm of old wives' tales and folk legends.

All this helps explain why people believe that they are pawns of heredity, traumatic incidents, and what their parents did or did not do. They are left with poor insight into their spiritual roots and do not know why they exist. The materialistic worldview insults our intelligence.

Principles of the Pre-Birth Paradigm

The Pre-Birth Paradigm is an inspirational, optimistic message worthy of review.

1. Individuals with expanded awareness recall life before birth.
2. Consciousness and memory go beyond the brain.
3. Sensitive parents are aware of Souls seeking birth.
4. Our life plan is designed prior to birth.

First Principle: Individuals with Expanded Awareness Recall Life before Birth

Rare are those who can remember their first breath or the doctors attending their birth. Memory is transient. Memories are so fleeting that all that surfaces are crude highlight reels of special moments here or there. People forget more than ninety-nine percent of their lives despite an intense desire to cling to the fading memories of the past. Is it a wonder then that most people forget their life before birth as if it never happened?

Whereas thousands of people have sought to retrieve pre-birth memories via rebirthing, hypnosis, psychoanalysis, meditation, submersion in water, and breathing techniques, a much smaller number naturally recall them. In 1989 our interviews began with individuals who recalled pre-birth spontaneously accessed since childhood. Pre-birth researcher Elisabeth Hallett describes this group of people: "There is an invisible tribe in the world—a tribe of people who have grown up with memories of preexistence. Whether they describe it as a place, a time, or a state of being, they locate it not just before birth, but before identifying with a physical body. They remember existing as soul."[3]

Part One includes interviews with people reporting significant pre-birth memories. Chapters 7 and 8 feature extensive memories stretching back to the pre-planning stages involving past lifetimes. Even rarer are individuals, such as Diane, Beverly, and Inelia who describe coming from a single Soul Source at the beginning of their existence analogous to a spiritual Big Bang when the physical universe was first forming. Chapter 18 in Part Three delves into why most people forget life before birth. Philosophers, theologians, and poets have acknowledged this "pre-birth amnesia" since time immemorial. Parallel theories arose in ancient Greece, Rome, China, India, and in all major religious and philosophical systems.

Expanded awareness is the basis of the ability to recall the journey into life. As an example, among those interviewed, several displayed unique brain waves indicative of a permanent, transcendental state during laboratory research. Evidence of higher consciousness leads the way to a greater potential for memory.

Common Elements of Pre-Birth Memories

What can people tells us about their existence before entering the fetus? Each person's pre-birth recall is unlike any earthly memory they describe. They easily distinguish the pre-birth experience from memories of events occurring after birth. They emphasize that pre-birth memory is their most powerful memory. Each person's memory of life before birth is as unique as a set of fingerprints and includes any combination of twelve elements. Further elements related to children's pre-birth memories are described in chapter 1.

1. Self-aware of their true blissful nature: the physical body is a garment, a cage, shell, a temporary housing for the Soul.
2. Eternal: they know that parents do not "create" them. They are brought to birth through parents. Birth is a change from "being" to "becoming."
3. Feeling at home: the heavenly world is their true Home, where there is a sense of belonging, meaning, and completeness.
4. Limitless love: love in the heavenly world is off the scale, intense and endless in scope compared to earthly love.
5. Soul families: Heaven is a place teeming with Souls. They exist with loved ones in groups. Beings of Light and beauty are their true family.
6. Telepathy: they report telepathy and instantly manifesting whatever they think of or travel via mere intention.
7. Spirit guides, angels, divine planners, Great Being, Creator: a Higher Being tells them they are going on a journey and will return Home one day. Guides assist in pre-birth planning and escort them to their mother's womb.
8. Preview and life plan: their upcoming life appears like a Hollywood movie or images on a computer screen. They are given options for parents and lessons to learn.
9. Pre-birth amnesia: they may feel parts of their pre-birth memory being erased as they descend on the way to Earth. Some are also aware of amnesia gradually taking place in childhood.
10. Interest in human experience: some are reluctant to be born, whereas others have a strong desire.
11. Awareness in fetus: once the Soul connects with the fetus in the womb, most Souls feel a loss of freedom, constricted awareness, a feeling of being in a cage.
12. No fear of death: some even look forward to returning "Home."

Tracking down pre-birth memories can be challenging since it is a rare topic of conversation, and a cultural bias exists against them.

Nonetheless, we project that thousands of cases exist based on our research and reports offered by other pre-birth researchers, such as Elisabeth Hallett,[4] Sarah Hinze,[5] and Arvin Gibson.[6] PMH Atwater cites pre-birth memories discovered in her children's near-death research.[7] Websites where people post pre-birth memories are also helping to document them.[8]

More than forty years of credible research in prenatal and perinatal psychology adds support on the science, including lifelong work by David Chamberlain and others. Chamberlain is a clinical psychologist, pioneer in prenatal psychology, and founder of a website for the Association for Prenatal and Perinatal Psychology and Health (APPPAH). Thomas Verny is the founder of APPPAH and author of *Secret Life of the Unborn Child.*[9] Breakthroughs in prenatal frontiers by Chamberlain, Verny, and others have revealed that babies are far more alert and have memories of prenatal life.

Pre-birth memories not only make for interesting stories, these abilities will change the boundaries of medical and psychological research, and even more importantly, change our understanding of who and what we are.

Second Principle: Consciousness and Memory Go Beyond the Brain

Memory science is catching up with other disciplines in understanding the power of human nature, even before birth. During the twentieth century, memory research advanced from the belief that a baby is born as a blank slate to acceptance of third-trimester or pre-birth memories.

Scientists were skeptical, until recently, however, that newborn babies or the fetus could remember. Due to the lack of brain development in newborns, they believed that human memory could not operate so early. In addition, they had mistaken assumptions of how memory works. From the babies' perspective, their own difficulty lay in being unable to communicate their abilities to doctors since they do not speak at birth and their screams seemed unrecognizable.

❄ Before 1950: psychology placed the beginnings of memory at age three based on the medical-psychological mind-set of Freud's personality theory.

❄ Late 1960s: psychologists posited bonding, a postbirth system of mother-child communications. Medical doctors traced early childhood emotional development back to the hours immediately after birth.

❄ 1980s (Dr. Gladys McGarey): the mother of holistic medicine in the United States, obstetrician, and family physician for over sixty-five years was the first doctor to encourage pregnant women to communicate with their unborn children. In difficult cases where pregnant women had emotional problems and chose to terminate their pregnancy, McGarey guided the women to talk to the Soul about leaving and returning at a better time instead of seeking an abortion.[10]

❄ 1981 (Dr. Thomas Verny): the beginning of the parent-child bond is pushed back into pregnancy. Verny, after conducting a comprehensive review of the published science at the time and evaluating the extensive research, concluded that the fetus sees, hears, tastes, and can learn from at least the sixth month onward in utero. An unborn child, for instance, grows emotionally agitated (quickening of the heartbeat) when the mother thinks of a cigarette, and the fetus is sensitive to subtle nuances in the mother's attitude and knows whether he or she is welcomed with love.[11]

❄ 1990s: prenatal and perinatal psychologists conclude that memory is nonphysical, as neuroscientists are unable to locate or isolate memory in the brain or in its biochemistry. Researchers theorize that memory storage is in a field of information such as a field of consciousness.

❄ 1995 (David Chamberlain, PhD): "Ultrasound observations of behavior in the womb reveal that fetuses can show strong emotion. Observations made between sixteen and twenty weeks of gestation during the procedure of amniocentesis have revealed fearful reactions including extreme fluctuations in heart rate and withdrawal from normal activity for a period of hours or even days. With increasing use of amniocentesis, women and doctors have witnessed aggressive actions toward the needle itself as babies attack the needle barrel from the side. Similarly, observation of twins via ultrasound have uncovered body language including holding hands, kissing, playing, kicking, and hitting each other. This communication before birth was not predicted in psychology and medicine."[12]

Evidence of pre-birth memories contradicts the materialistic mind-set that we have no consciousness or sensory abilities before the brain exists. In our research, several detailed cases were found where children's memories of conception were later confirmed by parents. Nan (chapter 4) and Rennie (chapter 5) recall observing from above the parent's sexual act and the unique locations of conception.

Third Principle: Sensitive Parents Are Aware of Souls Seeking Birth

The realm of unborn children is invisible to "normal" human senses. Like a scientist piercing subatomic particles with an accelerator, women with an expanded awareness transcend ordinary perception and see into a subtler dimension. Such mothers feel blessed to begin motherhood by welcoming and connecting to their children before birth. Pre-birth researchers Elisabeth Hallett, Sarah Hinze, and Fred Seligson document cases of pre-birth communications in their writings.

Reports from parents communicating with children before birth transcend the assumption that conception marks the first step toward creating human life and a newborn is a lump of clay to be molded by parents and society. Inelia, for example, was enjoying a walk in the countryside, when a beautiful blond blue-eyed eight-year-old girl appeared out of thin air and said, "My name is Daniela.

I am your daughter." Inelia's family thought her mystical vision was crazy since both Inelia and her husband have dark hair and brown eyes. Besides that, Inelia had already lost three babies due to miscarriages. Even when Inelia realized she had become pregnant two weeks after the mystical encounter, her family next tried to convince her to think of a boy's name as well and not to buy a pink cradle but a yellow one. Nine months later, Inelia gave birth to the same beautiful blond blue-eyed baby girl who had announced herself in the vision.

Chapters 9–13 explore cases of parents who communicate with their child-to-be at various stages on the way to parenthood. Children searching for parents appeared as sparkling, virtually invisible visitors in the form of spheres, bubbles, lights, cherub-like faces, tiny figures, and sometimes even departed relatives. Contacts with a child-to-be includes any of these five elements:

1. Souls emanate Love and Light; they preexist in a Higher World.
2. Souls choose parents.
3. Souls engineer the circumstances for conception with their eagerness for birth.
4. Spiritual blueprint: the parent sees their unborn child's face or body.
5. Messages and guidance: (a) Souls plan earthly life and convey what they hope to accomplish; (b) Souls convey a message or warning to benefit parents; and (c) Souls reveal their preferred names.

Chapters 9 and 10 present cases where parents met children prior to conception in dreams and visions. Chapter 11 features couples who were aware of the mystical side of conception. Chapter 12 shares experiences of parents like Judy who lost her twins early in pregnancy and mothers like Summer who believe the same child returned after a spontaneous miscarriage. Chapter 13 highlights pregnant mothers who received instruction, warnings, and guidance from their babies in the womb. Chapter 14 illustrates how Spirit-Children communicate with the indigenous men of Australia before their wives became pregnant.

Fourth Principle: Our Life Plan Is Designed Prior to Birth

Human birth is merely the beginning of our spiritual journey on Earth, a notion traceable in the West to classical philosophers in ancient Greece and Rome. This concept of a lesson plan is upheld by religions, philosophies, and small-scale societies. Shakespeare alluded to our life contracts when he said, "All the world's a stage"; all the men and women are merely players with their exits and entrances. This was the playwright's way of teaching us about pre-life planning. We come to the earthly stage with a pre-existing script.

Pre-birth experiences and memories transport us beyond the materialistic idea that heredity and social environment explain human life. Our life's drama is planned long before birth. Pre-birth experiences in Parts I and II illuminate the Soul's role in selecting parents and choosing to enter the stream of human life. Pre-birth reports in chapters 5 and 12 give insights into the healing power of challenges such as abuse, miscarriages, and accidents. Rennie realized why his life included the deaths of two wives and three children. Chapter 15 features pre-birth memories of medicine men who prepared for their life role via a dress rehearsal before birth. Chapter 16 presents pre-birth planning theories from various perspectives.

Cosmic Cradle Overview

Pre-birth memories and pre-birth communications deserve our attention.

Shifts in consciousness, like shifting gears in a five-speed transmission, hold the key to pre-birth experiences. People reporting pre-birth memories and communications with the Soul seeking birth have shifted from the mundane third gear of awareness or consciousness into the fourth and fifth gears of higher awareness. Pre-birth experiences are not so much due to social upbringing, educational background, or religious training as they are to an individual's innate awareness. Just as the physical world is experienced through the physical senses, pre-birth experiences become available through the eye of the Soul. Intuition is the gateway. Higher realities are grasped by a clear mind, open and without preoccupation, rather than a busy mind cluttered with fears, worries, and anxieties.

Though consciousness is a less familiar term in the modern world, the major spiritual traditions have fine-tuned their understanding of consciousness over the millennia. They elucidate degrees of awareness. Just as a thermometer measures hotter and colder temperatures, an awareness scale registers higher and lower perceptions of reality. When awareness grows beyond ordinary waking, dreaming, and sleeping states, an expanded awareness supports access to deeper memories and subtler perceptions. A general description follows of three ordinary states of consciousness and two expanded states based on brain-wave research of key frequencies (delta, theta, alpha, and beta).

- ❀ Sleeping: we have no awareness of the outer world or inner reality; large delta brain waves dominate; no brain-wave coherence.
- ❀ Dreaming: we are aware of worlds conjured up by the imagination; interchanging mental and restful activity with no brain-wave coherence.
- ❀ Waking: we are aware and experience the world via our five senses; fast beta waves without brain-wave coherence.
- ❀ Brief transcendental bliss: Abraham Maslow coined the term 'peak experience' to define this state of inner peace, energy, creativity, and bliss. Mystics call it *samādhi*. The Soul begins to wake up to its true nature. Brain scans show dominant alpha (alertness) with theta (deep rest).

❂ Permanent transcendental bliss: being alive is a peak experience of inner happiness, peace, silence, wholeness, wonder and awe, and awareness of higher truth. The Soul has awakened to its true nature. Everything becomes sacred and beautiful. Brain scans reveal mixed beta, theta, and alpha. Orderliness increases between the right and left hemispheres.

Pre-birth experiences are clustered at the upper end of the awareness scale. Reports from ancient Greek, medieval Catholic, Islamic, and Asian traditions, as well as Descartes, Wordsworth, and Einstein referred to higher awareness when they spoke of the all-seeing power of the superconscious mind. Ancient Greek philosophers recognized that when someone transcends mundane perception, he perceives "everlasting loveliness," "greatest joy," and "profoundly moving beauty."[13]

American Transcendentalist Henry David Thoreau speaks of a higher awareness:

> The millions are awake enough for physical labor; but only one in a million is awake enough for effective intellectual exertion, only one in a hundred millions to a poetic or divine life. To be awake is to be alive. I have never yet met a man who was quite awake. How could I have looked him in the face? We must learn to reawaken and keep ourselves awake, not by mechanical aids, but by an infinite expectation of the dawn, which does not forsake us in our soundest sleep.[14]

Chuang Tzu (369–286 BCE), the Chinese philosopher, clarified the lower end of the awareness scale: "We do not ask the blind about a painting, nor invite the deaf to a songfest. Blindness and deafness are not merely of the body: There are souls, too, that are blind and deaf."[15] Chuang Tzu acknowledges what happens when an individual attains the upper limits of the awareness scale: "You can't discuss the ocean with a well frog—he's limited by the space he lives in.

You can't discuss ice with a summer insect—he's bound to a single season. You can't discuss the Way with a cramped scholar—he's shackled by his doctrines. Now you have come out beyond your banks and borders and have seen the great sea.... From now on it will be possible to talk to you about the Great Principle."[16]

Cosmic Cradle offers an optimistic message of humanity's essential spiritual nature. Most people suffer from amnesia of their spiritual roots, and this is why the vast majority are unable to call up their pre-birth memories. Pre-birth experiences can teach humanity about new dimensions of human awareness. They stretch the boundaries of what people consider real and will change the way humankind approaches conception, pregnancy, childbirth, and death.

Cosmic Cradle inspires a strong interfaith message because it lays out a vision bridging major religions and linking a wealth of spiritual wisdom from diverse cultural perspectives. The ideas contained in *Cosmic Cradle* are unifying rather than divisive. We are all one family.

PART ONE

❦

Pre-Birth Memory

OULS BY THE BILLIONS PREVIEW the earthly abode. Like sparks of light dancing in a great theater before the curtain rises, each Soul will come on to the earthly stage to shine in a fleeting moment of glory and fulfillment.

Part One presents summaries of our interviews with children and adults who retain crystal clear awareness of their pre-birth memory. In some cases, their recollections stretch back to include interlife memories and past-life memories. Even more impressive are individuals who report far-reaching memories of being pure Light and coming for the first time into a physical body. Pre-birth researcher Elisabeth Hallett instructs us to imagine that the following ideas are true before we read stories about pre-birth memories:

> We are Souls that exist before we are conceived.
> Before conception, we can communicate with our parents.
> We participate in coming to an agreement: our decisions are mutual and can be changed.
> We can announce our arrival and make our presence known during pregnancy, even interact in ways that let our parents get to know us before we are born.
> As children, we may remember our pre-birth life and be aware of siblings yet to come.
> Family links are enduring; ancestors take an interest in new births and may act as guides and guardians of the arriving Soul.

1

We can see echoes of other lives together and perhaps plan the next act in the long-running play of our existence.[1]

CHAPTER 1

Children as Messengers

༄

CHILDREN'S PRE-BIRTH MEMORIES

We chose our parents and our children chose us.
There are no victims in the Preexistence, in that
place before here.
—JEANNINE PARVATI BAKER

*Children are aware and involved in the process of birth
long before conception.*

C HILDREN WHO RETAIN PRE-BIRTH MEMORIES appear to be a
rarity. Toddlers stop parents in their tracks when they utter
words like these: "Mom, I told you we choose our parents,"
little Catcher emphasized. Two-year-old Diane told her mother, "I
am an orphan. I did not come from you. I came from the Light; it is
much happier there."

A child who recalls pre-birth memories has a desire to share them
and assumes mommy and daddy have these memories, too. Unfortunately, a child becomes silent and frustrated if parents label their
memories as false or fantasies. Such a child can become insecure
about his or her inner world and self-image.

Are children trying to communicate with parents about pre-
birth? Should parents be open-minded? Prenatal researcher Dr.
David Chamberlain asserts: "Old myths, which for so long have
doomed babies to inferior status, are challenged here. The truth is,
much of what we have traditionally believed about babies is false.

We have misunderstood and underestimated their abilities. They are not simple beings, but complex and ageless—small creatures with unexpectedly large thoughts."[1]

Children's pre-birth memories challenge the old medical myth that birth is the beginning of life and that the newborn has a blank memory slate. Yet even science is verifying how evolved and developed babies are right from birth. Dr. Chamberlain says: "Babies know more than they are supposed to know. Minutes after birth, a baby can pick out its mother's face from a gallery of photos. Babies recognize the gender of other babies, even when cross-dressed, provided they are moving—something adults cannot do."[2]

How fetal brain development can support pre-birth memories is a scientific mystery. Thus pre-birth memories are naturally met with skepticism. They offer new territory to explore in childrearing research.

Indicator Signs: Real or Imaginary?

How can a parent know whether pre-birth memories are real or fantasy?

Pre-birth memories are poorly documented. Few experts know about them. How can anyone interview a newborn before it has learned to talk? A common misconception about pre-birth memories is that the parents have artificially influenced their child's pre-birth memory. Our interviews did not reveal any cases of parents coaching children. Nor did the child overhear anyone discuss this subject. Instead, the parents are puzzled about their child's matter-of-fact claims.

Insights on reliable truth-telling indicator signs from Carol Bowman are helpful in determining authentic pre-birth memories. Bowman, a children's past-life researcher and author, distinguishes a child's past-life memory from a wild imagination.[3] We can apply three of Bowman's criteria to check whether a child's pre-birth memory is real: matter-of-fact tone of voice, consistency over time, and knowledge beyond experience.

Chapter 1 presents children's pre-birth memories that meet Bowman's criteria. These accounts, based on our interviews with children and parents, are all the more impressive when we consider: children are still innocent and speak without social conditioning to censor them; children have no agenda and no bias; and children are not sophisticated or educated.

Two-Year-Old Philosopher in Love with Heaven

Catcher has been boldly saying that he came from Heaven since he was two.

Stacy: "Catcher has always been an observer, a listener, and a very cautious child. He is not a risk taker, at all. Catcher started speaking in full sentences when he was one. He walked at ten months. When Catcher was two and a half, he began to make interesting statements. One incident related to my friend Erica, who was pregnant with identical twin girls. She ended up losing Sadie, one of the twins. She was stillborn at nine months. Edie, the other twin, was in the ICU for six weeks.

"I had not said anything to Catcher about the stillbirth. At any rate, he tuned in. One day after Sadie's passing, I was nursing Catcher and thinking, 'I feel so bad that this has happened to Erica, because it is so heartbreaking.' All of a sudden Catcher pulled off my nipple and asked, 'Mom, when am I going to see Erica again?' I said, 'Well, that is interesting, Catcher, because I was just thinking about when we were going to see Erica. You will see her in six weeks.' Catcher seemed satisfied and popped back down.

"Later, when Catcher awoke from his afternoon nap, he said, 'Mommy, Sadie is in Heaven and she is fine. She is playing with her grandpa.' I called Erica straight away and told her, with tears in my eyes, 'You are never going to believe what Catcher said.' This was the first time Catcher woke up from a nap with a message. He had never heard about the stillbirth incident. We had felt that Catcher was clairvoyant; now he had validated it.

"Long before this, Catcher had started commenting about 'Heaven'. Now I finally understood what he was saying. I have no idea where he got the word *Heaven* from in the first place. Catcher is my first child. We live in the country, and the closest neighbors are far from us. He is pretty much isolated. We are spiritual people and say bedtime prayers every night. We do not attend church.

"When Catcher was two and a half, I became pregnant with a second child. He went to all my doctor's appointments and was so excited about the baby. He asked questions again and again. Early in the pregnancy, I started to miscarry. Once I started to hemorrhage, Catcher stopped asking about the baby. He did not push. He did not seek answers. I found it bizarre because we had been talking about the baby every day. He did not need to be parented. He was playing it cool and keeping it cool for everyone else.

"My miscarriage was rough. I stayed cooped up in my room during Mom's week-long visit. When I drove my mother to the airport, Catcher sat in the back seat. On our way home, I started to lose it. I was not bawling or shaking my shoulders. I had just started to tear up. Catcher said, 'Mommy, are you crying because you miss the baby?' I was shocked. I said, 'Yes, Catcher, Mommy is really sad because she misses the baby.' He said, 'Well, the baby's okay.' I thought, 'Well, I'm not.'

"The next time Catcher mentioned the baby was a few months later. Catcher took the TV remote control and playfully placed it on my stomach. I asked, 'What are you doing?' He replied, 'I am touching the baby.' I said, 'Catcher, we talked about this before. Mommy does not have a baby in there anymore.' He said, 'Yeah, you do, and it is a girl; it is a different baby.' Two days later, a pregnancy test confirmed I was pregnant. Twenty weeks later an ultrasound accurately determined that I was carrying a baby girl."

Hanging Out in Heaven after a Past Life

"Catcher's conversations when he was two and a half were so much more advanced compared to other children. He began to talk more about Heaven as the months passed. He was not asking me about Heaven; he was telling me about it. He said, 'Mommy, did you know that Heaven has really beautiful colors and there are lots of animals in Heaven?' I said, 'No, I did not know that, Catcher. If I have died and gone to Heaven, I do not remember it.'"

Wisdom about life and death continued to flow from Catcher's lips as time passed. "About a month before Catcher's fourth birthday, he had been quiet for some time as we were riding in the car. Then he suddenly said, 'Mom, did you know that before you were my mommy, I had two brothers and a daddy, but you weren't my mommy?' I said, 'Where was I?' He replied, 'You were in Heaven. You were waiting to be born.'

"The next night at dinner, I was feeling nostalgic and said to Catcher, 'It seems like it was only yesterday when daddy and I were dating and we did not have any kids. Now we have you and your baby sister. Well, it seems like yesterday that you were in my belly.' Catcher replied, 'I was not in your belly. I was in Heaven.' I said, 'What were you doing in Heaven?' Catcher said, 'I was waiting for you guys to be ready, silly.'

"I asked, 'What do you mean you were waiting for us to be ready?' Catcher said, 'That is what we do. I chose you. And Michael chose his parents and Mitchell chose his parents. We wait for you to be ready, but we have already chosen you. That is what you guys did, whether you remember it or not.' Catcher was so matter-of-fact. I said, 'Well, we made you.' He said, 'Mom, you did not make me; God made me.' I said, 'I remember making you, but if that is what you think, that's okay.'

"Catcher began talking more intently about Heaven when he started preschool. One morning before class he announced, 'Mom, I just want to keep dying so I can keep going to Heaven.' I said,

'Catcher, mommy and daddy have to die before you; I know that Heaven's a great place, but that is the order it needs to be.' He looked at me like, 'pff.'

"Since then it became hard on me. Catcher started this phase of telling me: 'I just want to die so I can go to Heaven.' I would say, 'Catcher, that's not funny.' I had no idea how to handle it. I do not want to leave my great friends and family. Catcher makes me feel like death is awesome. He comments on it like, 'It's no big deal.' Perhaps I've been given Catcher so I will be more accepting of death."

Catcher is an old Soul. When he was five, he started to become inquisitive and ask deep questions about Heaven. One day his mother overheard his conversation with her best friend Megan, whom he calls "Auntie": "Catcher asked, 'Auntie, what do you believe happens to people when they die? I believe they go to Heaven.' Megan said, 'Catcher, it is wonderful that you believe that. My faith is Baha'i, and it's not that black and white. We believe there are levels in Heaven.'

"Catcher was interested in knowing more about these levels. Megan explained, 'There are many stages of spiritual growth for the Soul. The amount of growth you do in each human life determines how close to God you are the next time you go to Heaven.' Catcher liked the concept of becoming closer and closer to God the more spiritual growth you do. Catcher was positive and accepting and said, 'Oh, yeah, that makes sense.' These are the kinds of conversations he has with Megan. He knows something about Megan that makes him feel safe."

Playtime with Auntie: Good versus Evil

Megan has visited Stacy and her son Catcher since his birth. So it was interesting to hear what Megan had to say: "I noticed right away that as a baby, Catcher was so emotionally connected and empathic with his mother. When Stacy was upset, he was down too and could not be soothed. When she was happy, he was as happy as can be. I thought, 'What is going on? They have the same emotions all the time.'

"Catcher fantasizes about life after death with me. He constantly tells me about Heaven, a place of unconditional love where everyone knows him and no one misunderstands him. Yet he also talks about how important it is to be here on Earth. He says, 'It's time for this here.' He understands that.

"Conversations about good versus evil come up during playtime. With every move, he will ask a question, such as, 'Why do you think this dinosaur chose to be bad?' 'What do you think it will take for this dinosaur to choose to be good again?' 'When will he change?' 'Will he ever change?' 'Auntie, what do you think?' I put it back to him and say, 'What do you think, Catcher? Do you think people can choose to change and get better?' 'Do people choose to go down the bad path and get bad?' Catcher will say, 'Yes, I think people can choose — it is up to them.'

"I do not remember having a 'me versus you' toy game without Catcher talking about 'who is going to win and why?' With Catcher, it's all about choice: 'Why is he the good guy? Will he become bad?' 'Why is he the bad guy? Will he become good?' 'Do you think they can change?' 'How long is this one going to be good?' 'How long is this one going to be bad?' Playtime with Catcher is much more dynamic than with a typical child's 'bad versus good' toy fights."

As these conversations during playtime with Megan reflect, Catcher thinks very philosophically about life, even at the age of three and four. Isn't this analogous to an adult who wonders, "Did bad guys like Hitler choose to be evil?" "Will Hitler ever change?" Paradoxically adults rarely ponder such deep questions.

In summary, Catcher displays the multiple elements of a prebirth memory noted in the Introduction. Beyond that memory, he recalls past lives and has reported after-death communications. Catcher is empathic, telepathic, clairvoyant, and expresses great compassion for other people, including animals. We are blessed to have him on planet Earth.

"Mommy, Why Are People Afraid to Die?"

Susan's son consistently talked about heavenly life.

Susan: "As a toddler, Kyle talked about God a lot. He said, 'When I talk to God, I am going to ask if I can have two brains. One brain can be busy doing one thing and the other brain can be busy doing another. I want to do twice as much. That would be cool.' He also told me, 'When I talk to God, I am going to ask: Why can't I be a butterfly?'

"When Kyle was three and a half, he stopped watching TV one day and asked me, 'Mommy, why are people afraid to die? I am not afraid to die because you go back to that place from before.' I asked, 'You mean that place that you always talk about?' He said, 'Yeah, it is really nice there. I don't mind going back there because that is where God lives.' I shared his statement with my mom, who believes that when we die, our spirits remain in the grave until the final resurrection. She said, 'Well, that is only Kyle's imagination as there is no such thing.'

"From the age of two, Kyle constantly talked about the good times he and four siblings had had before birth. He would momentarily stop playing with his toys and explain, 'Before I was born, we played games or walked in a park with trees, flowers, and happy sunshine. We could do anything we wanted. We could even fly.'

"These were not random, wild stories. He fixed the time of each event by pointing out each sibling who was with him in Heaven. His memories ranged from being with three to five siblings before being born. I noticed a pattern, a real theme. He said, 'Adam (his oldest brother) was not there that time. He was gone.' Another time Adam and Chris were not there because 'They were simply gone.' The missing sibling was 'gone' from Heaven because he had already been born on Earth.

"One day Kyle told me, 'Mom, another kid was there with me (during a specific incident), but I don't remember his name. I keep trying, but I can't remember it at all.' At first, I let it pass, until Kyle mentioned it the next day: 'Who was that kid? Do you have any idea?' I then realized that Kyle was talking about the baby that never had a chance to be born, a baby I miscarried before his birth. That had to be it."

My Most Treasured Memory

Thirteen-year-old Drew's parents regarded her pre-birth memories as fantasies.

A spontaneous meditation elicited Drew's pre-birth memories in early childhood. As she explains, "My memories were triggered when I had a day to think about what events happened in my life so far: 'What happened before that? And before that?' and so on. I traced back my pre-birth memories to before anything else. They are real, much better than a dream."

Drew first shared her memories when she was ten. "Mom gave me the 'eyebrow' as if I was making up nonsense to get attention. I said, 'I am not lying. I've been keeping this to myself for quite some time.' I trusted Mom might give an explanation, except no matter how many times I explained it, she turned her hearing off. I gave up. Dad was no different. I am frustrated when those closest to me toss it aside.

"My memories are special and give me comfort. I long to be in that boundless, blissful state again. I felt pure existence, freedom. Things were very black. I could not feel, and yet somehow I sensed things. I felt weightless.

"I heard a female voice speaking in a peaceful, content tone as if it were a mental thought spoken aloud. The exact words were: 'It is time for me to wake up now.' At first, I was not sure it was 'me' saying this. I felt happy to be 'waking up' after waiting an eternity in some type of slumber. I wanted to be existent again.

"Some other force was gliding me down to Earth. As I descended to Earth, I had a panoramic view of a beautiful, bright planet with a comfortable, appealing aura. I saw all its vast clouds and oceans. I felt somewhat confident of going.

"Time was in incredibly slow motion as I hovered there. Earth continued to move as I observed it. Then, for some reason, I was approaching this planet at an unbearable super-speed. I had to go quickly like an asteroid entering Earth's atmosphere. Incredible. Light speed, I suppose. I felt a slight shaking when I observed the planet, like a shaky camera lens when it tries to remain still. I could not control my movements and manipulate them by thinking 'left' or 'down.' I had no choice but to come down."

Drew's first memory in her body is at age two: "I was walking around the house. My body was not as light and blissful as I had expected. A human body has limits. Without a body, I had no such limits. As I grew up, learning how to do things felt more like a reminder: walking, speaking, being nice to people. When my kindergarten teacher pulled down a map of the Earth and said, 'You are living on planet Earth, California, in the USA,' this reminded me of its name and appearance. I had seen Earth before I was born. I thought, 'Oh, yeah, everything feels familiar. Having a mom and dad is familiar: waking up in the morning and being closest to one or two other beings.'

"When I was in fourth grade, my mom told me, 'You were an easy baby and very sweet. You were always cautious, obedient, and 'ready to serve' at any moment. When Mom told me that, I understood my memory. I realized who had said, 'It's time for me to wake up now.' The tone of the voice had that type of personality. It was, and is, me."

Reborn Straight from Tibet

Jan's children shared pre-birth memories as toddlers and remember them today as teenagers.

Two-and-a-half-year-old Robbie caught his mother's attention when he said: "I came from Turquoise Land. The music there was different from the music Daddy plays. My sister is waiting outside the gate, in the Pink Land. She will put a ball of white light in your tummy and jump in." One year later his sister, Anna Grace, was born. Robbie also told his mother, "My brother is further away in another land, the Blue Land. He will come later and be born in America."

Three years after Anna Grace's birth, she too began sharing memories: "Mom, I was up in Angel Land, the Land that I came from. I heard Dad calling my name, 'Anna Grace,' so I knew it was time to come." Indeed, several weeks before her birth, Anna Grace's father had suggested the name Anna Grace. Over and over again Anna lamented: "I miss Angel Land. I don't like it here. It's too hard. I want to go back." Her mother consoled her, "I love you very much. I know that it's different, but you can feel good here too. I'm glad that you are here. Everything will be okay." At other times, Anna said, "I have all the angels in my bedroom, and throughout the house are stars. No one else can see them because I can still see Angel Land, where I came from."

Besides remotely sensing her father choosing her name, Anna Grace understood life in England, although she had only lived there the first six weeks of her life: "Mommy, I knew all about England. I saw you there when I was in Angel Land, and I decided to come here."

Jan's son Robbie's memories stretch back to a past life. As a child, he had recurring dreams and woke up saying, "I came from Red Roshi Land. The people wore red robes. I saw a big fire in Red Roshi Land. We had to go away." At other times, he said, "I went back to Red Roshi Land. I remember a fire, and we had to travel over the mountains." Jan recognized Robbie's description of the flight from Tibet during the Chinese takeover. "My son looked like a little monk in his baby pictures. An intuitive told me, 'Your children came straight from Tibet.' I feel that Robbie chose me as a mother, knowing he would have contact with spiritual teachers. Even before his first birthday, he attended the fourteenth Dalai Lama's empowerment ceremony. He also received blessings from Buddhist and Hindu masters. At ten, Robbie sat in the full lotus posture during his father's Zen priesthood ordination. Later, at twelve, Robbie expressed a desire to become a monk."

Jan desired a third child and reminded six-year-old Robbie, "Do you remember saying that your little brother was coming to us when we moved to America?" He said, "Yes, but it's uncertain. He's in school in this other land. He's unsure whether he's coming." As time passed, Robbie kept saying, "Mom, I talk to my brother, and he talks to me. He's not sure whether he'll come. It's not determined." As it turned out, Jan and her husband divorced and did not have a third child.

I Saw the Snow before I Was Born

A New Zealand woman first shared her memories as
a toddler.

Three-year-old Shannon sat in the back seat with an older brother and sister. As they traveled along, her dad said, "We should go to the snow [the mountains] sometime soon." Shannon's older siblings chimed in, "We've never been to the snow. We really want to go." Shannon sat silently for a moment before announcing, "I have been to the snow." Her brother argued, "No, you haven't." Her older sister corrected her as well: "If we haven't been, then you haven't either." Shannon became annoyed and raised her voice, "Yes, I have been to the snow." Shannon's mother turned around and gently said, "We haven't taken you to the snow, so you couldn't have been."

Shannon felt frustrated and on the verge of tears. She yelled, "Yes, I have been to the snow. I was walking up a mountain, and there were three people in front of me. I was also down the bottom of a mountain. When I looked up I could see snow on the top. I saw a creek down at the bottom and lots of big rocks in it." The car became quiet. After a few moments Shannon's mother said, "That was me. That was what I saw when I went to the snow when I was pregnant with you." Shannon told her siblings, "See, I have been to the snow. I was in Mom's belly." After a while, her mother said, "You were only new in my belly, about three months old. You must have opened your eyes and saw what I saw."

Shannon now felt content that her family accepted her pre-birth memory of "going to the snow." She did not take the chance to share a second memory at that moment: "I was seated in a room with another person who told me that I was going back. The man said, 'You have two lives left to live. Choose the one you want first. One life will be hard. The other will be relatively peaceful.' I spent time trying to decide, weighing if I was strong enough to handle a hard life. In the end, I chose to live the hard life first so I could end my time on Earth with a peaceful life."

Ty's Transmission

When toddler Ty began to blurt out his pre-birth memories, rather than react with skepticism, his parents recorded these notes.

Chaos greeted three-year-old Ty and his parents as they entered Colombo, the capital of Sri Lanka, in May 1983. A civil war between the minority Tamil population and the majority Singhalese had just broken out. Ty's parents had traveled to Sri Lanka on business, and they were also exploring the possibility of moving from the United States to Sri Lanka. On arrival they immediately felt they were headed in the wrong direction. Crowds of people inside the airport were in long lines sprawled everywhere, fleeing from the turmoil. As Ty's family left the terminal en route to their hotel, their taxi passed by scores of armed soldiers and burning buildings. During their first week in Colombo, a government curfew was in place. No one was permitted to leave their homes. Ty spent days working out his feelings about the violence and destruction, verbally and in his drawings.

Several months later, the family flew to London to visit Grand-honey, Ty's eighty-six-year-old maternal grandmother. On this visit, August 11, 1983, for the first time Ty shared pre-birth memories. Ty began by explaining the meaning of the burned-out houses and buildings he had witnessed in Sri Lanka. The power of Ty's spontaneous "transmission" impacted his father, Len, who described the experience: "There was a strong sense of urgency in Ty's voice as he spoke, without hesitation and with clarity. It seemed as if our son was directly experiencing something from a higher source and trying to translate it into language. He was speaking with such authority that I grabbed a notepad and started writing down each word as fast as I could."

Len's notes from thirty years ago follow. Ty said: "Before I was born, first I was nothing. I was like the sky. I was like the Buddha. I was listening with my hands, and the whistling went right by me. When I was born with the sky [at the time of the Soul's creation as an individual spark], I was very little. When I was born with you, I was bigger.

"I went to all the countries before I was born, but I could not find anybody that I was going to be. Before I was born on Earth, I saw mom and I touched her head with my leg because I was very big when I was in the sky. [Ty's consciousness had evolved and expanded from the individual spark.] When I was born, I was much smaller." [Ty's Soul connected with his mother's body once he located her on Earth, an ability of his expanded consciousness. As Ty's Soul entered his physical body and was born, his consciousness became less expanded and he no longer had such an ability.]

Ty's mother, Anna, asked, "Where was I before I was born?" Ty said, "You were like me, up in the sky pushing [through space], but not with a body. Grandhoney was also up in the sky, and I was waiting for her to be born. I was looking up in the sky for her, and I was standing in the middle of the road when I was run over by a car." [Ty remembers how his past-life ended in a traumatic car accident.

He then searched for Grandhoney and waited for her to be born.]

Ty told his mother, "Before I was born, I was growing on plastic, cardboard, walls, roads, hardness, everything. You, Daddy, and Grandhoney also grow on the same things as me. Everyone grows that way. First, you grow on wood and trees and on dead animals. Then you grow on people, which are alive." [Ty is describing the Soul's evolution from mineral to plant to animal to human. See the parallel to Rumi's poem below.]

Ty next told his mother, "When you were born, you were transformed, and then you did not push out—you came out like that." Ty then showed what he meant in a drawing. His mother was born via cesarean section.

"There is all this whiteness and sky, and then there is form. [First, there is a field of invisible pure consciousness that is all-pervading. Then physical form manifests from this field like a jack-in-the-box.] If a piece of white paint is chipped off the wall, then it goes back to the sky. Or if it is blue paint, then it also goes back to the sky." [Everything emerges from the absolute field of pure existence and ultimately returns to it.]

Ty recalls his past life: "Before you were born, Daddy, I went with Mama to every country." Ty also cognized his father Len's past life: "Daddy was born in Alan's belly." [Alan, the father of Ty's friend in this life, was Len's mother in Len's past life.] Ty revealed his mother Anna's past life: "You were born in Tina's belly, mama, and you talked out of her mouth. Your voice was up here [pointing to his throat]." [Tina, the mother of Ty's friend in this life, was Anna's mother in Anna's past life.] Ty explained how his grandmother and mother were connected in a past life: "Grandhoney was born in your belly, mama." [Ty's mother Anna was the mother of Grandhoney in their past lives.]

"After you die, you go back to the sky. The whiteness sees your bones, and then it gives you skin and blood. The sky gives power movement to your body. After you die, first you get alive again. [After death, you are reborn in another body.]

"If you say something to me, then your/my power movement thinks about it. [A simple, straightforward statement of fact that when we are in the human form, thinking is how we interact.] When you are in the sky, it is not 'you' that thinks about it or 'your bones' that think about it; but really, it is the sky power movement. That is how it happens. [This suggests that in the sky (before form occurs) there's only 'sky power movement,' where there is no thinking, only pure consciousness or being. 'It's just sky power movement' where thinking does not exist, since that's not a dimension where thought abides.]

"That's all I know, but I'll tell you one more thing that I was not going to tell you because I thought everyone knew: everybody is in the sky twice." Anna, his mother, then said, "So everybody is in the sky." Ty answered emphatically, "Mama! Everybody is in the sky twice." [Ty is referring to his recall of his own past life as well as remembering the past lives of his parents, Grandhoney, and Alan and Tina.]

Cultural Parallels: Evolutionary Journey

The tragic events in Sri Lanka appear to have been the trigger of three-year-old Ty's pre-birth and his own past-life memories as well as memories of the past lives of family and friends. Ty also appears to recall being one with the Source (the Sky) and his evolutionary journey as an individuated spark. At no time had Ty's parents ever taught Ty about Buddhism, reincarnation, or pre-birth existence. Len: "We were, however, in a Buddhist country, Sri Lanka, so there was exposure to Buddhism in that way." Ty's parents were deeply touched by their young son's transmission because they could feel that it was authentic.

Is it possible that a three-year-old could understand the Soul's long evolutionary journey in the same way as the mystical poet Rumi? If Ty's vocabulary had been more mature, could he have written what Rumi composed in "I Died as a Mineral"?

First into the state of mineral he came;
And then, as vegetable, ages spent, forgetting all he felt
    as mineral.
Then into the state of animal he passed, oblivious of the
    vegetable state;
Ascending thus, stage after stage, he now is man, intel-
    ligent, knowing and strong,
Yet forgetful of his previous states.
From this stage of intelligence also he has to rise,
Since it is full of greeds and clingings to small things and
    jealousies.
When he has done so, then a myriad of paths of knowl-
    edge, wonder, and great mysteries,
Will open out before him endless ... till he laughs at
    Him-Self in ecstasy.[4]

Snippets of Children's Pre-Birth Memories

*Children enjoy speaking about what it was like before
they came here.*

Children's pre-birth memories tell us that the pre-birth world is
filled with bliss and peace. Children like to remember because
it is so wonderful. A toddler's direct statements are all the more
impressive since they are just starting to speak. In this innocent
atmosphere, they feel a compelling need to talk with Mom and
Dad about their birth journey. Nine pre-birth accounts follow.

Two-year-old Chancey's matter-of-fact tone of voice was difficult to dismiss when she talked about observing her parents before
birth. Chancey drew a picture of herself as a little angelic being
flying around in the sky with three human stick figures below
and explained the drawing: "I picked you to be my mommy, and
daddy to be my daddy. I picked Rick to be my brother." Linda was
shocked and immediately telephoned Chancey's Sunday School and

asked, "Did you teach her this?" The teacher said, "No, we would not teach anything like that. That is merely Chancey's imagination."

Four-year-old Derek shared knowledge of his pre-birth memories and said: "Mommy, I was a star in the universe waiting for you and daddy to become my parents. I remember when I was in your tummy. I did not want to come out because I felt safe and warm. It felt like peace and home. I could see even in the dark." Derek's birth seems to reflect his reluctance. His head was blue when he emerged from the birth canal, and the umbilical cord was wrapped around his neck four times. The doctor cut the umbilical cord and rushed the newborn to the ICU, where daily CT scans were done to determine whether he had brain damage. Derek has had no problem and is an excellent math and science student who likes to invent.

Pre-birth memories reveal knowledge beyond what anyone has taught the child. As reported in two earlier stories, Kyle knew his mother had a miscarriage before Kyle's birth. And Catcher described Heaven and the process of reincarnation without his parents ever having used the word *Heaven* or mentioning rebirth. The case of four-year-old Jordan is equally provocative. Jordan had never visited the neighborhood where his family lived when his mother was pregnant with him. One day he pointed out, "That's our house," as he and his mother, Rani, drove through the neighborhood for his first time. Rani said, "Jordan, how do you know that's our house? You didn't live there." He said, "Yes, I did." Rani corrected him, "No, honey, only your sister lived there. You weren't born until later." He said, "I wasn't born, but I was on the other side." Rani said, "No one had ever used that phrase *on the other side* around Jordan. He just knew."

Five-year-old son Eric said something profound one day— "something a five-year-old would not ordinarily have heard of, much less been able to speak about with such depth." His mother Ritamarie responded and asked, "How do you know that?" Eric replied, "I learned that in Baby School." His mother asked, "You've been to preschool and soon you'll go to kindergarten. What's Baby

School?" Eric asserted himself and replied, "Baby School is where we all go to school when we are in our mommy's tummy. My teacher was the heart."

As another illustration, the mother of three-year-old Steven and two-year-old Amy consistently witnessed the children's peculiar conversations as they played during evening bath time. Steven and Amy reminded each other about the big angels and little fairies who were "cute and had pretty colors" and lived in the place the children had come from.

Lynn's six-year-old son felt frustrated one day and told his mother why. Jason recounted his birth: "I came into my body too fast. I felt confused. I wasn't ready to be born." Lynn realized he was describing what had happened at his delivery. The umbilical cord was damaged and the midwife pushed on Lynn's uterus to speed up the process. Jason also shared his first thoughts: "When I looked at your face, I thought, 'What's going on here? The last time I saw this person she was my cousin and she was a boy.'"

One more aspect of a child's sensitivity is tuning in to children waiting to be born, as two cases illustrate. Inelia was puzzled by her three-year-old Mark as she was getting him ready for bed. He said, "There's a little boy in our yard. I was talking to him earlier." Inelia asked, "What did he say?" Mark replied, "He hasn't been born yet. He's waiting for his mommy and daddy to be ready. They live in one of these houses [nearby]."

Two-and-a-half-year-old Jeremy made a surprise announcement: "We could have a baby, Mommy; a little girl." "Really?" his mom replied. "Yeah, soon," he said. Jeremy's "telegram from her daughter's Soul" was Nancy's spark for a third child. Three weeks before delivery, Jeremy expounded on his sibling waiting in the wings: "Mommy, you will have a little girl. Her name will be Sheila, and she'll have orange hair." Nancy had a red-haired little girl. Jeremy called her Sheila, so the family honored that.

The Azure Palace: A Story for Children

*Pre-birth memories remind us of The Blue Bird.⁵ Here
we offer an adaptation of Maurice Maeterlinck's play,
considered the Peter Pan of his time.*

An ancient legend says a wise queen known as the Great Mother
watches over the world's unborn children. She dwells in a kingdom full of love, beauty, and harmony. Within her vast realm lies an
Azure Palace with thirty thousand halls housing countless children.
Many of her royal children left long ago to rule their own king-
doms. Those who remain behind are the children not yet ready to
leave Home. One child will be born in twelve more years; another,
in fifty years, four months, and nine days. Before their departure,
they devise the inventions, tools, and instruments they will use on
Earth. One child is designing a way to bring pure joy to people
through music. Another is creating thirty-three medicines to pro-
long life. Yet a third child wants to eliminate injustice.

The children choose parents and look forward to entering Earth's
school. At appointed times, the Great Mother summons the children whose turn it is to be born. As the little ones descend to Earth,
they cry out, "Earth! How beautiful and bright it is!" In response,
they hear a distant song of gladness and expectation coming from
the Earth below—the sweet song of the mothers coming to meet
them.

The Great Mother's heart melts as she watches her offspring
move out into the universe. In her love and mercy, she has granted
two gifts—an angel to watch over them, and temporary amnesia so
they will set forth with eagerness. She knows that when their memory awakens, they will find their way back Home.

CHAPTER 2

Memories of the Cosmic Cradle

Man is a stream whose source is hidden.
Our being is descending into us from we know not
whence.
—RALPH WALDO EMERSON

*Imagine that we exist in the Mind of God, as little more
than red blood cells swimming in an infinite ocean,
orchestrated by a higher intelligence. Just as a red blood
cell is part of our body, we share part of a universal
wholeness beyond ordinary perception.*

CHAPTER 2 PRESENTS PRE-BIRTH MEMORIES as told by four mothers with deeper insights into who they are and where they came from. Ever since childhood, they retained memories of their pre-existence as pure Souls. They realize that they are multidimensional beings coming from an infinite Source, and act in more loving ways to themselves, to others, and to the world.

Pre-birth memories serve as messengers of a place where only love and oneness exist. Our birthright is to remember our non-physical existence as love, joy, and awareness. Francine, whose story appears in this chapter, considers her pre-birth memory of a profound love that permeated the universe as a gift: "It was as if my pre-mortal Mother was preparing me for a journey and, to be sure there was no mistake or confusion, gave me the one thing that would be sure to bring me back to Her—the memory of pre-existence."[1]

Soul Born in Response to Collective Call for Help

Inelia has been sent to Earth on a specific mission from the highest intelligence.

Inelia Benz describes herself as an ascension coach, etheric warrior, and a light worker who was born in 1966 as a direct response to humanity's plea for divine intervention. She is a rare individual, born with gifted abilities and high consciousness. Even more surprising is that Inelia has not come alone—"slightly over one thousand" high beings like Inelia have also come directly from Source to raise the vibratory rate of humanity. Inelia says, "There are also millions here to raise the vibrational level of the planet. They come from all sorts of dimensions, planets, and states of being." Inelia's blissful nature is a constant companion even though her life has not been easy in many ways.

Inelia was virtually unknown until 2009, when she was directed by Source to go public and share her unique story. She had not been on the public stage before and was trying to figure out what going public meant. Even though earthly life was a bit strange to her, Inelia quickly set up a website, Ascension101.com, and began sharing her life's purpose, and today, millions have become acquainted with her global efforts.

An elevated being such as Inelia comes for one purpose and merges back into the divine, Nonsingularity, when their mission is over. Inelia explains Source: "The best description I can give for Source is 'Light and Love'. It is the best description because there are no human words, or expression, that can truly describe Source. We are simply too limited in awareness! If you can imagine a light beyond light, which at the same time is love beyond love, that would describe it better."

Inelia's pre-birth memory is one-of-a-kind: "I have not had an evolutionary journey for personal or Divine Consciousness evolution or experience either before or after this singular life existence.

The best description I can make of beings such as myself are 'soul constructs' designed very much like a program, or application, in computers: specific jobs to do, and then dissolve back into nonbeingness. Soul constructs have no attachment to being or existing, or evolving like other human Souls. In fact, there is an added subprogram, and that is a 'rejection of singular existence' of all levels of singular awareness, including being aware at a Divine Consciousness level, the first singular construct. This subprogram was probably added to keep us focused on the work, and not get distracted with attachments of survival, evolution, or experience."

First Thought and Repairing a Baby's Body

Inelia describes her peculiar Soul journey of descending through multiple vibratory levels of existence until arriving at her birth: "My full journey was from Nonsingularity, to Divine Conscious Awareness Singularity, to Universal Consciousness, to Sentient Collective Singularity, to Species Specific Singularity, to Human Collective Singularity, to Singular Human. Never identifying with any of them, as they are all illusions."

Inelia had her first conscious thought half an hour before birth. She describes how she entered this time-space reality matrix at the Singular Human level: "I actually came in just before the baby was born. As a singular entity, I had a job to do, almost like a program in a computer. When this happened, I had a sense of being a singular entity in a human body. After that, my point of awareness was flying over the surface of the sea, then into a city, a building with lights, and a room where a birthing was taking place. I could see the body intelligence waiting for the body to separate from the mother's body. The baby's body was meant to die a few minutes after birth.

"I have no recollections of anything before then. I imagine that there was a human Soul, and it interacted with the body and the parents before I came in, and I have no information on it. I had no awareness of choosing parents; at the same time, I have a knowing that my particular body was chosen due to its genetic material coming from two psychic lineages.

"We requested the body to stay. I speak of 'we' because up until I joined with the body, I did not have a personal identity, a singularity. So it felt like a 'we' asking the question. Once I entered the body, I became 'I' and no longer 'we.' When I try to pierce the 'we' identity, it feels vast. When trying to identify it, saying it was the human collective, or Gaia, or Source, feels limited. It was almost all combined, like a 'knowing' rather than a 'being.'

"The body was asked to do one more life in this form in order to house me. The body was reluctant, as it was done with its evolutionary journey, and was also battle weary, yet it agreed out of a sense of duty. The body was then 'fixed' enough to house a Soul; it had heart and liver problems. The body was also made lighter, slightly less dense on a DNA level. The body had to vibrate at a higher rate so it would not burn up. After that, I watched the body being born, and joined with it as it took its first breath.

"That was my first sense of singularity. I then became an 'I' rather than a 'we.' My body was like a hundred-million-dollar racehorse, and I was like somebody who had never ridden a horse before! It took a while for the body to get through to me that it was not a computer, not something to be programmed by me. We learned to function together. We are not our bodies, yet our bodies resonate very closely with our Souls. And we work and evolve together very well."

Inelia's entire life has focused on learning to function within human parameters and to communicate to others. Her global mission means she is on call 24/7 to help deal with emergencies anywhere on Earth. Inelia is involved in two types of Light work: to help people raise their own vibration, and to inhibit negative people who interfere with the efforts to raise the planetary vibration.

First Memories of Coming from Source

Inelia briefly panicked at the age of three when she began to realize her peculiar history: "As a child I knew that all the explanations of where I came from did not resonate with me, although I had no words to explain where I came from. As a young adult I even tried previous-life regressions and got some hits. Even so, they were not my Soul's. Some were my physical body elemental's previous experiences, and others were experiences of those people near me. One of the interesting aspects of the dissonance is that all singularities, whether they have had an evolutionary journey or not, also come from Source, and their trajectory in linear time is an illusion.

"The realization that my soul construct had come from Source directly, and that most other people's did not, was verbalized in intellectual understanding as an adult.

"Communicating to others within that 'illusion reality' has been the most challenging of all aspects of life. It is like stepping into another person's dream, and within the dream telling them it is time to wake up. And yet in their dream, they do not remember what the phrase *wake up* means, and when they do, they dream that they wake up. In other words, the person knows they are sleeping, and then continue doing things within the dream-world rules and regulations or keep the same dream story going. So, they know they are in a dream but are more interested in how I came to enter the dream rather than waking up. They ask me, 'Where did you come from?' I tell them, 'I came from outside the dream.'

"Then they try to find ways to explain how I came to exist inside the dream. And they tell me all the ways that people came to exist within the dream. I know I just popped in. But then I try out all the ways they explain, to see if I took one of them to get in, as I might have, after all. It is a bit like when my friends and relatives convinced me that my daughter Daniela might be a boy before she was born. [No one believed Inelia's vision of a daughter before conception.] So the 'knowing' was always there, it was the words that took a while to find that explain my origin without dissonance."

Falling to Earth from the Pure Light

*Pre-birth memories fade, just as a muscle atrophies from
lack of exercise.*

Summer, a thirty-five-year-old midwestern mother of six children,
recalls: "At the age of four, I experienced several incidents of lying
in bed and telling myself, 'I must remember my birth.' Forever after,
I mentally reviewed the memory so I would not forget, somehow
recognizing its importance. Despite that, my memories did end up
becoming 'second-hand' or dormant for awhile. I did not deliberately seek to remember them, but they just popped back up and
were refreshed after I did a six-month meditation retreat. They have
been remarkably clear ever since.

Summer remembers the inner world of Light, the Cosmic Cradle: "My memory goes back to a place of pure light, intermittently
between lives. My individuality was barely audible. That is the best
way I can describe it. All my senses became unified. Everything was
one. Still, I had a subtle feeling of 'my'-ness, identity, ego, or individuality. I felt the presence of God, of not being totally one with
God, but being in God's womb, so to speak.

"I was aware of other Souls close by. It is hard to explain because
there was no space and time, only the present moment and other
Souls coming toward and going away from me. When the time
came to establish my next life, I traveled through a tunnel filled
with lights representing the laws of nature and different people. I
had an ongoing dialogue with an angel, God, an aspect of God, or
Saint Peter. It is hard to say exactly who he was. I desired to achieve
the maximum in terms of clearing up karma and reaching enlightenment. We discussed what I needed and how to achieve my purpose with certain people. I saw my goals as well as all the choices
that I could make as if I were looking at a computer board, only
the computers seemed like stars. When I saw a quality I needed to
develop, like kindness or compassion, I pressed the corresponding

light. Then in a millisecond, I witnessed a panoramic view of roads I could take with different people in order to fulfill those objectives.

"It is not as if my consciousness said, 'Give me a good life,' 'I want to be rich,' or 'I want to be pretty.' Rather it was simply, I needed to establish the quality of kindness and compassion first, then the wealth would come. I emphasized certain choices more than others. Since enlightenment was a major goal, I made a special effort toward having my meditation master. There was no other path for me. I did not allow any leeway. And nothing in this life has ever interrupted this relationship with my teacher."

As part of her life agreement, Summer planned to be born into a family with Susan as an older sister. The sisters had evolved through many lifetimes together. A Soul magnetism brought them together again. In contrast, she does not recall selecting specific parents: "Yet I do remember that my parents needed to have a deep level of spirituality that did not fit into a little cubbyhole. They needed to be yogis in their own right. As it turned out, my parents are not dogmatically religious. My mother knows greater truths than those presented in traditional Christianity. Because of Mom's openness, as a child, I could say, 'Do you remember birth, Mommy? I remember mine.' She did not ridicule my beliefs. A lot of parents do. Without this upbringing, I would not have had the same spiritual experiences as a child.

"I recall the sensation of leaving the place where I had established my life plan and the descent into matter. I traveled through space and time, which literally looked like flashing stars. It was a very fluid motion of space and time, from death to life and life to death. Obviously I did not have eyes and ears. I had nothing physical to perceive with. However my senses were in play. I became all one sense. All the senses became one, traveling through space and time and coming into the womb. So there was some entity that was myself that had these tools at its disposal.

"I remember finding myself in this physiology, of coming into my mother's womb for the first time. I knew I was going to be born, recalled former lives, and knew I was coming from an intermittent place between earthly lives. Having a body felt pleasant. I stretched out and felt my body, even my hands and fingers. I thought, 'Great, I have a physiology again.' All my body parts had formed. I felt contented. Sometimes I heard the voices and sounds outside my mother's womb—my mother, siblings, and other children playing. My parents were happy. Of seven children, I was the only child planned. I was a product of a fortunate time. That is probably why I am so happy.

"I had no concept of time, of how long I waited in the womb. At one point, a click signaled that birth was underway. I sensed a hormonal infusion into my body. I remained alert and comfortable and felt my head moving down. But just as I reached the birth canal, I suddenly could not breathe. I heard my mother's scream, 'You are going to kill my baby. Get off me.' She was upset and terrified. I thought: 'Maybe I'm not going to be born.' I felt lackadaisical and consciously left my body. It was a gentle and slow pulling away from the body. There was a different sensual aspect to being out of the body, hovering above my mother on the table. But then, with a quick snap, I was, wham, right back in really fast. I thought, 'Well, I am going to be born.' I felt a burst of cool air on my face. An overwhelming coldness hit my body, and a rush of cold air entered my lungs. If I close my eyes right now, I can see the delivery room: the angle of the bed, the angle of the birth coming out, how the doctor lifted me, and the direction I faced. I looked around and saw the doctors and attendants, but their features were blurred. They wore hospital outfits without the surgical masks. Everyone appeared red. Yet there was no red lighting in the room. Maybe pressure on my eyes caused the redness or it came from opening my eyes for the first time. Since I was blue at birth—barely there—it may have been due to lack of oxygen.

"I saw everyone's face except mother's. The doctors had put my mother out [anesthesia]. I only remember that she was conscious until my birth. The nurses pulled me out into the cold, wrapped me up, and put me in the nursery. I felt a yearning, a sad feeling of being alone, a cold feeling in my heart. I did not know why I felt emotionally out of sorts. I did not really understand 'mother' yet."

Summer had questions about her birth. "When I was twenty-two, I told my mother, 'I heard you screaming and wondered why. I thought doctors put women out cold so they could not feel the pain.' Mom explained, 'I was not put under until right after the birth. I was screaming because the nurse sat on my knees and held my legs together, trying to slow down delivery. The hospital had blamed another nurse for delivering a stillborn by herself the day before. So this nurse became frightened when I began to deliver before the doctor arrived. I frantically fought her off.'

"Now I finally understood my birth. The umbilical cord had gotten pinched and interrupted my oxygen supply. I also had wondered why the doctors did not wear masks. Mom explained that the staff didn't have time to put on masks due to my fast delivery.

"A slow process of forgetting of my memories took place once I became a baby and part of this world. I grew out of the awareness that the whole universe is inside of me. My memory of other lifetimes gradually faded. Even so, I have never had any doubt that life is eternal. I was never without that feeling, the knowledge that you are reborn again and again. Death is an embracing thing—going back to God. The spiritual world is my real Home."

Today Summer is happily married and a fulfilled mother: "My memories are a gift. My traumatic birth was a set-up. And the set-up worked. I am glad I experienced it that way. My memories enriched the births of my children and inspired me to be a more sensitive mother. I knew that I was giving birth to an alert, conscious individual. Babies come in very wise, aware of past lives, and aware of what they are coming in for. But then within a few months, they lose this wisdom and become giggly, innocent, charming little babies."

Memory of Unlimited Possibilities

A toddler pined for the lost talents she had as a "super being" in her prelife.

Judy, a forty-five-year-old spiritual author, meditation teacher, and mother of two children, feels more "at home" in the upper dimensions and longs to return there. She reminisces, "Since I was three years old, I maintained the strong feeling that I did not belong to this physical plane. I never felt comfortable and did not enjoy the earthly pleasures like those around me. Every material thing became a disillusionment. I gradually learned to pretend interest and attraction to things so as not to seem odd.

"As I grew up I felt something was really wrong and was always alert to discovering the nature of my true origin. I could not believe how limited I was as a child. I knew from direct memory that in the past I was capable of unlimited potential, abilities known as *siddhis.* I was stumped as to why these abilities were not working as a child. It was very confusing. I wasn't sure if I was living a dream. I couldn't figure out reality. My memory was so strong. I knew what I was experiencing wasn't right. No one else seemed concerned. As far back as I can remember, I wondered: 'Why is it that we can't get what we desire immediately?' 'Why can't we walk through walls?' 'Why can't we levitate?' 'Why is this body so cumbersome?' 'Why can't I just flow through a room?' 'Why do I have to walk and bump into things?' 'Why is there pain?'

"Everyone else seemed comfortable with the way things were. I wondered, 'Is this a nightmare?' I felt like I was in a zoo with people who were happy in not questioning anything. I was three years old. I had this kind of thinking. Of course, I was not to the point where I could articulate: 'Well, mommy, why is this so weird?' I never verbalized, but I thought about it the whole time. I was confused and distraught.

"I was always amazed about how much emphasis there was on possession of material goods among my family and outside my family, too. I never got it. I felt it was a a cheap imitation of what I knew to be a thrill. I remember playing with a child who was thrilled with a toy ferris wheel. For me it would have been much more exciting to manifest a Christmas tree instead of buy one. Or why have a toy plane when you are used to flying through the air yourself?

"As a child, taking possession of things felt wrong or artificial: 'You mean I'm supposed to be happy because this toy is mine and not yours?' It made no sense because I didn't understand ownership. I felt like I owned everything and everybody else owned everything.

"Years went by. I never ran into anyone else who let on that there was anything wrong. I felt very much the loner. I got used to feeling like an alien. It was not until I started meditating and meeting people who knew what consciousness was that I was given the vocabulary to express my reality. This was in my late twenties. I resonated with teachings about higher consciousness because almost literally, that was my experience. I became friends with twelve people who also shared the same enlightened reality. Those connections made all the difference in the world. Here I was, thirty years old, and finally realizing I was not the only one on the planet who felt very alone.

"My life still does not match the memory I came in with of having this unlimited potential and using it. But I have picked up some understanding of why. This is a different dimension than the one I came from and so I feel at peace with that. I know that different dimensions have their own challenges, obstacles, and limitations. So as an adult, I am okay with it. But I still wonder, 'Why did I come here?' There is still some veil. I am still puzzled over that. I have forgotten why I have chosen this. I am not quite sure what this mission is. I trust there is a reason. I have learned to enjoy without knowing all the answers."

Cultural Parallels: Pre-Birth Super Powers

Judy's pre-birth memory of supernormal abilities parallels the abilities of the "between-being" or "intermediate being" described in Tibetan Buddhism. The interlife being exists between "the being in the dying state" and "the being in the state of being born."[2] Interlife beings possess heightened intelligence, extraordinary powers of concentration, flexibility to become whatever can be imagined, and super abilities such as clairvoyance and the ability to travel wherever they wish by mere intention.[3]

Tethered to Divine Love

Francine understands the healing power of pre-birth memory.

Francine, a sixty-year-old grandmother, has known her entire life that she pre-existed in a non-physical world of indescribable love and it awaits her return Home: "My very first thought was being suspended in outer space, in darkness, like a vacuum. I was surrounded by love. This love was monumental, dense, and complete.

"An all absorbing thought—*I AM*—came to my awareness and captured my attention. I was only aware of my existence as Consciousness. I was only aware that 'I AM' I had no perception of time, but if I had to put it into context of what we know as time, it seemed like years or even longer, an eternity. I had no sensory experiences of sight, smell, touch, taste, or hearing. I just floated as if suspended in space or in a void; there was no feeling of a body. I became the 'I AM. It became part of me. 'I AM.'

"Then an outside feminine voice spoke to my consciousness saying: 'Remember this; it is very important because by remembering this, you will find your way back.' The loving voice told me this several times; I soaked in everything I could.

"At one point, I became aware that others around me off in the distance had some interest in me—like people interested in seeing someone's new baby. I was aware of them, and they were aware of me. Then I returned back to being totally by myself again; next thing I knew, I was a little girl.

"When I was three or four, I heard the voice again, 'Remember that place; it is important.' It was very soft, calm, and gentle telepathy. I concentrated on every detail of what that place was like and practiced remembering it whenever the Voice reminded me. Later on, when I was ten years old, the voice said, 'Remember the place; you will become busy in life and forget. Later on, you will remember it again.' After I got married at eighteen and started raising a family, I did not think about it for a long time.

"My memories puzzled me as a child. When I was brave enough, I told Mom. She did not understand. Later my Catholic priest said, 'Don't talk like that.' No one could give an explanation. The subject was taboo. When I checked with the Protestants, they said, 'We don't know what that is.' I finally got an explanation when I contacted the Latter-day Saints. I was forty-five.

"I see a continuing thread as a result of my memory. That voice continues to advise me telepathically. That is what happened in 1984. My husband said, 'If we're going to have more children, we need to have them soon.' After birthing Paul, who had been eleven pounds, I resisted, and thought, 'I'll gain thirty pounds again, and childbirth isn't any fun.' At the same time, every night as I tried to sleep, a message kept coming: 'A child is waiting.' I said, 'Let it wait.' After this continued for a year, I made a deal. 'Okay, I will give you three months. If I am not pregnant by then, you can give the baby to somebody else.' I had the IUD taken out and immediately became pregnant. Nine months later my son Robert joined our family, along with our seven-year-old daughter and six-year-old son."

Paul Waves Good-Bye

Doctors initially counseled Francine about her autistic eldest son, "Paul will never walk, talk, or be a useful human being." For years

Francine and her husband cared for Paul, an all-consuming responsibility: "Paul was the love of my life. He was the sweetest, most loving being in the world; such a high, pure love. He would run up to me with a big kiss, sit in my lap, giggling and laughing and hugging me so tight."

By the time Paul was fourteen, he was living in a group home for children with special needs. One day at the end of a visit, Francine waved good-bye to Paul as usual. "Paul looked up with a beautiful smile and waved. Never once in his whole life had Paul ever lifted his arm and waved back to me. I waved three times, and each time Paul waved back.

"Three days later, I had a premonition on my way to visit Paul. The voice advised, 'Don't go.' I thought, 'Okay, maybe my visit might upset Paul since it is so close to bed time.' I headed home. Minutes later I received a call. Paul had been taken to the hospital. Paramedics were screaming in the background. By the time I arrived, I saw 'Full Arrest' on the EMT log. His doctor said, 'We tried everything.' Despite the grief, I felt a protection, a buffer. The voice had prepared me beforehand to soften the blow.

"If I had gone to visit Paul that night, I would have interfered with God's plan. I would have gotten him to the hospital quicker, and they may have saved him. God gave Paul the ability to wave good-bye on my last visit as a confirmation that his leaving is part of His plan. That's the way God chose to take Paul home. My son fulfilled his purpose."

On the loss of her autistic son, Francine became an advocate for disabled children and organized a parents' support group. Perhaps this was the gift that her son's loss brought to the world. Without the loss, none of this would have happened.

"Paul's passing allowed us to concentrate our love and support on our youngest son, a very troubled Soul. Robert's challenges began at thirteen: alcohol, drugs, DWIs, jail. Now twenty-eight, he has three children out of wedlock. My husband often asks, 'Why have we had these problems with Robert? We have prayed for him and helped him start three businesses.' I tell him, 'It is the will of God. It is God's job to do. Our job is to pray and let God do his wonders.' Today Robert is serving a short-term jail sentence and has discovered his gift in life: drawing. He feels he is beginning to learn his lessons."

The Voice Said, "Walk"

"A few years ago, my doctor told me, 'You have a four-inch tumor on your right ovary.' I knew, 'This is not permanent.' I felt an unusual peace and calm. After surgery, I overheard the doctor say, 'This is a fifty-seven-year-old woman with stage 3 ovarian cancer.' Again, I felt engulfed in peace. I heard the voice say, 'Don't worry about it.' Sure enough, ten days later, the doctor said, 'Your pathology report indicates that it was stage 1 and curable. When you complete treatment, your cancer will be gone.'

"I walked in for my last chemo in March 2010. The radiation damaged the nerves in my spinal column, and I could not walk afterward. I became frustrated with my lack of progress after nineteen months in physical therapy. My doctor recommended, 'Increase physical therapy to three times or more per week; after four months, you may see improvement.' I asked, 'What about walking again?' He replied, 'I don't hold much hope for that.'

"I did not increase my physical therapy. Two weeks later, I heard the voice say, 'Walk!' The voice said, 'You can walk.' I felt an electric charge, a healing energy, throughout my body. I walked from one end of the kitchen to the other without holding onto anything. I sat down to rest and walked around the house several times.

"Today, six months later, I am getting better and better. I walk independently half of the time and rely on a cane or a power chair the rest of the time. My rehab specialists are amazed. My inner strength comes from my ties to my pre-birth memory. I could not have coped with all the trials of this life without knowledge and belief in a Higher Power. I approach problems with love rather than lashing out in anger. What do I call this entity, this voice? I don't know. It has been with me my entire life, and I feel it every day. I feel peace and happiness every time I remember. This is the way I will eventually find my way back Home. I trust and have faith that God is all-powerful."

Parallels: The Void

Francine's pre-birth memories are similar to the crystal clear consciousness of the after-death realm as reported in near-death experiences (NDE). During an NDE, a person is instantly thrust into a higher spiritual awareness due to being "clinically dead." The individual perceives that his awareness is separate from his body. He can still think, feel, and sense, and recalls his personal identity and life circumstance.

Francine's "I AM" experience and being suspended in darkness, like a vacuum, mirrors NDE reports cited in Dr. Raymond Moody's research:[4]

* ❀ I was in an utterly black dark void. I felt as if I was moving in a vacuum.
* ❀ I was so taken up with this void that I did not think of anything else.
* ❀ This was the most wonderful, worry-free experience you can imagine.
* ❀ There was a feeling of utter peace and quiet, no fear at all.

CHAPTER 3

"I Was in Your Tummy Twice"

◡

IS REINCARNATION REAL?

For are we indeed old wine, having brought the
flavor with us from many past incarnations. Each
lifetime, however, presents us with a new body, a
new environment to work with—a new wineskin.
—GLADYS T. MCGAREY, MD[1]

*A toddler's memories challenge whether a brain is
essential for memory.*

A s a precocious toddler, Elizabeth shared memories
with Lezlie because she wanted to get something off her
chest about the rocky journey to birth. Elizabeth's memories popped up out of the blue as her mother, Lezlie, listened carefully to past events, including a miscarriage. The toddler spoke as if she had been an eyewitness. At first, Lezlie was surprised because Elizabeth was too young to have heard about the miscarriage. Elizabeth's words came as a revelation and explained why a baby boy had died three years earlier.

One Soul, Two Bodies

*Today, at twenty-eight, Elizabeth shares her memories of
the rebirth.*

Elizabeth's Soul was hanging out in the fetus that suddenly perished: "Mom was taking a shower. She had her hands on her head shampooing her hair. The last thing I saw was her looking down at me; then I went down the drain. I did not feel pain. I remember the strong thump of hitting the shower floor, shaking everything within my core. I recall falling out of her body in slow motion and the emptiness and vastness. I felt exposed, no longer being in the womb, feeling unprotected. The drain was dark; it slowly started closing up, and at that point, I died. Everything stopped. I ceased to have awareness of that experience.

"The miscarriage explains why I did not like to hear the toilet flushing when I was young. That sound triggered memory of going down the drain. I asked Mom to flush the toilet, or I freaked out and ran once I flushed the toilet. And to this day, I will not step on a drain. If I take a shower at the beach, I wear shoes. I also prefer baths to showers. I recognize where this comes from. Mom did not discredit my memory. Otherwise I might have found myself as a strange person with this phobia, trying to cope with it, not knowing what it was.

"As soon as I could speak, I made a matter-of-fact, casual statement to my mother, 'I was in your tummy twice. The first time, I washed away. The second time, I came out like a zipper. I was a boy, and I decided to come back as a girl.' Mom had done studies in past life therapies and was open to someone being able to remember.

"As my vocabulary grew, I could articulate what happened and the intent behind the miscarriage. I was aware that my parents got into a huge fight about whether to circumcise the baby in the womb if it was a boy. I knew that I was a boy. Neither Mom nor Dad would compromise their opposing positions. This issue threatened their marriage, and I needed them to stay together to fulfill what I came here to do. So I chose to leave."

Elizabeth explains why she felt impelled to share her memories with her mother at an age when most toddlers are playing with toys: "Often when a woman has a miscarriage, she feels it is because there is something wrong with her, that her body was not capable, or that she had done something wrong, ate the wrong food, etcetera. I did not want Mom to think the miscarriage was her fault. I needed to let her know that I had made the decision to leave and come back. I felt Mom's relief when I told her."

Soul Triggers Miscarriage and Rebirth

Elizabeth describes the heated argument between her parents as if the Soul was in the tiny twelve-week-old fetus: "I heard every word, and I felt the emotion it stirred in them. I want to claim I was there in the room; however, that is unclear. The strongest part of their argument was the emotion. Emotion overrode everything else. A pregnancy that had been filled with love and joy was suddenly rocked with fear and pain. I did not take sides. I knew this issue threatened their marriage. My mother was probably thinking of divorce. I may have seen that alternative timeline open up. Or maybe I sensed the universe reworking itself regardless of Mom's thinking. In any case, I could not risk a divorce. My Soul's plan was with these parents, and my future was threatened. After the argument, I questioned how events might unfold. I second-guessed the course Mom and Dad would take as a couple. I had to make a quick decision or else it would interfere with my Soul's plans. Mom miscarried the next day.

"I always told Mom, 'I left and came back.' One challenge was my window of opportunity to leave without changing everything. The decision needed to happen right away. I am glad that my parents' fight occurred early in the pregnancy. Otherwise I would have been committed to birth as a boy. My parents would have divorced before they changed their minds about circumcision."

Formless Form Spirit Guide

If Elizabeth stayed to be born as a boy, she risked a divorce and losing the set of parents that she needed. A divine planner helped Elizabeth decide the next course of action: "A Formless Form counseled me about my options. When I say I counseled with 'a Formless Form,' that divine energy did not have boundaries. The divine energy did not need a physical form to have an identity, a uniqueness, or a self. This energy was in front of me, inside of me. Even so, it was not me. I perceived it as distinct and personal, a direct communication without words—telepathy.

"Counseling with the Formless Form was a formality. A time limit existed for choosing what I wanted to do. I was presented options to be born to the same parents or to opt out. The Formless Form showed me five choices in grading order, such as A, B, C, D. My choices were A++, B, B, B, and C. In my case, whom I chose as my parents was a no-brainer. Mom and Dad were my A++, my absolute first choice because only this particular couple could provide what I needed, not what I wanted. I had other choices, but I never gave them any consideration.

"My choice was not based on material satisfaction: 'Where am I going to have the happiest home?' 'Where will I have all of my needs taken care of?' My decision was based on the spiritual growth and fulfillment I needed and for setting the foundation to become whatever I will become in this world or something spiritual later on. The decision was one hundred percent mine. I had my own idea of what I wanted to become. And it was crucial that this set of parents raise me."

Meeting My Unborn Sister

After Elizabeth made her decision to come back as a girl, she met her future sister in the spiritual realm. "I remember the presence of another being waiting to be born. She appeared as a five-year-old child. She needed to be a second child with an older sibling. That limitation was based on the way she needed to be raised. Irritated with me, she was to be born as my younger sister. In retrospect, I suspect she was ticked off since she needed to wait three more years to be born. She had to adjust her plans accordingly. I messed her up—it was a timing issue. I felt bad that my choice set back the

process for my sister. The doctor advised my mom to wait one year after the miscarriage before getting pregnant again. I was born as a girl in 1984 rather than as a boy in 1981. If I had been born in 1981, my sister could have been born in 1983 rather than 1986. She was born twenty months after me. Because my sister was born behind schedule, there was a strange animosity between us until recently, as if I owed her something."

From the Blissful Womb to Breech to Caesarian Trauma

Elizabeth recalls fetal life in Lezlie's second pregnancy: "I was completely aware of everything going on for the entire nine months. I heard voices and Mom and Dad talking to me. I felt their love. I knew when my time in the womb was growing short, and I was not ready. I always told Mom that it was one hundred percent my fault that she went into labor seventeen days late. I needed a specific birth date for astrological reasons.

"Six hours into labor, I made a decision to flip and became breech. Perhaps I was trying to hold onto that blissful experience of being in the womb. As a result, I was born via an emergency C-section. That is why I told my mother, 'I came out like a zipper.'

"Coming out via C-section forced me into a shock, a traumatic jolt. I sensed the doctor cut Mom's stomach. Blinding light came in and the slit became larger and larger, like opening a curtain on a bright, sunny morning. A cool draft invaded my space. I felt exposed and cold. I had a feeling of abduction as my body was grabbed and handled. The feeling was a different vibrational level compared to the blissful womb."

Sensitivity in the Womb

Elizabeth's sensitivity to Lezlie's feelings during the argument is supported by medical findings. Leading physicians and researchers in prenatal and perinatal medicine and psychology support fetal sensitivity to the mother's emotions and thoughts. Research findings over the last forty years have revealed such awareness in the growing fetus. A number of researchers have published books on prenatal awareness.

* David Chamberlain, PhD: "Although prenates have never been acknowledged for their psychic senses, they do demonstrate at least clairvoyance and telepathic sensing and attunement with parents whether they are near or far from each other; they know whether they are wanted or not, and discern the emotional disposition, and character of those around them."[2]

* Dr. Thomas Verny: "Evidently the child's emotional radar is so sharp that even the slightest tremors of maternal emotion register with him."[3]

* Dr. Gladys McGarey reports cases of miscarriages where a fetus senses its mother's difficulties and decides to depart, then returns in a later pregnancy when the mother's life is smoother.[4]

* Wendy Anne McCarty, PhD: a Soul-like transcendent awareness operates before and after conception. "One of the most powerful understandings and frequently reported findings in the prenatal and perinatal clinical literature is the ability we have from preconception on to perceive information about our parents ... that appears holographic ... including all levels of the parent's being—conscious, subconscious, unconscious, super conscious ... and memories."[5]

Childhood Dreams of Rainbow Child

"I made the right choice in returning to be born to my parents. For the first eight years, they provided a loving, nurturing home and did everything they could to cater to me. They gave me anything I needed to explore my desires. I loved everything and jumped from one infatuation to another. Mom called me a 'Rainbow Child.' An important part of my path was to learn about everything I explored, academically as well as spiritually. Dad was a student of Transcendental Meditation and Mom was a student of past-life therapy. I was not born into a specific dogma. I have a broad understanding of spirituality and the nature of God and the human condition because of the way my parents raised me. My eyes were opened at an early age to subjects not taught in school.

"Dad exposed me to political and social topics that a child does not need to be exposed to. We had a competitive relationship. He challenged me to intellectual debates. I loved it. That's how I learned to challenge my teachers. When my fourth grade teacher gave me an assignment, I said, 'Can we renegotiate? Can I read this other book instead?'"

Elizabeth's childhood became less than ideal in her preteens. "Dad became involved in drugs. He is a Vietnam vet and was a Green Beret Special Forces medic. He served two tours and saw the worst of the worst and suffered severe post–traumatic stress disorder. So our family life became rough. By the time I was fourteen, I worked to help pay rent. Given that it was not easy, there was lots of growth. And I do not feel resentment or anger, as shoddy as my life was for many years. I am grateful. That experience made me who I am today.

"I am not bogged down by the dogma of the educational system or society telling me who I should be and what I should do. I broke out of that conditioning in high school. I was hospitalized for two months with viral meningitis in my freshman year. The high school did not cut me any slack when I missed a midterm. I hated high school, and it took little convincing for Mom to yank me out. So I home-schooled myself. I acquired all the credits at a quicker pace. I graduated at sixteen and started college. I wanted to study the cosmos. I wanted to find God through science. My plan was to get a PhD in astrophysics."

Parents' Divorce

"Meanwhile, I began to face painful circumstances at home. Dad became disabled and in pain. He coped with his PTSD the best way he could. He became suicidal. My parents divorced when I was sixteen. Dad has got help now, and we are the best of pals: a lesson in forgiveness, tolerance, patience, and lessons I am still working on. My parents' divorce was a key to my development. I dropped out of college because Dad was in the hospital and I worked to support our family. Plus I met my future husband at that time and became involved in studying subjects like martial arts.

"I have enough credits for two college degrees. I have a hard time with the system because it fails to teach us how to think critically. Instead it teaches input-output response, how to answer questions. This is what molds people. I would not gain much from that other than a piece of paper that says, 'You can follow the rules.' My parents shaped me into who I am. I lost my innocence at an early age and am a better person because of it. I saw the world for what it was earlier than most children who live in a bubble and go to high school with the prom being the most exciting thing in their lives. I started working at twelve and have worked for the last sixteen years."

Today, twenty-eight-year-old Elizabeth and her husband are excited about starting a family. "We have been visited by our future children already. Knowing from personal experience that a baby is conscious from the moment it is conceived will affect what I do during pregnancy and how I treat our children. What a pregnant woman exposes herself to is important. I will follow my mother's lead. She did not watch intense movies or horror movies. She knew a baby is aware and feels whatever the mother feels.

"My pre-birth memories are deeply rooted within me. They are my strongest memories. I cannot deny them. Even when I explored Christianity for a while, I reconciled my memories the best I could. I did not give them up because they are true."

Elizabeth also retains memories of infancy: "My parents moved a lot, and I can describe the houses we lived in when I was three months old, six months old, and eighteen months old. I have been diagnosed with dyscalculia—the left and right hemispheres of my brain are not separated. The direct link of the brain's hemispheres gives incredible memory and ability to retain information. Today, if I make a conscious mental note of something, I remember."

From a spiritual angle, Elizabeth is likely an old Soul who brought to her life deeper insights into her evolution. Elizabeth sought parents with specific qualities to fulfill lessons she needed to learn on Earth, and sharing pre-life memories has been a vital part of her Soul's journey. Elizabeth had thirteen out of the fifteen common elements of a pre-birth memory as noted in the Introduction and in chapter 1: self-awareness, eternal, feeling at Home, Soul families, telepathy, divine planner, preview, interest in human experience, awareness in fetus, no fear of death, matter-of-fact tone of voice, consistency over time, and knowledge beyond experience.

Elizabeth's memories lead us to question the relationship between brain function and memory. The biological basis for pre-life memories is a scientific mystery because clearly such memories indicate that no human brain is necessary. We need to look into our deepest core, the field of consciousness, for answers.

Confirmation of Pre-Birth and Rebirth Memories

Pre-life memories are controversial and poorly accepted. Accounts where mothers validate a child's memories are the most convincing.

Lezlie had a clear psychic vision before she became pregnant at twenty-four: a little blond-haired boy with his sister two or three years younger. Lezlie intuited that children were part of her destiny despite the challenges that began as early as her own fetal life: "I was born as a three-month preemie. I was a DES daughter: my mother took the hormone diethylstilbestrol (DES) when she was pregnant with me to reduce the risk of miscarriage. Side effects occurred in numerous DES daughters. So there were no guarantees I could bear children when I became pregnant. Dr. Anderson, an obstetrician specialist, closely monitored my pregnancy. I had menstrual spotting and nothing more serious.

"Then, twelve weeks into the pregnancy, while showering and shampooing my hair, I felt something fall out from between my legs. I saw a white blob go down the drain. I thought, 'That's the baby.' I heard the fetus hit the shower floor with a clear 'thud.' It was two and a half inches long. I had no pain or cramping. Dr. Anderson confirmed the miscarriage and performed a D and C to prevent infection in November 1981. Dr. Anderson cautioned me, 'Wait a year before becoming pregnant again.'"

Unlike miscarriages involving shock, grief, anger, and guilt, Lezlie's miscarriage was less traumatic: "I felt initial disappointment. I didn't know whether the miscarriage was because I was a DES baby or because there was something wrong with the fetus. In the end, I sensed the miscarriage did not happen by accident, and I consoled myself with the thought, 'Nature takes care of something when it is not right.' I moved forward with my life knowing that I would get pregnant when conditions were more favorable."

As the months passed, Lezlie had a psychic vision: "Two girls close in age, long hair, light coloring, and big eyes appeared in my mind's eye. They were committed to being together in this lifetime." While shopping one day, Lezlie fell in love with a statue of two little cherubim holding hands. She purchased the figurine, put it on their bedroom dresser, and humorously told her husband, "These are our girls."

A year after the miscarriage, Lezlie's doctor gave the okay for a second pregnancy. When she and her husband were ready, Lezlie had a telepathic conversation with the unborn child: "We have moved into a bigger home. Dad's work is settled. Now is an opportunity to come back. I am ovulating. My window is open. Meet me in the bedroom now." Lezlie recalls: "I had no trouble conceiving that day and knew it was the same Spirit in my womb. I suspected a girl because of my vision of the two girls holding hands. I never saw the little boy again."

Lezlie's pregnancy culminated in the birth of a healthy baby girl in January 1984. Elizabeth began to walk and talk at an early age: "Since Elizabeth was teeny-weeny, she told me unprompted, 'Oh, yeah, Mom, I was in your tummy twice. The first time I washed away. The second time, I came out like a zipper.' I had never mentioned the miscarriage to her.

"Later, when Elizabeth was seven, the subject came up about losing the first baby. We were driving through Coronado, a part of the city Elizabeth had not been to before. As we passed the Coronado Bridge, Elizabeth pointed out an inconspicuous building and said, 'I was in that building.' I replied, 'That was the building where my doctor's office was when I was pregnant with you the first time.' Elizabeth said, 'I remember the miscarriage, Mom. That was me. I was a boy, and you and dad had a fight. I chose to leave and come back as a girl.' Her memory blew me away. How did she know about the fight the day before the miscarriage? I knew exactly what she was talking about."

Lezlie describes the disagreement and why it happened: "I had done extensive past-life training and regression work. I knew the fetus and a newborn are aware. I was determined that our child's birth be mellow and peaceful. I had sensed that we were going to have a boy because of my vision of our son. So one night my husband and I discussed what we would do if we had a son. My husband was adamant about circumcision. He said, 'If we don't circumcise, he'll be regarded as odd by the boys in the locker room.' I felt just the opposite: 'I will not put my baby through that torture. Under no conditions will I allow our child to be circumcised.' Neither of us was willing to budge. My husband was upset and did not grasp how important it is not to create birth trauma. That argument happened when I was twelve weeks pregnant. I had the miscarriage the next morning. At that time, I didn't link the argument to the loss."

A Mother's Validation of Rebirth

Like other parents, Lezlie had no expectations of Elizabeth's pre-birth memories. Lezlie chose not to suppress her daughter's memories or dismiss them as fantasy. Lezlie was the mother Elizabeth needed, and that is why she chose to be born to Lezlie. What Elizabeth said, as a baby girl, challenges the medical myth that a pregnancy is not influenced by the incoming Soul. Elizabeth told Lezlie that she had made a split-second decision with a Spirit Guide's help to abort the pregnancy after the parents' argument. Lezlie felt exonerated about the miscarriage, since mothers who miscarry tend to feel guilty, as if there is something wrong with their body.

Lezlie confirmed seven of Elizabeth's pre-birth memories: (1) first pregnancy, (2) visit to clinic in Coronado, (3) parents' argument, (4) miscarriage in the shower, (5) Elizabeth's return in the second pregnancy since Lezlie felt the same Soul had returned, (6) breech, and (7) C-section. Dr. Anderson confirmed that Lezlie was pregnant and that she miscarried. Lezlie's validation of Elizabeth's memories bonded the two together more than most mother-daughter relationships. Four of Elizabeth's pre-birth memories were unconfirmed, despite being plausible: (8) miscarried baby's gender as male since Lezlie had a vision of a boy, (9) parents' argument as Elizabeth's reason for the miscarriage is accepted by Lezlie as the cause, (10) Elizabeth consciously going breech, and (11) Elizabeth meeting her unborn sister, whose birth was to follow.

CHAPTER 4

Scanning Soul Plans: Contemporary Pre-Birth Memories

~

The human soul is a silent harp in God's choir,
whose strings need only to be swept by the divine
breath to chime in with the harmonies of creation.
— HENRY DAVID THOREAU

*Once our Souls select a life plan, we are prepared to go on
stage, on cue.*

CHAPTER 4 HIGHLIGHTS MEMORIES FROM six people of their behind-the-scenes planning before birth. Their pre-birth memories overturn the old viewpoint that a random process brings parents and children together.

Earth: A Place Set Up to Heal the Mind

*Knowing where we come from and why we have come
here keeps us on track.*

Teresa, a forty-five-year-old mother, is the founder of a spiritual center open to people of all faiths. Teresa's memories came to her before she was able to talk: "I was just a baby, fresh out of the womb, when I heard my parents deciding what name to call me. Dad won the debate; mother was not one hundred percent pleased, but she was acquiescent and went with what my dad wanted."

51

Baby Teresa was aware of her teeny body and still could not figure out how she was attached to it: "I knew it was definitely 'on' me, like experiencing mud on my face for the first time. I could not figure out what my body was, or what to do with it, but I knew one thing I could not seem to get out of it.

"I would lay there in the crib and try to recall why everything was so blank. 'Why am I an empty slate? Who am I?' I knew there was more to this than what was happening at the moment because what was happening was very strange to me. I could not grasp the concept of a body. So that is when I laid there in deep peace. The deeper and stiller the peace was, the more beautiful it felt. I was lying there in that peace at all times. I knew that this was God, but I still felt separate from Him because the body was making me feel separate.

"So I began to try to remember back, trying to figure out where I was and what was going on. I wanted to know, 'Where am I?' and 'What is going on?' 'What happened before this?' I remembered a divine planner—a tall, stately gentleman who stood in front of a device similar to a podium, but it was more like a computer on the top. I remembered what happened in Heaven before birth. I was confused about good and evil and why we cannot judge someone. I had a strong desire to be more special to God and receive more of his love. I did everything I could to get love from the Supreme and be more special.

"Now, in Heaven, I had seen someone do an action, something I perceived as less than worthy. I said, 'That person should not get away with such a despicable thing. Surely I am better than this and deserve more appreciation from God.' I was dwelling on thoughts that were less than loving. All the beautiful divine beings around me advised, 'Oh, no. Don't think this way. Let those thoughts go.' Then I began to push it: 'Why can't there be good and evil? Why can't there be specialness? Why can't I judge?' I was dwelling on those thoughts and forcing them into belief to see what would happen. The more I thought about this, the more miserable I became. I realized that when

I judged another, I had actually judged myself. I felt ashamed and did not want God to know.

"I had failed my Divine Creator by having unloving thoughts. I had worked myself into a corner by thinking evil was possible and my brother was 'less than.' I curled up in a ball like a little scared animal hiding in a hole. That is when I met this divine planner, somebody who could help me. He was calm, cool, and collected. The divine planner explained, 'Earth is set up for the purpose of healing the mind. Earth is a world built out of specialness. Specialness is the opposite of Heaven, where God loves everyone equally. Specialness is when you give someone special favor over another, when you judge others. Earth is where we see the result of the attitude or thought of specialness.'

"The divine planner talked about going to Earth, experiencing my thoughts and feelings and acting out everything I wanted to the absolute extreme, no matter what it was. The divine planner said, 'You can think and act any way you want to the maximum. You will not be judged or condemned. Your life will be an experience of what you think and believe. You will see the results of that method.' I thought, 'There has to be a catch.' He replied, 'No catch, and any time you want to get out, you can come back.' I thought, 'This is the best deal in the world: think the way I want, act any way I want, and if I want to come back here, I can come back.' I said, 'Okay, I'm in.'"

Male or Female, Rich or Poor, Single or Married, Injury, Death

"The divine planner began to ask questions: 'Do you want to be male or female?' I said, 'Of course, I want to stay female.' He warned, 'You will be persecuted because you are female on the planet. That is part of the deal.' I replied, 'I don't care. I want to be female. I love the energy too much.' So he punched in something on his keyboard. It was like going up to a bank teller: you are not sure what the teller does on the other side of the window except that you get your money.

"The divine planner posed the next choice, 'Rich or poor?' I replied, 'I prefer not to work hard, to make a serious effort. I prefer to be rich.' He advised, 'It will be twice as hard if you are rich. You learn from challenges.' Also it had something to do with attachment. I stuck to my decision. I liked the idea of wealth and not having to grovel or starve.

"Then we talked about family. I asked, 'What's the best family?' He said, 'The highest is Brahmin.' I thought about that for a minute, 'No, I don't want that.' I did not know a lot of about the structure of the Earth, yet I visualized the Brahmin lifestyle. I wanted a cushy world, not a hard resilient world. The Guide explained, 'Brahmins are one hundred percent devoted to the worship of God in all their actions. Being born in a Brahmin family is a great fortune, worth more than money.'

"It was my choice, and I preferred a wealthy family. The divine planner said, 'You will be born in a Christian family in America, and your parents will believe in God. Being born in a family with faith in God is positive, although not quite as good as being born in a Brahmin family.'

"The divine planner next chose a person who would be a key person to help me learn the most. He was hyperactive. We stood next to each other. We could see exactly what someone was all about by looking at his heart chakra—compassion or lack of compassion. This being had one thing that I totally detested: absolutely zero compassion for children. And the instant I showed lack of interest, he had no interest in me.

"Then I realized, 'If I don't do this deal with him, I will not reach True Thought, my goal (to learn why I don't want specialness, why I don't want money, and why I don't want to judge my brother).' I turned, looked at him, and proposed, 'Let's make a deal. If you help me with my mental salvation, I will help you with your children.' There was something in it for him, so he was interested. 'Deal,' he said.

"The divine planner asked my partner questions: 'Do you want to be rich or poor?' He replied, 'Very rich.' The Guide talked about his family and birthplace. The Guide set it up so that we would meet. The divine planner gave him everything he asked for.

"Since this Being was to play a major role in my life, the divine planner held his face close, face-to-face. The Guide inserted the memory imprint of his face so that there would be no question of identifying him on the planet. The Guide told me, 'He will be younger than you.' My ego liked that: 'Oh, a younger man.' The Guide asked, 'Do you mind having sexual intercourse with this man?' I replied, 'No, I would love to do that.'

"The divine planner added more details. 'This man has a choice, yet most likely he will choose the path of drug abuse.' I saw a vision of a man sitting on the ground, with folded knees, his head resting on his knees and his arms wrapped around his legs.

"Next the divine planner asked, 'Do you want this man to physically harm you?' I said, 'No way.' He explained, 'You learn the divine lessons quicker when these things occur.' I said, 'I don't want the guy to hit me.' (My husband has never physically abused me. For the personality he has played [a drug addict], that is amazing. I have pushed his buttons; fortunately, it is not in the Divine Plan for him to hit me.)

"I resisted the next choice: 'Choose an injury.' I replied, 'I don't want to get hurt. Forget it. I'm not choosing an injury.' The divine planner told me, 'You will learn from these things.' I finally agreed, 'Okay, my hand.' He was disappointed that I picked something minor, but made the entry into his 'computer.'

"I broke my hand five years ago. I was a black belt in martial arts school. A man was goading me because I didn't practice with him. After he teased me three times, I put on the pads and decided to have a round. He went blank, as if in a meditative state, and his punch broke my hand. The injury was part of the Divine Plan. He felt terrible. This is what the ego does. The ego causes pain for us as well as for others.

"The divine planner finally told me, 'You must choose a death.' I said, 'Now, wait a second.' He explained, 'You do not really have to die. You simply have to choose one. Remember, you can get out of this anytime you want.' 'Okay,' I said, 'I want it to be quick and easy.' The first thought I had was a car wreck, a head-on collision with a van."

Attaining Mental Salvation the Hard Way

"I was born into an environment where I had opportunities to attain mental salvation, my original goal. As a child, I could go outside and ponder and contemplate a lot. I had a tremendous strong, beautiful experience of God. I had a divine experience because my thoughts were so open. Then when I was introduced to the world's concept of God and spirituality, I had a bad taste in my mouth and became very confused. I did not want anything to do with it. I saw that it could only cause misery. By the time I was seven, I shut down the memories, put them on the shelf, and tried to forget about them because they did not fit in the world. Nobody had these same experiences. Nobody was talking to God. Nobody was following the voice of God. I chose forgetfulness as a temporary path to relieve me from the burden of my memories. Literally this is what I did for thirty-two years. I guessed what I should do next instead of asking God and getting the answer. I did what I wanted and made mistakes. I got involved with the materialistic world—my physical form, appearance, dating, education, what car to drive, and what kind of house I should have. Because I did not follow the divine planner's advice and chose a wealthy life instead, I slowed down my spiritual growth. I took a long time to wake up. If I had to choose all over again, I would pick the ideal spiritual parents my Guide first offered me.

"When I was thirty-two, I had a memory recall and realized that everything that happened to me as a child was real. My pre-birth memories were not an illusion. Those things happened. Everything fit. My husband even looks like he did in Heaven. My family fits the divine planner's description. Mom was a Christian missionary. Dad was a minister who spent his life thinking of nothing other than Jesus. Jesus was every other word. Every time he signed his name it was,

'Love in Christ.' He had a fellow traveler's mission. He picked up hitchhikers off the street, gave them clothes, a place to stay, food to eat, and sent them on their way.

"My grandfather set up a trust for my father and left it alone. The trust grew and grew. By the time Dad returned to Heaven, he left me and my siblings a significant inheritance even when the IRS took half of it. I was placed in a family where I experienced special-ness in a way that caused me not to desire it. That is my purpose on the planet: to see why everyone should be loved unconditionally, and to understand the principle of why God loves everybody the same. I am here to get back to who I really am and my true thoughts of love and truth.

"When we don't follow God's Plan, we are attacking ourselves and others. I went to church, even though I was not committed to God. I took too long to get back to who I really am and to love everybody. In order for me to believe that evil cannot exist, that specialness is not what I want, that judging my brother is not what I want, I needed to experience what happens when we think evil toward our brothers and judge them.

"When I was in Heaven, I traveled anywhere at any time with merely a thought. While I was cruising around trying to figure out my mental salvation, I talked to one of my buddies. She was sup-posed to be born ahead of me. I told her, 'I prefer to have money when I get to the planet. I don't want to grovel and make an effort.' This was distasteful to her. She quickly said, 'Oh, no. If you don't work for it, you don't get the feeling of appreciation.' She wanted to go the route of hardship, effort, and hard work. I wanted to go the route of a little bit easier job.

"Twelve years ago, I ended up meeting this friend, and we became instant buddies as we had been in Heaven. We were obviously sis-ters, yet we had never seen each other before on the planet. This woman has had a hard life. Sahara lives the way she wanted to walk on the planet. These are challenges and triumphs to her. This is how she wanted to do it, and boy, has she done it that way."

Sex at High Noon

Nan remembers her own birth more than the births of her children.

Nan, a forty-five-year-old mother of three sons, has been a clairvoyant her entire life. Nan is the founder of a non-profit organization dedicated to sharing and preserving the wisdom and healing ceremonies of tribal elders: "My memories stretch back to a period long ago when I existed as a conscious being in spirit form. It was like a grammatical comma, a temporary break from the physical dimension. I remember isolating myself in a Soul form, long before I prepared to be born this time. A quietness permeated that spirit realm—a quietness that totally restores. Everything was in balance. I floated in a vacuum, feeling safe and protected.

"Once in human form, I missed that love, joy, peace, and comfort. I am unable to consciously go there. The experience is so beyond, yet there are times when I spontaneously reexperience it. All of a sudden, I can be totally spread out everywhere, like turning into a million stars. Part of me craves it, but my ego is frightened because it is hard to find my focal point: 'Oh, no. I am going to lose my attachment here.' My mind tries to make sense of it; it is part of the great mystery.

"In the pre-birth state, the family patterns were clear to me: positive and negative. I saw the blessings and the burdens. Each family member was to play a special role in my life. I had strong connections to my sister, father, and maternal grandmother. My grandmother and oldest sister were 'seers,' so my family was familiar with higher sensory perception. I felt safe coming into a family who understood my gifts. My sister would support me if my mother tried to shut us down. And that is what my mother tried to do. Our abilities terrified her.

"The problem is my grandmother had been a seer, and my mom did not appreciate anything but ordinary everyday behavior. You see, my maternal Grandmother was labeled insane because she would literally see writing on the wall. She foresaw the death of her two-year-old son. My mother was terrified of that: 'I don't want to see. What if they told me one of my children was going to die?' Due to my mother's fears, my sister and I could only discuss our clairvoyant visions privately."

Nan remembers conception. Her Soul was hanging out nearby: "My daddy came home, and Mother was cooking lunch. Dad said, 'Drop everything, and let's go into the bathroom.' Mom said, 'I have to put on a diaphragm.' He replied, 'No, it'll be okay this time.' I can remember that. I thought, 'Now is my chance. Here is my door.' I went in. So it is no accident that I was born with eating disorders, a food obsession. I was conceived at the noon hour, and sex interrupted lunch. Dad could never eat enough, have enough sex, or live enough.

"I waited until I was an adult before I told my mother because she was fearful of my clairvoyance. Mom screamed, 'How could you know this? We did have sex in the bathroom at lunchtime. That was the only time we didn't use a diaphragm.' She freaked out.

"At the same time, I told Mom that I was aware that Dad and my mother's sister had had a sexual affair during Mom's pregnancy. She said, 'Yes, they started their affair when you were in the womb. I didn't know about it until five years later.' The fact is, I knew about it all along. I tried to babysit Dad through it by coming in between him and my aunt at church and at family gatherings. I felt angry toward Mom for being unconscious about the affair. She coped with it as soon as she could.

"At the time of the affair, Mother felt terrified. I also watched Dad crying during Mom's pregnancy with me. His death urge was up. He was thinking, 'What are we doing having a fourth child? I'm not even comfortable with the family that I have now.'"

Nan recalls birth and the trauma resulting from her mother taking medication: "I entered the birth canal. If Mom had given three pushes, I would have been birthed and free of the canal. Instead, she took twilight drugs and had an out-of-body experience. She did not have the soul-urge to push me out. I was furious. I had a strong thought: 'If things get rough in this life, do not lean on her. She will leave.' I created that thought form around my mother despite the fact that she was a loving mother. My mother was out for two days after my birth. Later in life, she told me, 'I floated right out of my body. I can't express how great it was.' It wasn't good for me. Yet I know it had a role in my birth script. I may have already had that thought form, 'You cannot trust women' before I was ever born. I definitely have had challenges with women in this life.

"I remember how good it felt to finally come out despite being so cold and wet. All of sudden, there were all these foreign noises. I missed my mother's heartbeat so much. I was angry. Without a mother to bond with, I felt an emotional vacuum; later I found life jarring and unsatisfying."

Nan had an NDE at two and a half and "died" of double pneumonia: "I lost color in my eyesight. Everything appeared in shades of gray, black, and white. I knew if I kept going that I would go into a brilliant light and the colors would return, except that I would have to leave my body. Archangel Uriel came and asked me if I would stay."

Cultural Parallels: Remote Sensing and Conception

Nan's memory of conception is in agreement with Buddhist and Jewish teachings. Conception is a holy moment, pure and sublime. From the Soul's perspective, parents are creating what the Soul seeking birth needs—a body. There is no sense that sex is something to be kept hidden.

* Buddhism: for conception to occur, the *gandhabba*, the being to be reborn, has to be present when the parents unite. The intermediate being witnesses the sexual act of the parents with whom it has a karmic affinity. The being unconsciously jumps in and finds itself nestled in a womb.[1]

❊ The Tibetan Book of the Dead: this text outlines the incarnation journey between death and rebirth. Visions of the world one is to be born into arise. One glimpses their potential parents in sexual union and feels attraction to the mother if born male or fondness for the father if born female.

❊ Kabbalah: if a couple perceives an image of the Soul *(tzelem)* hovering above during lovemaking, intercourse leads to conception.

Snippets: Souls Watching Pre-Birth Movies

Our destiny may be chosen long before conception.

Vincent, a young man from the Netherlands, recalls when pre-birth visions flooded his mind at the age of four. Vincent realized that he existed before he came to Earth. The little boy felt overjoyed that he was allowed to remember: "Do you know the feeling of all human emotions bonded together to form an explosion in your mind? It was a big 'wow' feeling. So intense yet feeling good, indeed a tear or two escaped at that moment." He recalls that his Spirit floated in an empty universe with no stars or planets, the Void. From a distance, Vincent could see his fetal body surrounded by a light, pinkish-red energy inside his mother's womb. "I saw my body that was growing for my Soul."

Prior to birth, a "guided tour" of images of his parents announced what to expect: "This is what you get for your money. You've made a choice and there is no way back now. These are your parents. This is what they will look like. Good luck."

"I Choose to Be a Boy"

Mat, an electrician in his mid-twenties, has preserved deep memories of his pre-life: "I remember before I came into the womb. Everything was dark. I felt empty. I was waiting for something to direct me. Then my consciousness suddenly clicked on. I became aware that I existed. A thought, from seemingly nowhere, asked, 'What do you want to be?' Those exact words entered my mind. I knew the answer: 'I want to be a boy.' I instantly left that dark space and came into light.

"My pre-birth memory has stuck with me. I can differentiate it from memories of everything I've gone through in my body. This happened before I became 'me.' I assumed everyone picked gender. When I was five, I told my friends, 'I remember being born.' They looked at me like I was full of crap. I'm twenty-three now and shared it with Mom a few years ago. Mom said, 'It's odd that you wanted to be a boy. Even after four sonograms, the doctor told me you were a girl.'

"I am blessed to remember. Even when negative things happen, there will be a happy end when I return to whoever asked me, 'What do you want to be?'"

Cosmic Contract with Strings Attached

Rob, an art professor and meditation teacher, conversed with a Guide before birth. He was given two options: "I remember being in the space between life and death, and on the other side, and being given a choice whether to incarnate in 1948 or to wait twenty years. If I incarnated in 1948, I would be a spiritual pioneer, paving the way for others on the path to enlightenment. I would incur good karma by taking this difficult path and removing roadblocks for others. If I waited twenty years, my life would be easier. I chose 1948 and also picked to come in with my father. I remember being almost impulsive about my decision. My Guide explained that choice involved a packaged deal—it included my mother and brother and karma to be worked out with these people. Part of me looked with chagrin at being with my mother and brother. Still, I thought, 'I will be strong enough to handle anything.' The positive factors of being with my father outweighed the negative.

"As a young child, I was drawn to my father. I yearned to have a strong bond with him. We had a positive relationship. Unfortunately, he was uncommunicative and distant, too removed for my liking. We never spent time together. We did things as a family unit.

"We did most of our bonding when Dad got cancer. I was sixteen and old enough to drive Dad back and forth to the hospital, and relate to him as a man. We shared some closeness for two years. My desire to establish a bond for a longer time never came to fruition. The fulfillment of my desire was a bud just starting to open, and then it got stopped. He was fifty-six when he died, and I was seventeen. Life doesn't always have closure. It is a never-ending story."

Grandmother Lily's Protection

Matthew: "I was adopted as an infant by Hispanic parents. One day when I was eighteen, I was lying in bed wondering, 'Who are my real parents?' Suddenly in my mind's eye, I saw a three-dimensional flashback: I was inside my mother's womb listening to her heartbeat, and I felt a closeness and bond to that heartbeat. She was four months pregnant with me. I felt a heated discussion in the room. I could smell tortillas and homemade beans. A black-and-white TV was turned on. My five-year-old brother was playing with toys in the corner of the room. Mom was sitting on a couch. Grandmother Lily was standing over me and saying, 'You better take care of this child. You have a very special child in your womb. You must find good parents for him. His life is in danger.' Mom asked, 'What do you mean by special?' Lily said, 'Your child has spiritual gifts. He needs to have them nurtured.' Grandma felt me to be in danger when my mother's husband got out of prison because I was the child of another man.

"While I never met Lily in the physical, she came to me with messages and started protecting me when I began my healing work. She has helped me help heal many people since then. She also brought my ancestors to help me: Red Cloud, who invited me to sit in his fire and see more of my past through his portal in the fire; Grandfather Geronimo, who told me to be still and listen for the answers in my heart; and Sitting Bull, who said to be proud of who I am and never let myself be humiliated by my own negative thinking. She told me, 'I prayed for Christ to touch your life when you were in the womb, and so did your Grandfather. He put "medicine" in your heart. You received a full hit of medicine from all your ancestors.'

"I was born in San Jose in 1967. I would like to find my birth family. I have no information about them. I only have my pre-birth memories and what Lily told me: 'Your birth father is very tall, and your half-brother is short and chunky. You are related to the Aztec, Lakota, and the Ocean [Hawaiian] peoples.'"

Today Matthew is an intuitive healer and a massage therapist who works in hospitals, convalescent homes, and social service offices. "I am still engaged in unfolding my understandings from my family, the Karuk Nation, and my Lakota Sun Dance leaders. I am learning from the land, as my ancestors did, sharing my knowledge with the rest of the world, and hopefully I will leave a mark on this planet before I go Home."

CHAPTER 5

Welcome to Planet Earth

෴

Pre-Birth Memories of Courageous Souls

I walked a mile with Pleasure
She chattered all the way
But left me none the wiser,
For all she had to say.
I walked a mile with Sorrow
And never a word said she
But oh! The things I learned from her,
When Sorrow walked with me!
—Robert Browning Hamilton,
Along the Road

*We are beings in the magnificent dream of the Creator.
The Grand Designer makes His motion picture very
complex, full of contrasts of good and evil.*

D O HARDSHIPS AND PROBLEMS FALL within our pre-birth options? While contradictory to what we may think, many Souls believe that harsh conditions are part of their lesson plan. Chapter 5 presents pre-birth memories of five people who accept that all experiences offer opportunities for growth.

Such pre-birth memories offer insight into the purpose and value of the toughest life scripts. These courageous Souls have known illnesses, deaths of loved ones, abuse, accidents, and near-death experiences. They have found their way out of the depths of suffering gifted with an understanding of life that fills them with compassion and love.

Path of Earthly Thorns, Smell of Roses

If everything were a piece of cake, life would be dry.

Rennie (1929–2004) was destined to become a military pilot in this life; in a past life, he may have been among the legendary fighter pilots in World War I. His inner desire to fly was so strong that at fifteen he taught himself to fly airplanes. Rennie's fascination extended over fifty-nine years in the cockpit and setting aviation records. Besides flying military jets, Rennie kept a Piper Cub until his passing. During his interviews, he shared flamboyant stories of his U.S. Air Force career flying jets and serving as an intelligence officer. His pre-birth memories depict a deep part of him that was not understood by his family and friends.

Rennie: "When people fuss and curse their parents, that is unjust, because they have themselves to blame. It really irritates me when I hear people complain and curse their parents. I want to say, 'Look, you damn fool, you chose your parents. You are to blame, not them.' But you don't do that because if you are not careful, people mark you down as a kook."

Rennie believes we choose our parents because he recalls making that choice: "I remember this as a young kid. It kept coming back to me through the years. I spoke to my mother about it when I was seven. I said something about where I came from and those other people I was with. She said, 'What are you talking about?' I asked, 'Was I placed with you and Dad when you were in the front seat of a car?' Now, my mother came from an old German family where you didn't talk about that stuff. She cut me off posthaste, 'Where did you get that idea? That is indecent.'"

Visit from the Virgin Mary

"I kept quiet after that, but it kept going through my mind. Later on, when I was in my twenties, I prayed for an answer. A divine entity appeared on my right at the foot of my bed one night. It was a small, short person, eighteen inches off the floor. She was looking down at me: a young woman in a purple cloak with a white veil draped over her head, and a very bright glow around her. The Light lit up the whole room. She looked like the Virgin Mary, but I am not Catholic. I had an [airplane] instrument desk in the corner of that room where I was working on altimeters, and I had lost one of the pieces. That glow [from the Light] was so bright that I could look on top of that desk and see the missing piece sticking in a crack. The divine entity stayed for several minutes, never said a word, and then faded away.

"I got out of bed the next morning and looked with a flashlight and pulled that [missing] little wheel out of the crack. That proves that I really saw what I saw. If I had been Catholic, I would have built a shrine in that room. I could not accept that. After this, I decided to go and confront my parents. I wanted to put a few things at peace in my mind."

Eyewitness to My Conception

Rennie flew home to confront his parents in 1954. He wondered if his memories were true. "If I found out it was some quirk in my mind, I would let it go. I asked Mom and Dad, 'Do you know where I was conceived?' Mom said, 'I have not thought about that in years.' I asked, 'Was it on the front seat of that 1917 Overland car?' When my parents turned beet red, I knew I was on to something. Mom looked at Dad and said, 'Gus, you haven't been talking to this boy, have you?' He said, 'No, Hilda, you know I wouldn't talk about that. Did you say something to this boy?' She said, 'No.'

"I asked, 'Can you think of any other details?' They said, 'That was so long ago.' I said, 'I know what happened. Suppose I supply some details. Can you confirm them?' My parents said, 'Yes.' I started out by saying they were partially disrobed and 'monkey-messing.' They opened the car door, and my mother looked over the back seat to make sure my sister was sound asleep. All the details had been branded in my mind as if it were yesterday. They verified everything. Nowhere did I find an error."

Rennie's parents believed him and asked how he knew this. He told them he had memories like a videotape of seeing it happen. His parents were embarrassed. "My mother and daddy had a better-than-average relationship despite their peculiarities and shortcomings. I can easily conceive them doing this kind of stuff.

"My father was a romantic, and my parents were affectionate with each other. It kind of ran in the family. At the same time, there was never any show of public affection in these old German families. My parents were married fifty years. I saw Dad kiss Mom twice. In our family, sex had never been openly discussed. My parents kept quiet about the facts of life and kept us from even joking about sex. Following our discussion, the subject was never mentioned again."

Looking-Glass Portal: Three Couples Observed During Sex

Rennie's memories stretch back to being in an assembly of Souls and observing Earth through a bird's-eye portal. "I was up in this high place, and I could look down. It was like looking down from an airplane or a dirigible. It was like standing on a long ledge, and you looked down at the Earth. There were Souls to my right and Souls to my left. They looked like human beings. The only difference was they were not dressed like people on Earth. Everyone wore full-length white kimonos. They were making the same decision that I was making. Conversations were going on all around me. Souls were pointing down to Earth and selecting parents.

"I knew who the directors were by their attitude and actions. My Guide stood on my right and held me by the arm. He had superiority over me. I felt like a student, and he was a full-fledged teacher. What is so amazing is that I visualized that I would return to this place in the hereafter. We go to Earth as children. Before that we are mature spiritual beings up there. When I looked down, I was given a choice of three couples having intercourse:

1. Wealthy couple: this couple was in their early forties or late thirties and on the pudgy side. They got after it right away. They entered the bedroom, disrobed, and got on with the program. In those days, it was fashionable to have a walnut bed with spindles on the elevated head and footboard. They had a matching dresser and chest of drawers. My Guide explained, 'If you are born into this family, you will breeze through life and encounter the least trouble. Your reward will be the smallest.'
2. Middle-income couple: the youngest couple did a little kissing and caressing before intercourse. The wife was stout and the husband was a large, tall man. Their bed had a three-foot-high metal headboard and footboard with vertical metal spokes. My Guide advised, 'In this family, you will have minor problems. You will earn an average reward.'
3. Poor couple: the third couple was driving along a country road, smooching and caressing each other. Pretty soon, they stopped the car, and the woman looked in the back seat to verify that a child was sound asleep. The little girl was lying on her back with her arms up above her head. Her feet pointed toward the driver's side. The husband laid his wife on her back and the car door opened. They got into other things. I remember the smallest details of it. My Guide said, 'If you go to this family, you will have many trials and tribulations. You will never reach your potential. It will be in the cards to experience frustration.'

"I asked, 'If I take this couple, my reward will be equally as great, right?' He said, 'Yes, except you will have a hard time, and it will be frustrating to pass God's test. Part of your trial will be to fall short of achieving what you are really capable of. With the other two couples, you will just about have it made. Decide on the couple you want.' I answered, 'The couple with the greatest trials.' He asked, 'Are you sure?' I said, 'Yes.'

"I had no special feelings toward the wealth of each of the couples. We are born on Earth for Soul growth. It is a matter of choosing what degree of salvation we want. I desired to shoot for the top, maximum salvation. I wanted to prove myself.

"As soon as I chose my parents, I entered a huge, round tunnel. I flew down that tube at a terrific speed. Lights coming from a narrow band flashed by. The lights wrapped all through that tube, like a red stripe on a peppermint candy cane. The light circle never broke. It was dark except for the band of light."

Four Lessons of Rennie's Pre-Birth Memory

"My memories first came to me when I was four years old. My parents had returned from the funeral home and explained death to me. 'Auntie went to Heaven to be with God and the angels.' As soon as I heard that, I recalled the assembly of Souls and this place I had come from. I knew that was where Auntie went. I wondered, 'What world am I in now?' I was in a different place, and that confused me.

"My memory taught me four lessons: (1) life begins at conception; (2) we choose our parents; (3) there are degrees of salvation. We can get in at the bottom or higher up the ladder, depending upon how we fare with earthly trials. Those who succeed, solve, or overcome get the biggest rewards; and (4) God gives us free agency. We make choices throughout our lives."

Rennie's Cosmic Contract: Seeking the Greatest Spiritual Reward

"I have never forgotten my Spiritual Guide's instructions: 'Your tribulation will be to fall short of expressing your full potential.' Usually, people forget what happens before birth. In my case, the eraser did not work. Someone forgot to shut my computer down, so I am ten steps ahead. I view challenges as opportunities for growth. I face pain with patience, tolerance, and love.

"I have been at the edge of fame many times. I had two careers with the government: first as a military intelligence officer, and second as an agent with the Federal Crime Commission. Other people achieved the notoriety and got the limelight even though they did very little. I was on the team, even if I didn't carry the football. None of that ever bothers me because I know why I was on the sidelines.

"I lost many opportunities for fortune. I invented a medical device; a doctor stole my idea and made millions. I played a character in the movie *Sugarland Express* and declined director Steven Spielberg's Hollywood offer to be in movies due to family ties and obligations in Texas.

"My life included countless traumas and chancy experiences. Luckily I came out smelling like a rose. I was shot several times. I was knocked off a bridge and fell thirty-six feet—landing on a slant and sliding down saved me. One other time I bailed out of a military jet at three thousand feet. Officers notified my wife, 'Rennie died in a plane crash.' I called home moments later. My wife handed the phone to the officers and asked, 'Do you want to talk to a dead man?' I walked away without a scratch. I also buried three children and two wives who passed away due to illness. My third marriage ended in divorce.

"Major health challenges began in 1962. I was hospitalized for a stroke and paralyzed on the right side. I had complications and they removed half my colon, small intestines, and stomach. Doctors also did heart surgery and gave me a pig valve. Once I recuperated, I was admitted back into the hospital after a second stroke paralyzed the left side. Doctors put me on morphine for pain. I dropped from 255 pounds to 128 pounds. When I was discharged from the hospital after fifteen months, I was unable to walk, stand, or hold my head up. I lay in bed and stuck my legs and arms up in the air and moved them until I fell asleep. Whenever I woke up, I started all over again. Doctors gave me two years to live. At home, I broke myself of the morphine habit—cold turkey."

Love: Unfinished Business on Earth

Thirty years later, in the 1990s, Rennie underwent nine surgical procedures over a two-year battle with cancer. During the first cancer surgery, he had an NDE. "My heart stopped for four minutes. I floated out of my body. I looked down and saw the body that was 'me.' I saw huge carpenter's clamps holding me open so the doctor could operate on my intestines. The doctor was screaming at the nurse and anesthetist because a particular machine was not set up properly. I floated through the wall. I saw my family and the preacher in the waiting room. I had no desire to return. I never felt so good in my life. Material possessions meant less to me than a burned cigarette. My deceased son, Glen, appeared and said, 'Papa, you must go back. My children will need you as they grow up. I cannot be there; you can.' Glen asked me to do a favor. He talked about his Lionel toy train set, a prized possession from childhood, and some antique doll family heirlooms: 'Papa, give them to my children after they grow up. I hid them in the airplane hangar. Look for a box in the northeast corner of the kitchen cabinet. I left a message in the box explaining what to do.'

"I wanted to ask about my first wife; however, my son pointed to a dark oval archway and said, 'Papa, you must go back. Know that you will come again. I will meet you, and we will go over to the other side together.' I have always been family-oriented. It was up to me. I elected to satisfy him. Family was more important than the peace of mind I had at that time. I would have that peace one of these days anyway.

"I observed a second scene as I conversed with my son. The doctor was raising hell with the staff because my heart had stopped. The nurse tried to start my heart with adrenaline. I had no reaction: no heartbeat or respiration. I saw all of this on the monitor. Next, they placed a big balloon over my face and pushed both sides together to get me to breathe. The doctor rushed around trying to hook up a machine to give electric shocks. He put on rubber gloves, laid a wet towel on my chest, and gave me three shocks. The third time, I got a heartbeat. That is when my deceased son started to fade away. I felt like I was slipping down the side of a hill with nothing under me. As I descended, I felt pain. It became more intense as I neared my body. I hovered above my body; my feet entered first. I 'locked back' into my body. All of a sudden, I was looking the doctor in the face.

"One week after my NDE, I walked out to the airplane hangar at the ranch. Without my knowledge, my wife was following. She was worried because I was still so weak. I found the items for my grandchildren where my son told me. Inside the box was a note. 'Dear Papa, please save these things for my children. Explain the history of it.' I sat down and cried. My NDE was not my imagination. My wife threw her arms around me and said, 'So this is what you were talking about when you came out of anesthesia and we did not listen.'"

Validation of Pre-Birth Memories and Near-Death Experience

Rennie's gift as a more-evolved Soul who recalls life before birth is highlighted by his parents' validation of his conception: "I proved my [pre-birth] memory with one hundred percent accuracy. This was not a dream. It would take a pretty good dream to be one hundred percent accurate, wouldn't you say? How could I imagine these things happened when my parents conceived me? If my parents had said that they did not know where I had been conceived or denied my memory, I would have decided that there was a quirk in my mind. The truth is, they verified what I saw in explicit detail, such as my sister lying on her back with her arms up in the back seat of that old car with her feet toward the driver side. They confirmed that they had stopped on this country road and had sex in the car before they got home."

Rennie's descent via the Tunnel of Light was identical to an experience he had of weightlessness when he trained the first NASA astronauts in an Air Force jet: "I took the jet up to a certain altitude and suddenly descended to allow astronauts to simulate the weight-lessness of space. We could hear the astronauts hooting and laughing in the padded interior in the back. I told the copilot, 'Next time, you take over. I am going to check this out.'" Weightlessness was like flying down the light tunnel into the fertilized egg.

"I proved my NDE encounter with my deceased son was not a figment of my imagination. I found the gifts for my grandchildren. How could I imagine that the box of toys was hidden in the hangar with the note from my son? My son had leukemia and knew he was going to die. He put these toys in the box and kept it a secret so his wife would not throw these things away.

"Once I regained consciousness in the hospital following the NDE, I asked, 'Where is my brother, my daughter, and the preacher? Why aren't they here?' My wife asked, 'How did you know those people were here?' I observed them when I floated out of my body through the wall of the surgery room. I also later confirmed that the doctor had really used furniture clamps during surgery because my body is extra big."

Darkness Cannot Exist Where There Is Light

"I chose the most demanding life plan because there is another victory that really counts: whoever is able to succeed, solve, or overcome will get rewards. I won a fifteen-month battle with cancer. While my two wives and three children died, I never quit. Certainly I miss my loved ones who passed on. Despite my tough losses, I can look ahead and have a positive outlook. Optimism is a big key to survival. When negative things happen, I have a positive attitude and joke about them. I intend to leave the world a happier place."

Rennie's life was mostly about love: giving and helping people. "I do not concern myself with selfish ambition and material pursuits. I try to fill my life with generous thoughts and unselfish actions. When I see people who have a genuine need, I help. I do not walk around with blinders and say to hell with everyone else and I am number one.

"I chose a life with the greatest spiritual reward and not a cushy life of material success. Even though I chose the tough road, I wanted to know why I had so much trauma. One night I prayed for an answer. An angel appeared and said, 'God needs good Jobs [the biblical Job] in this world, and you are one of them.' God needed to test my character to see if my commitment to Him would bear up under adversity. I trust that He saw what lessons I needed to learn."

Forgiving My Mother's Abuse

Misfortune gets our attention to face our demons and "deal" and "get real."

Lania's nineteen-year-old mother got married to a man in his forties in order to get away from her parents. Lania: "My mother was diabolical and could fly into a rage at any moment. I sensed these emotions and drama, manipulations, forcefulness, and intensity the moment I entered the womb. I felt such abject terror, total contraction, darkness, and fear that I began to forget 'Home.' I felt trapped, annihilated. I did everything I could to stay in the womb. I felt overwhelmed. I had no option, no escape hatch.

"When the nurse brought me to my mother after my birth, I felt a devastating slam of energy. I wondered, 'What am I doing here? Did I make a mistake?' I was fully conscious that Mom did not want me. I lost trust in myself. I thought, 'My choices are bad.' I wanted to go Home. Earth was not the appropriate place for me. The stork dropped me on the wrong planet.

"Mom's purpose for having a baby was to manipulate Dad, who was a traveling salesman. She wanted him to stay home more. That failed to work. Dad was away on business even at my birth. That totally enraged her. Her manipulations had not worked. I had not fulfilled what I was supposed to do."

Lania's relationship with her mother did not improve with time. As a child, once, while standing in the grocery checkout with her mom, Lania knew that the woman ahead of them was unhappy because she could not bear children. She was struggling with the idea of adoption. Lania knew that if this woman chose to adopt, her life would blossom. Little Lania tugged at the lady's dress, looked up into her eyes, and said in a whisper, "You're going to be happy when you adopt your child." The woman's face turned red and she sputtered, "How did you know?"

Unfortunately, Lania's mother did not appreciate that her daughter knew, heard, saw, and understood things that no one else noticed. She did her best to destroy Lania's gifts, nearly killing Lania in the process. Her mother's worst punishment was to force Lania to eat Tide detergent whenever she did something wrong. It became more and more difficult for Lania to eat food as the acidic compound burned away her intestinal tract lining. Her mother's tactics worked. Lania soon learned to turn her back on her gifts. Lania's relationship with her mother set up major psychological patterns. "I started believing that I have no value. I take up air that someone important could have. It's dangerous to ask for help and voice my opinion. I can never be taken care of. I began to go into a pleasing mode and gave my power away. Loss of self-trust and belief in outer validation became so interwoven into my consciousness that I acted on automatic pilot."

Mother's Script

"Why did my mother abuse me? The answer depends on how you view physical reality. If you see life as being real, then it makes no sense. Nevertheless, it makes perfect sense if you recognize life as an illusion—like a movie that you create and step into. From that perspective, these were things that had been set up before I came into this body in order to learn how to validate myself, trust others, speak out, and know that I was responsible for only myself. I wanted to come back to Truth.

"Before I came into this life, I chose to go through hell. I picked my mother for that reason. As my primary caretaker, she tried to destroy me, wanted to shut me up. Even so, didn't she do the greatest thing for me? If that woman tortured me and could not stop me, who could? If I blamed my mother for playing the role I asked her to play, I would do myself a disservice and keep myself in bondage. As easy as that sounds, I did not simply forgive my mother and let her off the hook. First, I needed to release anger, rage, and hurt. I talked to therapists twice a week for four years. Mom died before I completed therapy. Even though she was no longer alive, I came to appreciate what my mother really did for me. Who did my mother have to be in order that I might accomplish what I came here to do? Sure, she was the villain. In any event, is that who she really is? From another perspective, wasn't she the greatest angel that ever lived for me?

"Why? My mother was the taskmaster, baddest of the bad. She put me through a torture camp from the time I was born. Hitler could not have done any worse. And still I love. People may wonder whether my mother incurred negative karma for abusing me. She would have incurred karma if she refused to play the role. The better my mother portrayed her role, the more ability it unlocked in me. And my mother's strength and determination held her role in place like the finest actress.

"I needed to transcend her abuse. When I did, I developed a core of steel and inner strength. I had come into this life to resolve certain issues and move forward. Now no one can stop me from bringing forth the conversation that I am here to bring. What was the overriding factor that allowed me to do that? I was able to find the love. Love is at the core essence of All That Is. Love is the message of Jesus, Moses, Muhammad, Buddha, and Krishna. And lack of love has held torture and torment in place.

"When I was in my early thirties, I had a car accident. I was not able to work. I felt depressed. One night, I cried and put out a call for help. My mother came in my dream. She had passed away seven years earlier. Mom said, 'If you had not done all the work to forgive me and learned to realize that you have inherent value, it would have been impossible for me to come tonight. I want you to realize we set this up before you were born. You asked me to play this role. I played that role so that you could resolve the conflicts that stood in your way. Now I want you to see who I really am.'

"My mother revealed herself as a glorious, radiant being. She enfolded me in her all-encompassing love and said, 'I came to help you recognize the vastness and power of love, that you might stand tall above darkness.' I was shocked at her loving presence. My mother had played the total villain in my life. She gave me the greatest gift.

"I woke up crying. The dream changed my perception of who I am, what I am here for, how I interact with others, as well as how I can resolve and overcome conflict and restore personal dignity. Human experience has nothing to do with what is 'real.' In the end, it gives us the opportunity to discover that in our own time and in our own way."

Interlife Memories

"Before I came into form, I reflected on what beliefs, attitudes, concepts, and traditions had kept me forgetting who I really was in former lives. I realized, 'Well, it didn't work in that life. Or I accomplished a little bit doing it this way in another life. Or I maneuvered it around a little this other way.' In one lifetime, I had been born as an only child. My parents suffered a fatal accident. I lived with my uncle who did not like children and had no idea what little girls needed. He became angry that he had been saddled with caring for me. He abused me.

"As I grew up, I became bitter, sinister, and could not function. I lost the love I had inside. Prior to that life, I had actually planned to be with my uncle as that little girl. In a previous life, he had lost his beloved in a devastating occurrence. His heart had been broken. I promised, 'I will be with you in your next life and open your heart back up.' He agreed, 'Yes, of course. I want my heart to be healed. What better way to do it than to be with a little girl who just wants love?' However, I could not follow through on our agreement. The stage had been set. We had an opportunity to shift things, yet I lost the power to materialize that. When I was in the in-between, I had forgotten how intense it is to be in physical form. I didn't realize how much focus it would take to turn my uncle's heart around. It was too much, too big of a slice."

Lania saw what was needed to ensure total success for her current life: "I wanted to get the most gusto out of this life. My goal was to learn self-validation. I chose to experience the human condition from a horrendous perspective, doom and gloom, and atrocities. Then, if I found my way back to Wholeness from total annihilation of self, look what I would have accomplished.

"Human experience works like a pendulum. If I had picked an easy ho-hum life, the pendulum would not swing far. Those experiences don't give a big evolutionary push. If I had a mediocre life, how motivated would I be to do something about it? I wanted the pendulum to swing to the other side and break through. If something was tearing me limb from limb, I would crumble and retreat or get my act together.

"In planning my life, I made certain that I had the proper players to pull me through: the support and the villains—devastation, heartache—to motivate me. Of course, once I came into form, I forgot so that I could do it. That is the game, one of the rules I agreed to. Before birth, I only knew total connection with God, and I accepted the illusion that I would be separate once I entered physical form.

"The purpose of each life is to remember what brings us ultimate joy. When we acknowledge our Self, we are in alignment with God's will for us. All there is, then, is love, joy, expansion, and being present in our Self. We have this dramatic story we play out; it is the only way we can see and find ourselves. When we are in the Oneness, there are no distinctions. We do life in order to remember Unity while we are in the physical."

Lania fulfilled her pre-birth plan: she grew past her mother's abuse, thereby finding forgiveness, love, and her Self. Today, Lania teaches self-empowerment workshops, helping people to live their full potential.

Learning Lessons in One Life or Three Lives?

Pain and problems are a means to teach truth, humility, and freedom from egoism.

Lorenzo (1935–2008) is a former Wall Street advertising director and the author of *Mouth of God: Your Cosmic Contract.*[1] During interviews with Lorenzo, he shared pre-birth memories: "As the Soul that is yet to enter into physical form, I saw my whole life, including past lives." Lorenzo's birth was unexpected. "Mom called me 'ghost baby' because I was not supposed to be born. I was purely an accident. My parents had not been sleeping in the same bed for years. Mom was not supposed to have a second pregnancy because my sister's birth shattered my mother's pelvic region and Mom nearly died. She was in a body cast for six months. She was barely able to walk after nine years."

Did Lorenzo engineer his parents' coming together for conception? Lorenzo: "Probably, sure. I am a creative director. When you ask that question, the first image that comes to me is the charm that my parents radiated. Dad was a talented artist. Mom taught classical piano. Together they could charm the world. They were sweet people, just a little out of balance here and there. Before coming into the womb, I recall them as environments of male energy and environments of female energy. And that does not mean one coming from male and one coming from female; they both interacted and interchanged."

Lorenzo's selection of parents was not by chance: "I saw this whole life, and I accepted it and the lessons, the peaks and the valleys. For those highs and lows to be what they were, I needed to be guided by energies, called 'parents.' So it was not specifically this human and that human, rather that energy to serve this peak or valley and the other energy to serve a different peak and valley."

Vortex of Creation

Lorenzo came through "the Vortex of Creation" into this world. This journey involved "interdimensional manifestation" rather than travel or movement: "Imagine all your senses just rolled up into one sense of being. You do not hear. You do not see. You do not taste, smell, or touch. Yet everything exists for you. And you are totally unattached. It is an experience of Unity: *tat twam asi*— 'Thou art this. Thou art that.' Everything was part of the Oneness. I was aware of everyone and everything and everywhere else. That is also what happens when you die in this lifetime. At least that has been my experience in three NDEs. I went through the vortex again and came out on the other side. So an NDE is like being born anew in the same life."

Lorenzo's memory and experience of "Thou art this. Thou art that" means he realized that every Soul was his own Soul. He cognized the existence of an underlying unity that he was a part of. Lorenzo had no feelings of separateness, exclusiveness, intolerance, or hatred.

Supreme Witness Awareness in the Womb

Lorenzo refers to his broad womb-time awareness as being a Supreme Watcher or Witness: being aware of the Higher Self while simultaneously witnessing his thoughts and actions. Due to this heightened awareness, Lorenzo recalls coming into the fetus, witnessing the dramas in his parents' lives, and exiting to other planets: "Earth would be blessed if people located that beautiful place inside themselves where the Supreme Witness takes over, where people become aware of who they really are.

"I cannot pinpoint when my Soul entered my mother's womb; however, I recall the special process, or divine infusion, that took place as my Soul infused with the "matter body" or "matter-being" [the fetus] in the womb. The connection was made in the initial spark of self-love. We cannot be born without self-love, without self-acceptance.

"The Soul has a contract with the matter being, i.e., the union of egg and sperm, so that it can fulfill its life's lessons in that particular body. The Soul brings parallel life memory and karma on the Soul level with it; the 'matter-being' [physical body] brings genetic memory and karma on the physical level with it."

Lessons Begin in the Womb

Lorenzo's mother played the piano so he "grew up in the fetus" listening to the classics. "My favorite was Sibelius's *Valse Triste,* a sultry, seductive, haunting, metaphysical piece. That is how I appreciated it. On the contrary, whenever my mom felt sad, it created even more melancholia in her. I felt her despair. It took me a while to grow out of that. So it is important what a mother 'feeds' the fetus."

Besides listening to his mother playing classical music, Lorenzo enjoyed "celestial music and voices in the womb. Evidently the 'Mouth of God Energy,' the subtle energy induction center at the base of the skull, is prominent for me in this life. This important energy center is located at the medulla oblongata. The Mouth of God is an opening whereby energy from the divine comes in. Vibrations and expressions of a divine nature continued to come through that channel after birth. The Mouth of God Energy experience is like one huge beauty parlor hair dryer sitting on my head. The hum is always there."

Emotional ups and downs in his parents' lives were due to the local politics of Lorenzo's grandfather Don Giovanni being a Mafia peacemaker. Lorenzo felt the disagreements and turmoil disrupting his parents: "I became less aware of it when I became more physical, more a part of the illusion.

"Mother's womb was perfect. My script was being read and played out before ever leaving the womb. I learned that I did not have to be totally there: if an activity was not supportive, I could check out. Mom was not totally happy with her surroundings. So whenever I sensed negativity, I felt no disharmony with the disharmony. I came and went as I pleased. I played anywhere I wanted. Lots of playtime took place on Jupiter, the planet of growth, and Saturn, the karmic teacher. That is where most of my lessons come from. That is where I hung out. I still do."

Lorenzo shared further details about Jupiter and Saturn: "They are Jovian, nonterrestrial planets. Every galaxy has solar systems with Jovian planets. (Uranus, Neptune, and Pluto are also Jovian planets.) They are seed planets. They have no core like Earth, no rock, nothing solid. Jupiter and Saturn are fire and ice, and gas and lightning. And that is my nature—silent, rumbling, and thunderous. Between lifetimes, I visit the Jovian Core Galaxy, a spiritual spa, a playground for gods, goddesses, gurus, and spiritual teachers. That is why all the rumbling is there. Undertones and a transcendental dialogue go on there all the time. It is a huge library of information. It is my Home and one of the original galaxies in the universe."

Remember, O Mind, Remember from One Lifetime to the Next

"In the Isha Upanishad, there is a verse, *'Krato smara kritam smara.'* That means: 'Remember, O mind, remember what has been done.' Those of us who have recited that phrase from one lifetime to the next bring that spiritual information with us and realize we have the latitude to travel; we do not have to stay put. We can learn lessons elsewhere, not just in this little womb. By maintaining that concept, the ego does not become attached to the illusion as quickly. In other words, if we do not bring all the past-life spirituality into the fetus, we can get caught up in our parents' lives when we grow as a separate living being. That becomes a real boundary."

Flight to Birth from the Jovian Planets

"I wanted to be born at an auspicious time: Navaswan—the gap between night and day, about 4 a.m. So I returned from Jupiter and Saturn in the nick of time to enter Mom's uterus to formally come out. I can see the delivery room through my perception. At the same time, it is hard to say I was actually on Earth because it is as though Jupiter and Saturn were right in the room.

"My first breath must have been significant. I was told an ejaculation took place. I remember it as a brilliant flash of light." Newborns are not expected to have the powerful kundalini energy shoot up a subtle spinal channel; nevertheless, this phenomenon may occur in advanced babies. Seekers of enlightenment spend years of meditation practice to attain awakenings like this; Lorenzo's kundalini experience at birth is an additional indicator of his advanced Soul status.

Did Lorenzo bond with his mother at birth? "Let me condense this for you. Up until I was four years old, it was just Jupiter and Saturn and a whole bunch of light and levitation. My awareness of my parents was love coming from a specific direction, as opposed to every direction. I do not recall bonding with my family because I always bonded with celestial energies. I feel that when I came into this life my parents had done what they were supposed to do. After that, I wanted them to leave me alone. As things turned out, my parents had other ideas: too much fuss—much to do about nothing."

Planetary Lessons and Near-Death Experiences

Part of Lorenzo's plan for this life was to end the curse of samsara: "Rebirth, rebirth, rebirth, who needs it? That is the reason for three NDEs in one life. I accelerated so that I do not have to be born three more times."

Lorenzo's window for learning "planetary lessons" opened at age four: "My perception was extremely celestial for the first four years. Everything I saw was totally infused with everything else, a Unity experience. I was never separate or apart from anything that existed. Then a moving van 'grounded' me. After being 'anointed' in the head by a huge truck, I went through the Vortex of Creation and was thrust back into my body with a thud. Earth lessons were starting. Nature was telling me it is time to be grounded, to be on this planet. Afterward the awareness of Unity was there, yet a feeling of

Earth started to prevail because I encountered fear for the first time. My parents found my body lying in the street. I saw them hovering over me, their faces full of fear. Prior to that, I had no fear. One day when I was a toddler, Mom stopped me on the top of our six-story building. I was ready to fly off.

"My family called the truck accident a tragedy. I saw it as a catalyst, a spiritual bridge. The accident was a blessing because I was a stuck-up little spiritual snob prior to that. I had a sharp intellect ready to annihilate anything that brought discomfort—to dissolve it, to move it away conveniently, including my parents. The NDE was part of my contract, a planetary lesson. After the accident, the intuitive aspect grew, the feminine approach. To have compassion and detachment is to have both worlds.

"My planetary lesson is to stay grounded. More lessons followed with each NDE every eighteen to twenty years." Lorenzo passed through the Vortex of Creation in each NDE: in 1971, a nasty auto accident, and thrust back with a thud; in 1991, intestinal cancer surgery. "I was out of the body and went through the Vortex of Creation, yet maintained body consciousness. 'Hey body, I will be right back. Hang in there.' It was the first time that I experienced being on this Earth totally. And that is in fifty-six years on the planet."

Earth Lessons and Amnesia

Lorenzo describes the energy downshifts on his way to birth. Each time he passed from one energy level to a lower one, it was a shock. First, he went from the subtlest energy realm to the womb: "Let's face it, Mom's womb is alive and a whole universe unto the fetus—totally self-sufficient, self-referral space: 'My space, my space, alone.' Then, I was dynamically thrust from a subtle energy plane of being in the womb to a thick, dense, hard rock consciousness energy plane at birth. My memory did not immediately stop with birth. I felt divine energy and perception at one and two years old. And there was never a concern about happiness or unhappiness until my mother said we are supposed to be happy about certain things. I could not understand. I always felt the presence of light and well-being."

Lorenzo describes pre-birth amnesia: "Forgetfulness started when I accepted mind conditioning and the world appearance from authority figures who wanted me to get involved in their drama. I then saw that this third-dimensional presentation on Earth contradicted my experience. So the more ego I developed, beginning with the fetal life in the womb and then after birth as the confused child, followed by ego lesson on top of ego lesson, the more I was pulled into my parents' emotional activity. They became giants, and I felt too small to fight them. I was drawn into the drama, and heavy lessons began. On the other hand, it was the grounding point, part of my Cosmic Contract.

"We need to pay attention to discomfort. The valleys can be as accelerating as anything else. Both negativity and positivity are exhilarating when we have no attachment. A car moves forward due to its battery's negative and positive poles; so too our peaks and valleys give us permission to evolve fully. As Nietzsche said, Be careful about casting out your demon, you might be casting out the best part of you. We tend to deny our negative side. This is a mistake. Both sides are important. If we release ourselves from attachment to good and bad, we expand our being. All lessons are born through the coexistence of opposites."

Guide: "Are You Absolutely Certain?"

Rebirth planning is like watching a thriller movie.

Henny, a European woman in her mid-fifties, has no doubts about her pre-birth memory: "When I was seven years old, I suddenly told my mother about my past life memory and choosing her to be my mother. I had kept it to myself long enough. I had to express it because it was true. Confirmation was not necessary. At the same time, I was glad when mother validated it.

"I recall getting ready to die in a hospital in a past life. Ill and bedridden, I could only move my head. A nun dressed in white attended me. On the other side of my bed, a door opened. A slim eighteen-year-old woman entered. She was five feet tall with dark blond curly hair. She wore a brown coat with large buttons and a small pair of eyeglasses. The nun lifted my head, so that I could see the woman. I said, 'Yes, this is the woman I want for my mom.' I was happy and felt her sweetness. I was ready to start a new life.

"A long time passed before I found myself standing in front of a long vertical cylinder filled with white light. A video screen with images projected events to happen in my new life. An all-embracing invisible voice, who felt like the 'boss,' asked me, 'Are you sure you can deal with it?' 'Yes, I can,' I nodded confidently. There was time to think about whether I would be able to handle this new life. Once more, the voice asked: 'Are you completely certain you can handle it?' 'Yes,' I nodded. I was ready to go to a new life. Moments later, the voice asked the third time: 'Are you absolutely sure that you can deal with that?' I thought about what they showed me of my current life. Again, I said: 'Yes, I am certain, I can handle it.'

"According to my mother, she wore glasses and owned a camel-colored coat with large buttons before my birth. She also styled her hair exactly like I remembered it. There was no way I could have known any of this."

Henny's life has been tough. "Mom passed on when I was thirty-nine after an eight-year battle with cancer. When I found her dead body, a primordial scream came out of my mouth. I saw an invisible thread, a nonphysical umbilical cord, snap as if it were cut through." Henny saw the subtle umbilical cord between mother and child, affirming her elevated awareness. This is one reason mother and child share a life-long connection. "Ten years later, my husband died of cancer in February, and two months later my father died. Dad was handicapped, and his condition had been deteriorating for years."

Déjà Vu: Dysfunctional Family, Abuse, Cancer, NDEs

*Cheryl soared above the horrific conditions arising from
her pre-birth choice.*

"I have had this memory as long as I can remember of being in a
different time, space, and dimension. I was in the presence of a great
Light, a wonderful warmth. It was a place of the high hum of the
Universe. I was with little Light beings like myself who were not
totally solid as people. We were filled with innocence and exhilaration like children excited about Christmas or a birthday—that awesome wonder and thrill. We were all One. We were the Light, yet
distinct from the Light. Looking from where I am now, it would be
more like a wonderland that surpasses what we know here on Earth
as love. Everything was more pronounced, more beautiful and titil-
lating, like roses opening up. I don't have a description in my being
to properly describe the Love. Just to think about my memories
raises me up in my heart chakra, like I'm floating, a very high feeling. Wouldn't it be wonderful if everyone allowed themselves to
remember when we get to 'this side?' Most people get caught off or
cut down if they talk about it.

"Our Souls were gathered together, looking down at pictures, at
Earth. We had an opportunity to come into families. I peered down
and said, 'Look! I can come into a family that does not want me.
Oh, how wonderful that would be. Maybe I could even turn that
around. How exciting.'

"There is a whole different perception when we are choosing.
On this side, I would never have chosen this family. My parents
didn't have any money. Dad was going to college. The big problem
was my mother was Rh negative and my father was Rh positive. An
Rh negative mother cannot hold an Rh positive baby in her womb.
Her body rejects the fetus. Mom was able to bear my older sister
because my mom's antibodies were still building up. After that, she
miscarried a second baby. My parents were Irish Catholic and did

not use contraception. She was forced to stay in bed most of her pregnancy with me. I am Rh positive. Mom was allergic to me. My daddy was so anxious and stressed out with my pregnancy that he lost all of his hair.

"I was born in January, in below-zero temperatures. I developed whooping cough and 'died' at six weeks. I came back into my body. I needed to be in that family, no matter how much I was not wanted. My NDE reminded me of my pre-birth choice: my life may not be easy, and I was here to overcome challenges. I chose a family who was striving to be better, and they were successful at it. My parents grew up as poor farm children. During the Depression, Dad was one of eight children with no father from the time the oldest child was five. He had no role models for what a loving father would act like. As children, he and his brothers were lent out to harsh disciplining relatives as farm slaves to milk cows and shovel manure. They had no shoes, twenty-degrees-below-zero weather, and twenty-foot snows. Mom's family lost their farm during the Depression. By the time she was four, it was her job to go out with a rifle and kill squirrels to feed the family. My parents came from nothing. This was such a ripe ground for me. I knew before I was born that I would be getting little boosts because my parents were going to teach me how to overcome obstacles. Mom was a good teacher. Her attitude served us well. She taught us to cook, clean, study hard, participate in sports and social activities, be conservative, be creative, take care of our money, and to make our family proud. Mom was fiercely on our side as children. Nobody could say anything negative about us, but she never learned to be huggy or kissy. We knew she cared about us, but there wasn't much holding or embracing in my family. When I was eleven, I told her, 'I want to become a nun and live in a convent.' She said, 'That is not the direction you are going in. You are going to get married and have children.' I cried incessantly, repeating over and over, 'You don't understand me.' She wasn't able to comfort me very well. She patted my leg and said, 'There, there, it will be okay. Your dad and I love you.'

"Mom's favorite expression was: 'Pick yourself up by your boot-straps and keep on keeping on.' Those were words I heard all my life. They helped me be at the head of my class and overcome economic or health-related setbacks. I grew up with asthma and often thought, 'It would be easy to die right now.' But I was constantly reminded of my pre-birth choice: 'I am not here to die young. I am here to overcome the challenge.'

"Mom died at seventy-one. My sister, Linda, and I were at her side. She enjoined us, 'Take care of each other, like I took care of you when you were small children.'" Cheryl recalls a typical scene from childhood: "When my sister was four and I was not quite two, my mom put me in the baby carriage, gave Linda the grocery list and money, and sent us off to the grocery store. She expected Linda to return with the groceries and correct change, and to bring me back without problems.

"On my mother's deathbed, she also told me, 'You know, Cheryl, you needed more love than we could give you. Your daddy and I gave you all the love that we had for you. I am sorry if that was not enough. You needed more than what we had. We did our best. It was hard times. You came when you were not convenient.' It did help when Mom told me that. It was comforting.

"I look at my dad as my dark angel. He taught me places I did not need to go and things I did not need to do. I could look at his life and say, 'Maybe I should take a different path and be a little more loving, kind, giving, outgoing; more godly.' Dad changed after Mama died of cancer. He lived another eleven years and learned to be more loving and caring. Dad read psychology books and attended spiritual workshops with Edward and me. He learned how to hug and to enjoy getting hugs. It was difficult, but he softened. He wanted to heal. I was my daddy's little girl until he died at ninety-one. He waited for me to return from Washington to tell me he loved me and for me to tell him the same. I spent the night with him in the hospital. Dad died in the morning when I kissed him good-bye.

"I am so happy I chose my family. My parents taught me to be fiercely independent. I thank them both for that. It helped me survive when I broke my neck and had a concussion, and it helped me survive my marriage to a schizophrenic violent alcoholic, and it gave me strength to run away with two small children and start a new life. I was an abused wife. My first husband died an alcoholic death in his mid-thirties. I was pregnant with our third child. Our eldest daughter, rightfully so, had mental challenges. She was in a lockup mental institution for a few years. Our son attempted suicide at eleven. This forced us to do counseling and created a situation where it was a norm to reevaluate. I got a chance to delve into myself and look at goals, feelings, and expectations: 'Why I am here? Where do I want to go? How can I get help to get there?' I had to go within. I had to look at my Creator and say, 'I cannot do this myself. I need help.' The counseling also benefited my children. My son and daughter overcame all their challenges and are successful, caring adults today.

"I became a welfare mother after I ran away from my first husband. My parents did not help. Remember, my mom's favorite expression was 'Pick yourself up by your boot straps.' There was no room for weakness in her life. There were no victims in my family, only success stories over obstacles. It gave me the strength to go back to school to become a doctor at thirty-eight, right out of the pit of welfare. I learned how to ask for help and was not to be ashamed because help is here in the form of angels, if we only ask. My big lesson was to get over humility and become humble. Humiliation is an ego thing. One of my teachers was an African American woman working in an office that gave assistance so people did not freeze to death in the winter. In the middle of filling out the application, I said, 'I can't do this.' She told me, 'You know what? You have two little children. You can't afford to be so egotistical. You have to forget yourself and get help for your children. One of these days, you'll make lots of money and pay all this back. Right now you need help. So let's get you some help.'

"Around this time, I also had a lucid dream, a transcendental experience more real than life. The Dali Lama visited me and set me on a different path. He said, 'You started out to become a doctor; you need to be a doctor.' I was working as a loan officer and on welfare. I asked United Way for help: 'I'm planning to go back to school to become a doctor.' The advisor cocked her head to the side and told me, 'Sweetheart, we don't help individuals. We help organizations, like the Red Cross.' As she was talking to me, the tears starting streaming down my cheeks. She bent over, patted my leg, and said, 'It is okay. We'll help you.' They paid my outstanding bills for heat that whole winter. From that time forward, I absolutely got it: my angels were real.

"Next, a friend offered me $11,000 with no strings attached except that I treat him free of charge when I became a doctor. He reminded me, 'You have been telling me how angels appear in the form of people. You would be doing me a great disservice if you did not accept my help.' He provided the means for me to become a chiropractor.

"My life has been like that. Angels came out of the woodwork. That is why I was excited before birth. A life full of challenges and successes over those challenges has all come to fruition. I am blessed with an amazing husband. We are cancer survivors. We have both been through three NDEs. We are now in our sixties getting advanced degrees in a new career. Success is to choose [before birth], work within the confines that you are given, break out of those confines, and contribute more to bringing things around."

CHAPTER 6

Shirley Temple and the Blue Bird

~

A SOUL'S RELUCTANT SOJOURN TO EARTH

I did not want to come. God, however, instructed
me, inspired me to undertake the mission [to spread
righteousness and chastise the wicked].
— GURU GOBIND SINGH

Incoming Souls face a paradox: remain in an ideal world,
or opt for a challenge.

PRE-BIRTH DRAMAS CHOSEN BY THE Soul may be acted out in
life even in Hollywood lives and movies. Did two famous
child stars, Judy Garland and Shirley Temple, select pre-birth
scripts to play the lead roles in two movies, *The Wizard of Oz* and
The Blue Bird? Young Judy Garland, with her gifted singing talent,
seems to have been born as a perfect fit for the role of Dorothy in
the *The Wizard of Oz*, and Shirley Temple wound up in *The Blue
Bird*. Our greater interest is in *The Blue Bird*, 20th Century Fox's
1940 Technicolor feature starring Shirley Temple, who finds herself
in the world where children wait to be born. In a twist of Hollywood fate, Shirley was given the lead role in *The Blue Bird* after losing out to Judy Garland, who starred in MGM's 1940 blockbuster
The Wizard of Oz. While *The Blue Bird* was a famous box-office
flop, it was nominated for two Academy Awards after once being
called the *Peter Pan* of its time.

In *The Blue Bird,* Shirley talks to a young man who laments: "I am going to Earth soon. I don't want to be born." "Why is that?" asks Shirley, a curious visitor to the Kingdom of the Unborn Future. The tall youth explains, "There is so much happiness up 'Here.' We are free. When we are born, some are born free, but many are born into slavery, greed, cruelty, and injustice. I will teach people that they need not fight, that it can be the same on Earth as up 'Here'—free, equal, united. Still, I fear they will not listen." Shirley replies, "You must make them listen." The reluctant youth prophesies, "They will destroy me."

Meanwhile, Father Time arrives, armed with his scythe and hourglass. Father Time presides over the departure of the children whose turn it is to become the future inventors, doctors, presidents, and Hollywood actors. He summons the youth who dreamed of setting everyone free: "The hour has come. They want a hero to fight against injustice; you are the one. Come, quickly or you will miss being born. The galley is waiting and already flapping her sails." The pensive youth sighs, "That's me." Shirley replies, "Good luck." Little did she know that this tall gangly youth would become Abraham Lincoln.

This movie script mirrors pre-birth memories of people in chapter 6 who recall the love and communion of their spiritual abode and hesitate to leave. At some point, birth becomes involuntary, and a Soul moves into physical reality as if being swept up in a swift current. These pre-birth memories parallel the paradigm of ancient Greek philosophers, Sufis, and Gnostics: the physical body is a tomb, a prison, or a cage until we wake up and remember who we really are. We also find this motif of the reluctant Soul in the Jewish Kabbalah, where the Soul hesitates to enter a physical body.

What Happened to My Baby, Mary Ellen?

A baby's Soul waiting to be born was a silent eyewitness to its birth.

Dr. Creekmore was summoned to the King's Daughters Home for unwed mothers in Natchez, Mississippi. Lillie Mae, who came from a family of poor white sharecroppers, was in the final hours of childbirth. The doctor assumed the fifteen-year-old was simply another naughty girl.

Susan: "As I watched my birth process, I didn't like the fact that I was going into a body. It had been fun where I was, with lots of other baby Souls: a dimension of sheer joy and peace. Knowing that I would meet these Souls again in human form made it a little easier to be born." Susan sensed the distressful situation she found herself in at birth. Her birth mother, Lillie Mae, was barely more than a child and facing childbirth without any family support.

Susan: "While being born, I zipped in and out of my baby body in my mother's womb at least four or five times. I felt elated each time I zoomed out. As I came into the womb, a heaviness of body constricted my joyful self in spirit. Every time I exited the womb, I either went to the ceiling near the window or above the lamp hanging over the delivery table. I recalled there were high ceilings in this old mansion, with tall windows almost from floor to ceiling." Going in and out of the womb was nothing new for Susan. She had been doing it throughout the pregnancy. "It was like playing and being not accountable. It became cramped in there after a while. I wanted to stretch out. I was getting used to the physical body and still wanted the 'other' too—to integrate them."

Susan's 360-degree Soul vision captured the entire birth scene and outside surroundings: "I had a perception of the river outside. I recall seeing out of those long windows. I also knew that it was windy, raining hard, and it was dark. At the same time, I could see the bright light of the lamp hanging above the table. I sometimes hovered above the light, like a moth. Or if I looked down at this young frightened girl with a pretty round face, I was suddenly pulled, against my will, back into my baby body, where it felt claustrophobic, an uncomfortable feeling of suffocation. I heard the moans from the woman whose womb I was exiting. Whenever my mother had the most intense pains, I was yanked back into her womb, knowing that my time was getting shorter each time I was pulled back in. I was last pulled into my body when it was being pushed out of the birth canal. I could not get back out. I was stuck."

When Susan, who was named Mary Ellen at birth, was only three weeks old, she was separated from unwed Lillie Mae, who gave up her baby to an orphanage. As the station wagon taking the newborn babies drove away, Lillie Mae cried as she wished Mary Ellen would find a good home and have a good life. Five months later, Mary Ellen was adopted and renamed Susan. Several years passed, and her adopted mother explained, "We adopted you. You were the best child we found, and we chose you." The toddler felt positive about adoption because unlike everyone else, "I got picked out." Today, as an adult, Susan feels her Soul found the family she needed since her adopted mother was unable to bear children.

"As a two-year-old, my pre-birth memory stood out in my mind. Then I began to realize, 'Oh, these memories are fading away—I wish they wouldn't. They are so enjoyable.' One day as I stood right below Mom's skirt level, I felt prompted to say, 'Before I came here, everything was pink, blue, gold, and like clouds.' Mom humored me, 'When you grow up, you can be an actress on the stage.' Mom didn't fully appreciate my memory.

"The colors of pink, blue, and gold that I recall were bright. Sometimes, I had glimpses of a brighter light, almost white. It seemed to come and go between the colors. When that happened, they paled against it. The white light was grander, more magnificent. I never forgot; knowledge of my life before birth has confirmed that Eternity exists even when life has the most awful experiences. My memory has been a tremendous comfort."

Susan always desired to meet her birth mother. After Susan's adopted brother took his life because he had a brain tumor, her dad advised, "We feel it's a good idea to find your birth mother. You may find other siblings. We're old, and it will be good to have some family after we're gone."

Susan: "Locating my birth mother was like digging to find a bone in the dirt. After many years, in 1978, I got the number of a witness who signed my adoption certificate. I eventually tracked down my birth mother, who lived four hundred miles away. I will never forget the day we spoke the first time. It was the end of a long journey that I had started when I was fifteen. My friend Kim left a phone message for my birth mother: 'Mary Ellen, whom you have not seen since 1948, would like to talk to you. Please call her at this phone number.' I arranged for Kim to make the initial call in case Lillie Mae wanted to reject me. After Kim made the call, I lay down with a throbbing headache. Ten minutes after, my phone rang. I jumped up, still with that headache, and listened. Kim came to tell me, 'Your birth mother wants to talk to you.' I picked up the phone and said, 'This is Mary Ellen.' My birth mother said, 'Wonders never cease.' Finally, we hung up agreeing to meet in Jackson, Mississippi, the next week."

Susan and Lillie Mae reunited after thirty years. "Tears? Not really. Nervous? Yes, indeed. I loved my birth mother, but she did not have the 'love in her face and eyes' that my adopted and 'real' mother did. Our reunion was surreal. Lillie Mae had married a multimillionaire and had gone from rags to riches. She had a quick beautiful smile, the looks of a Hollywood star, and a charismatic personality. We were identical twins. She was just fifteen years older than me. It was like looking in a full-length mirror at myself. Lillie Mae was happy to hear about my wonderful upbringing. I will never regret my search and the woman I found.

"Lillie Mae told me, 'I always wondered what had happened to you. I had been in a difficult situation. An older man raped me soon after I turned fifteen. My mother tried to abort the baby. She ordered me into a horse trough of boiling water; one other time she forced me to take a large dose of aspirin. Nothing worked. I ended up being in labor from early morning until late at night. It was a terrible ordeal. Everyone talked about it and asked, 'Who birthed a baby last night? Her screams kept us up until almost midnight.'"

Lillie Mae confirmed all of Susan's birth memories:

❀ King's Daughters Home for unwed mothers: "No one ever told me that was where I was born, yet I always remembered the dark red brick antebellum home covered with green ivy situated on a bluff on the great river. When I located the home in my late twenties, the mansion was white and did not fit my memory. Lillie Mae confirmed that it had been red brick with ivy. The building had been painted later. Lillie Mae confirmed the exact home I remembered—the shape, the size, and the lawn."

❀ Delivery room: "An old-fashioned tin plate lamp with a bright light hung over Lillie Mae on a delivery table; wind rattled the tall windows so hard that the glass panes sounded like they would break; raining and nighttime."

❀ Doctor: "The doctor was tall and thin with a stern menacing look. Lillie Mae said, 'Oh, that was Dr. Creekmore. He was horrible. He scolded me and warned me that the next time I decided to be a bad girl, maybe I would remember this. He was angry and gruff. The nurse was as nasty.'"

"After I shared all these details with Lillie Mae, she told me, 'Everything you remember is true.' Now I knew for sure that I had not imagined it. Since I met my birth mother who had been raped at fourteen and gave me up for adoption, I felt she was a 'vehicle' for my birth, yet not meant to be my 'real' mother." Susan felt blessed with her adopted parents and that she had ended up after all with the right mother despite the circumstances. Lillie Mae died of breast cancer six years after their reunion. Today Susan is a freelance entertainment journalist and writer.

Soul Has 360-Degree Vision without a Body

Kathy knew Earth was not her real home and she did not originate here.

Kathy is a fifty-one-year-old mother of twins and an owner of a medical boutique catering to breast cancer women: "My pre-birth memory is strong. I remember it flawlessly. This memory is the one comfort that I can come back to. It is a gift from God. I may get frustrated and upset when I see the horrors mankind is capable of, or I may feel grief at the loss of fourteen family members and loved ones in the last two years, yet this powerful memory has given me peace and insights into the mysteries of life. I know that there is life before birth and after death. Death is like an awakening from a dream. I have no fear of death and this allows me to live more freely.

"My memory is more real than anything else and has shaped me into who I am. Explaining it is another story. How can one explain something that has no comparison in this world? My very first memory is of being in space above the Earth. I was a Soul without a body. I was part of the All That Is, yet I was still uniquely me. In this state, there was a peace that does not exist on planet Earth. I felt the presence of my heart and my mind, those things that make me *me*. I could see, with my mind's eye, 360 degrees around me at once. I enjoyed calm like I have never felt since. I was connected to everything and everything was a part of me. I could pinpoint where there was pain and where there was joy. If there was sadness, I would know it. Joy, I would know that too. I just needed to put my attention on something and all the information learned by the 'Whole' would be mine. I knew it could be as complicated or as simple as I chose to make it. I thought, 'Simple is better.'

"Suddenly, I began to come together, as if every cell in my body came from every direction, from the deep reaches of space, racing toward my being, creating a tingling sensation like billions of tiny bubbles coming together. Prior to this, I was not in a position to physically feel. My hands now pressed against my thighs, and I felt my skin. I felt constricted in this form. I could no longer see all around me, although my heart and mind and Soul were still connected to everything else. I assured myself, 'It's okay. This is just a different form of being.'

"As I floated there, I looked down at this stunning planet, a beautiful gem in the universe. The brightness of the blue against that inky blackness of space was incredible. Even with similar planets in the universe, Earth was a prime piece of real estate. I wanted to take the planet into my arms and take care of all humanity. I also wanted to protect it because it seemed so fragile.

"Then pretty quickly, I began to experience dread because I knew where I was going. It was not going to be easy. At any rate, I volunteered: something I have cussed myself for during moments of frustration. I knew that dying would be like this feeling, and I have yet to fear death. We are all here to learn and grow. I had agreed to come to this planet. I had a sense of purpose and duty. As if finally accepting what I had come to do, I began very gently to descend, back first, toward this beautiful blue planet.

Pre-Birth Memories of Finding a Baby's Body

"As a child, I assumed everyone had memories of coming here. When I was four, my father sat me down at the kitchen table and asked, 'What's the very first thing you remember in this life?' I told him as best I could about coming to the planet and getting a body. Dad's jaw dropped a little bit, but I never understood why. He never said anything and I went back to playing with my toys. Periodically, Dad asked me to recount this again. He never pooh-poohed my memory. As I got older, I could explain it a little more as my vocabulary increased. Dad wanted to make sure I had written it down. But I didn't need to; it is ingrained in me like my fingerprints. Later on, when I was eight, man first walked on the Moon in July 1969. Mom was so thrilled. She pulled me to the corner of the living room and made me sit in front of the TV. She said, 'Watch this. It is history in the making. Look at that. That is where we are.' My mother really puzzled me. I said, 'Why are you making a big deal about this?' I wondered, 'Didn't Mom see Earth from outer space before?' The black and white, two-dimensional image could not compare to what I had seen.

"I did not know my memory was weird until I was playing in the driveway with my friends one day. I grew up in a neighborhood with a bunch of boys. When I was about eight, I got confused when they did something mean to a kid who had just moved into our block. I asked, 'Why are you doing this? Don't you remember before we came here, when we were all connected?' They stopped and looked at me. I assumed everyone knew we were all part of the One and that we affected each other. I thought, 'I am not explaining myself very well.' I said, 'You know, before we were born.' There was like a pause and then all of a sudden, it was: 'Oh my God, Kathy thinks she remembers being born.' This was my realization point. I fell back into myself and felt extremely alone. I kept my mouth shut after that.

"I remember sitting in my room and thinking about this. I got angry. When you are a kid, the last thing you want is to be different. I had quite a few conversations with God. I went outside and talked to the stars. I was mad and yelled to the sky because I knew I came from somewhere out there: 'Why did you have me remember this?' Why did you put me here? I am alone.' You should take me back now.' I heard a powerful, 'No' like a parent admonishing a kid. It made me cower.

"I finally realized, 'If I don't tell anyone my memory, how are they going to know I am different?' I also saw that so many people were afraid to live because they were afraid to die. I had knowledge that many people didn't have. How special that is. I felt it was my own private little gift from God. I felt extremely humbled.

"My life has been difficult. My mother, although sweet and even a bit psychic, had ongoing serious health problems that eventually led to alcohol. She was also a beauty queen. My ex-husband had health challenges for years. The doctors would conclude, 'There is nothing wrong with him.' That is, until the next thing sent him back to the hospital again. He was finally diagnosed with Asperger's syndrome."

Cosmic Twist: Girl Meets Boy

Since childhood Kathy recalled two male beings from Heaven whom she had been searching for: one was her "other" and one was her "brother." On the same day in 1995, Kathy hit the jackpot on the Internet, finding both Souls. Floyd is one of them, and they plan to get married. It is an inspiring love story. As Kathy got to know Floyd, she rejoiced in having someone she could talk to about life before birth for the first time in her life: "I can't tell you the comfort I have felt in finding someone who understands me. Pre-birth memory is too beautiful a secret to keep to myself." Floyd's memories are in chapter 7 in the story "Soul Reborn from Tibet."

Love Overcomes Trauma at Birth

Janice handpicked her parents and siblings.

"If you have ever had the opportunity to feel the Holy Spirit, that is the best description of the pre-birth state, or Heaven: love, in its most condensed form; goodness; happiness. It was a wondrous place filled with comfort, security, and understanding. Before birth I chose parents and one sibling after another. My Guides expressed a humorous reaction to the number of siblings I chose—seven. I felt a deep love toward my family and took comfort in the fact that these Souls would be with me."

Janice recalls embryonic life and birth. Fetal life felt "heavy, terrible, and awkward. I entered the womb for a while and then went back to Heaven. I gradually became accustomed to my body by increasing the time spent in the womb as pregnancy progressed. Delivery was an adrenaline rush. After the initial excitement and swoosh of traveling through a tunnel [the birth canal], feelings of confusion, panic, and pain enveloped my body. I thought, 'I cannot take this earth world. Why wasn't I warned about this harshness?' When I was about to give up, I took my first breath."

As a child Janice talked about her memories to siblings and friends until she was about eight years old. "My brother said, 'That's just a dream.' My memories did not enter my mind again until I was a teenager." Her mother explained, "You were born in a reputable hospital in Boston. Of my eight children, your delivery was the hardest. The umbilical cord was wrapped several times around your throat. No matter what the doctor did, you were not coming out. Then, in a panic, he threw his hands up and ran out of the room. The nurse chased him and pleaded for him to come back. She returned alone and calmly told me, 'We are going to deliver this baby, even if we have to do it on our own.' The nurse was able to unwrap the cord. The doctor never returned. The next day I caught the doctor sneaking past my room as if to say, 'Oops!' I said, 'You SOB. You had better duck.' He apologetically said, 'Well, you're all right now.'" When Janice's mother finished this story, memories flooded back into Janice's consciousness—panic, pain, inability to breathe. "Now I understood why I have never been able to wear a scarf, turtleneck sweater, or a necklace. I had always wondered, 'What's wrong with me?' It was good to know there was a rational basis for my strange phobia. I felt vindicated.

"I chose my life, and I thank God for my memories. They have given me a sense of security and well-being—an inner 'knowing' that everything will be okay in the end. I remind myself when I go through a hard time, 'You picked this, girly,' or 'This was picked for you, so go through it, learn from it, and do the best you can.' Life would be a lot scarier if I didn't have these memories. I know there is a reason for my being here. Certain attitudes come easier for me because of my pre-birth memories: Don't worry; be happy! We need to forgive more, and not be so quick to judge. Life is all about love and being the best person you can be."

Reluctant Sojourner Recalls Light at Birth

Angie recalls a great reluctance to be born before cervical dilation.

"Before my birth I felt bathed in peace and safety all around. A bright, soft light appeared in the darkness. I kept fighting; I knew it would be so very cold if I went to the light. As I was thinking about what was about to happen, I heard a male voice say, 'You must go to the light now. You are only going for a little while; you will come back. Trust me that everything will be okay.' I didn't want to leave. I felt like this being was right there with me. I felt safe with him and went to the light. And just as I already knew, it was cold. I saw the doctor, a nurse, and my mother. A woman singing to me warmed me up and placed me on a scale. I was afraid that I might fall off. Mom's voice calmed me down, and everything felt okay after that.

"I am twenty-seven now and remember this like it happened yesterday. The moment has never left me. I shared memories as a child. Mom thought I was making up a story. But one day recently, as I held my baby's hands, I told Mom about when I first noticed my hands as a baby: 'I was lying awake in something that made me feel locked up (my crib). I looked at my hands and thought, 'Wow, it has two sides, and I can control them too.' I was happy to have something new. Mom said, 'Babies do not think like that. It is impossible.' But I know what I remember, and I was only one month old. For a long time I was confused because Mom denied my memories. I wondered, 'How can I make Mom believe me and help me understand my memories?' I asked, 'Did someone sing to me when I was born?' Mom gave me a funny look and said, 'Yes, a nurse was singing to you. You must have overheard me talk about it.' But I never heard that; and why would my Mom have mentioned to anyone that a nurse was singing to me at birth?"

Angie recalls a special event during infancy. "I was resting flat on my back on a table and was thinking about the male being's voice telling me to go to the light. I thought, 'What am I doing here? Is this really me?' Then my mom repositioned me on my side. I became upset and filled with fear. I thought, 'I am going to fall off the table.' I cried and I didn't understand why no one took the fear away. I told Mom about this when I was six. She brushed it off as if it was nothing: 'I do not understand how you could remember that. I never told you. How could you know?' Mom had a different response when I broached the subject four years later: 'That was the day I put you on the table at Great-Grandma's home to show you off and take photos.' She showed me my picture as a two-month-old baby lying on the table and asked, 'Is this what you're talking about?' I had never seen that photo before. Mom believed me then, yet if I were to ask her today, she would say, 'No, that's impossible.'"

We Are All Beams of Light

Tim planned his last lifetime on Earth.

For the past fifteen years, Tim, has been an EMT–fire fighter until his injuries from his Army career prevented him from working. Tim now helps people recover their earliest memories. Tim: "I remember where I was before I was born: I was 'Home.' I loved everyone deeply and knew they loved me the same. We are all Souls traveling, coming and going. That place is Home for all of us. I met my Spiritual Guide before birth. I was lying in the grass under a tree in this heavenly world. I was thinking about the thrill of coming into the physical world. I knew without any doubt, that after this life, I would stay back Home for good. I felt a sigh of relief. I reflected on past lives like flipping through 3-D images in a Rolodex file. With each blink of my eyes, I saw one life after another: 'bam, bam, bam.' I thought, 'Oh, I remember that,' or 'Oh, there's that possession I missed.' I suddenly stood up and told my Guide, 'I'll do it.' Next thing I knew, I was slammed into Mom's belly. I felt the physical world—loud gushing sounds, heartbeat, and bowel tones. I yelled, 'I want to go back; I don't want to do this again.' I moved around and jerked. This may be when Mom first felt me kick. I squirmed until a familiar voice said, 'It is all right. I'm right here.' I said, 'Where? I can't see you.' My Spirit Guide said, 'I'll be right here.' I calmed down. I trusted him.

"I heard Mom's conversations while I was in her belly. One time Mom was excited and talking to someone. I felt joy coming from the two of them. I saw sunlight coming in through her stomach. Years later, I told Mom, 'You were excited about where to put a couch. I think you were talking to Great Grandpa.' She said, 'No, that was your dad. We were standing in front of the window discussing where to put the couch. We had recently moved into our new home. I was close to my due date. You were born the next day.'

"My vision was blurry at birth, and I felt cold. Then mom held me, and I felt safe. I recall the comfort of my mom, being close to her, and the voices of everybody. After that, it was wet diapers, dry diapers." Years later Tim's mother validated his birth memories of the delivery room: sea-foam green walls, a bright light above, stainless steel tables. Tim saw lines on the wall. His mom explained, "Oh, yes, I gave birth in the doctor's basement office. Those were cinder block walls. I couldn't wait to get out of there."

Tim was born in September 1969. He recalls his first Christmas as a three-month-old. "I was sitting on the floor gumming a yellow kangaroo squeak toy and enjoying the taste of the sweet air inside when suddenly, boom, my brain started clicking. I thought, 'Wait a minute, where was I before?' I realized, 'This is something I should remember.' I looked at the toy in my hands. I scanned the room. I knew what the TV was. I saw colorful lights dancing around the room coming from a silver tree covered with lights and shiny objects. I heard my brother banging on his toys in the other room. Mom and Dad were on a white couch with shiny reflecting plastic covers. I thought, 'Mom! Dad!' I wanted to get up and embrace them, but I couldn't walk across the room. I concluded, 'I must remember these things. They'll be important in the future.' Now I wonder, how could a three-month-old think like this? How did I already know what a kangaroo or a TV was?" Tim's mother later confirmed that 1969 was the last year they had that aluminum Christmas tree. The next year they bought an artificial plastic tree.

Tim relates an event when he was four years old: "Mom was getting ready in the bathroom. I asked, 'Where are we going?' She replied, 'We are going to church to see Jesus.' I was excited; I remembered who Jesus was. I knew him in Heaven. When we got to church, I looked all over, as people were mingling and greeting each other, but I did not see Jesus. Then I got shuffled off to a class, where the teacher kept us busy coloring pictures of Jesus in a coloring book. I thought, 'Mom said I was coming here to see Jesus. This teacher says this is what Jesus looks like, but this is not Him.' I told the Sunday school teacher: 'I'm not here to sit in class. I came to see Jesus. This is not Jesus.' She asked, 'What does he look like?' I told her, 'He's always smiling, and has a bright shining face, white hair, no beard, no mustache. He's my friend; I've always known him.' I was dismissed from class. I ended up in my grandmother's class across the hall.

"My memories have been a comfort. I have no fear of death. I know where I am going when I die. I know where everyone else is going. I have always lived that way. I have had that kind of mentality."

Reluctance to Exit the Bliss: Parallels to Near-Death Experiences

Susan, Kathy, and Tim who felt reluctant to leave their pre-birth Home and to enter a body mirror reports found in NDEs. During an NDE, people encounter mystical worlds filled with such love and bliss that they actively resist going in the direction of pain and returning to their bodies. In both pre-birth memories and NDEs, the Soul is apprehensive about leaving an unearthly world and journeying to Earth, a lower, thicker tone.

Here we offer an NDE illustration from Reverend Howard Storm as a parallel to people who were reluctant to be born. During his NDE, Howard told his Guides that going back to Earth, a world filled with hate and competition, would be cruel. Howard listed reasons why they should not send him back: (1) he would forget their teachings about love and compassion and would act mean again or hurt somebody; (2) the spiritual world offers everything he desires, whereas human life is filled with problems; (3) he could not exist without these beings of great love and light; (4) he does not know how to connect with these divine beings when he is on Earth.

The Guides gently explained why Howard should return: (1) they assured him that mistakes are an acceptable part of being human. Mistakes are the way he will learn. If he makes a mistake, he should try not to make the same mistake again. (2) the world is a beautiful manifestation of God, and depending on where we direct our mind, we find beauty or ugliness; (3) every aspect of creation is fascinating, and to explore this world with wonder and enjoyment is a great opportunity; (4) our love can come to you even when you are on Earth if you become quiet inside and ask. With that, Howard ran out of arguments and agreed to return to his body.[1]

Pre-birth memories and NDEs share another similarity in regard to Earth Lessons. In the pre-birth world, Souls are informed they must go to Earth for a while. They preview their upcoming life. In chapter 8, for example, Beverly compares this life-planning process to choosing an actor's role in a Hollywood movie. In an NDE, the person experiences the reverse process. Instead of previewing their upcoming life, they review their life already lived like a videotape replay. During Mellen-Thomas Benedict's NDE, for example, he witnessed a holographic life review going back to the period in the womb. He saw his father beat his mother and felt his father's fists pounding on her belly. He sensed her fear and depression. Mellen realized that this event was the first trigger of his brain cancer. Mellen was born "pissed off" at his father.[2]

As a second case, P. M. H. Atwater's NDE revealed: "I expected some kind of theatrical showing of my life as Phyllis or perhaps something like a television replay, but such was not the case. Mine was not a review; it was a reliving. For me, it was a total reliving of every thought I had ever thought, every word I had ever spoken, and every deed I had ever done; plus the effect of each thought, word, and deed on everyone and anyone who had ever come within my environment or sphere of influence whether I knew them or not (including unknown passersby on the street); plus the effect of each thought, word, and deed on weather, plants, animals, soil, trees, water, and air. It was a reliving of the total gestalt of me as Phyllis, complete with all the consequences of ever having lived at all.... If there is such a thing as hell, as far as I am concerned this was hell."[3]

At the end of a typical NDE review, a guide informs the individual that it is time to return to the physical body. There is more to do on Earth. Thus, we find that in NDEs and pre-birth memories, the Souls realize they have a purpose on Earth and surrender to fulfill a particular life plan.

CHAPTER 7

Our Soul as a Tiny Spaceship

INTERLIFE MEMORIES

What we call birth is merely the reverse side of
death, like a door that we call "entrance" from
outside and "exit" from inside a room.
—LAMA ANAGORIKA GOVINDA

Life is fluid and continuous from one lifetime to the next.

ANOTHER TWIST IN RESEARCH ON pre-birth memories are
cases that stretch memory back beyond the pre-birth realm
to include past-life memories. This research suggests the
underlying Soul connections linking past-lives, rebirth, and pre-
birth memories, since pre-birth may overlap with rebirth. Such
combined reports are not new since the research by psychiatrists
Dr. Ian Stevenson and Dr. Jim Tucker discovered them among three
thousand cases of children's past-life memories or rebirth.[1] Dr. Stevenson spent over forty years investigating and verifying children's
past-life memories largely in Asia where Eastern cultures are more
inclined to believe in rebirth and accept children's memories. Dr.
Tucker's research has focused more on identifying rebirth cases in
the United States.

Chapter 7 highlights five past-life memory cases that are coupled
with pre-birth memories. Prashant was reborn in India after a lifetime where he was a monk in a Christian monastery. Stephana's

first child chose to be reborn after his former life suddenly ended. Raghavan recalls his rebirth in India after a traumatic death. Floyd was a Tibetan refugee in his past life and underwent a unique inter-life journey based upon his belief system. Diane was a healer in many past lives and chose to be reborn in a family with a genetic predisposition for healing.

Dr. Stevenson emphasizes that it takes more than a good memory to remember a previous life. He cites an interesting link between past life memory and spiritually evolved persons: "the longstanding belief in Buddhism and Hinduism that spiritual development, through meditation and meritorious deeds, clarifies the mind and enhances memory." Stevenson explains that the *tulkus* of Tibet remember being spiritually evolved lamas in previous lives who lived rather ordinary monastic lives and died naturally. One might suggest that "although the events of their lives were not memorable, the persons who had lived these lives were remarkable and may have carried the mental clarity they attained by their spiritual practices into another incarnation."[2] This meditation-memory link is relevant to a number of persons interviewed for this chapter.

Dr. Jim Tucker's research goes one step further, suggesting that meditation practice in a past life may increase an individual's ability to recall a past life. Dr. Tucker writes: "The more the previous personality meditated, the more detail the child subsequently used in describing events in another realm."[3] Dr. Tucker cites a small, yet statistically significant link in thirty-three of eleven hundred children's cases between memories of another realm and if the previous personality meditated. In this regard, it is interesting that chapter 7 includes memories of Prashant and Floyd who recall being meditators in previous lives living within spiritual communities. Before presenting the unique set of memories of these five people, let us review two other well-documented and validated cases.

Surveyor Moves on to Become a Monk

A validation case investigated by Dr. Stevenson highlights the inter-life and rebirth memories of Sayadaw Sobhana, a Buddhist monk and scholar born in Burma in 1921.[4] At the age of two, Sayadaw recalled his past-life as thirty-six-year-old surveyor Maung Po Thit, who died in 1920 of an appendicitis attack. Little Sayadaw, remembering that he had left one child and a pregnant wife behind, was delighted to locate them living nearby three years after his death as their father and husband. Sayadaw's past-life family confirmed the youngster's past-life memories. The boy's new playmates were the two children that he had fathered in a former life. Sayadaw addressed them as if he were their father. He recalled events in that previous life going back to the age of twelve, including details of former relationships, friends, property, and debts.

Of special interest to us as pre-birth researchers is how Sayadaw's memories of what happened after dying in his past life dovetail with events on Earth. First he met an ethereal sage dressed in white who escorted him from the after-death paradise to his current mother. Next, they visited the home of Maung's widow. The sage went inside while Maung's spirit waited outdoors. The widow was likely grieving for her departed husband and the sage telepathically consoled her in a dream that Maung was being reborn nearby. Then the sage escorted him to his new mother, a neighbor. The sage accompanied Maung's spirit into his new home and announced that she was to have a child. Mrs. Sobhana gave birth to Sayadaw in 1921.

Sayadaw's interlife memories are all the more impressive because they dovetail with announcing dreams of his rebirth. On the seventh night after Maung's burial, a sage dressed in white appeared in the dreams of Maung's widow and his new mother. The sage told the widow that he was sending her late husband to the village headman's house. The sage appeared in a dream informing Maung's new mother that Maung wanted to live with her.

Sayadaw grew up to become the Venerable Sayadaw U Sobhana. He never forgot his interlife memories. He is convinced that the spiritual helper who guided him to his family corresponds to the sage in the announcing dreams of his former wife and present mother. Dr. Stevenson investigated two hundred and thirty reincarnation cases in Burma. He cited that in nearly half of the rebirth cases the parents had announcing dreams of the child prior to birth. Sayadaw's story is more rare because his interlife memories coincide with the dreams of two people.

Pre-Birth Memories and Rebirth of a World War II Fighter Pilot

The famous contemporary case of young James Leininger presents another combination of past-life and pre-birth memory validation.[5] Motivated by two-year-old James's nightmares of being shot at by Japanese warplanes and finding himself in a burning plane, his parents Bruce and Andrea researched and confirmed the boy's memories of flying fighter planes and his past-life ending as World War II pilot James Huston, Jr. The reborn James is Bruce and Andrea's only child together after leaving previous marriages.

One more surprise buried in this boy's memory emerged when his father picked the boy up into his arms, kissed and hugged him, and told James how happy he was to have him as a son. Four-year-old James responded in a matter-of-fact adult tone of voice that he had picked Bruce to be his father because he knew he would be a good dad. Bruce was dumbfounded by his son's statement and queried the boy further. James surprised his father with details of how he found them. The little boy mystically knew they would be good to him. James explained that he found them in Hawaii at the big pink hotel on the beach eating dinner at night. More surprising is that the parents had never mentioned their fifth wedding anniversary celebration to James. In 1997, Bruce and Andrea stayed at the Royal Hawaiian, the pink hotel on Waikiki Beach. They had a moonlight dinner on the beach. James described it perfectly. Five weeks later, James was conceived and born in 1998. Bruce had "no idea what to make of it. He was confused and frightened. Bruce ran into the house and told Andrea, but she was already convinced that James possessed knowledge that no one could readily account for. It was just one more thing."[6] This case offers a link between James's past life and his current life separated by over fifty years. James Huston, Jr. was a pilot who was lost in a battle near Iwo Jima in the Pacific in 1945. In this life, James Leininger found his parents in Hawaii.

A Soul Googles Earth Seeking Rebirth

Before birth, Prashant saw a market scene in New Delhi.

Prashant is a forty-year-old Indian author, freelance journalist, businessman, lawyer, Christian, and seeker of truth. "My first memory in early childhood was a deathbed vision of myself as a seventy- or eighty-year-old Caucasian monk dressed in a robe. My death was peaceful and painless. I was lying in bed in a monastery room illuminated by candles. I intuitively knew that I was somewhere in Europe in the fourteenth to sixteenth centuries CE, probably in Italy. A young monk sat at my bedside. One moment I was looking at this young brother holding my left hand and crying as he said in a language that must have been Latin or Italian, 'Good-bye, Father.' The next moment I was floating out of my body and looking at my own self lying on the bed from a vantage point of four or five feet off the ground."

A light in the corner of the room attracted the awareness of Prashant's Soul. "The light was like an opening of sorts—the upper right corner of the room opened up and a bright, whitish light with a tinge of pink, blue or both came through. I instinctively knew this is where I must go. I started to move towards it and eventually got sucked into it. There was absolutely no pain or fear. I would say it was comforting.

"Next I recall being high up in the clouds descending toward Earth, like Google Earth, where you zoom in and get closer and closer. I'm conscious that I don't have a body. I'm a point of consciousness descending on the Earth. I approached until I was one hundred feet above the ground. I noticed a market or bazaar. My attention was drawn to a happy couple holding hands and singing. The man was wearing a light blue sweater and blue jeans; the woman was dressed in a traditional Indian orange sari. I zoomed in closer and closer to the woman and entered her womb. While I entered my mother's womb and looked up toward her, I was not seeing the inside of her body as such; I saw her as if seeing someone from inside a swimming pool—like looking out through a fluid of sorts, but the fluid was not a liquid. Rather it was like a luminescent fluid. I observed a reddish color of the fetus as it developed. I have a vague recollection of my mother's heartbeat and seeing the umbilical cord. However, I saw my fetus as an outsider would, kind of the way I saw my dead body as a monk. I don't remember birth, but I do recall being a tiny infant in the cradle. I felt very distinctly conscious and a bit frustrated at being confined and unable to sit up and stand. There was definitely some memory of being able to do these things in an earlier existence, another sign of reincarnation.

"I have had this pre-birth memory as long as I can remember. At first I thought it was a dream. When I was seventeen, I shared my memories. I told my parents that they were singing and described the setting and their clothing. They looked at each other in shock and couldn't believe their ears. My parents verified the events. I was also shocked that they remembered what I remembered. They confirmed that when my mother was four months pregnant, they had attended a friend's engagement ceremony wearing the exact clothing I described. The only time that they held hands and sang a song in public was in the New Delhi South Extension market on the day of a friend's engagement ceremony. What a time for my Soul to enter.

"I am a Christian born into an Indian Christian family. I lived in the United States from the age of three to ten. I never knew about reincarnation until I was thirteen when my father gave me a copy of *Autobiography of a Yogi* by Paramahansa Yogananda. This book opened up my spiritual outlook. I also read the Bible regularly and found references to reincarnation in the New Testament, such as when Jesus told his disciples, 'Elijah has come already but you knew him not.' The disciples knew that Jesus was referring to John the Baptist. Also there is a reference to the blind man being 'born blind because of his sins.' Obviously those sins were committed in a former existence. My dad believes in reincarnation. My mom and wife are inclined to believe, but aren't sure. However, my experience has convinced them to a very large extent."

Phoenix Rising from the Ashes

Unexpected Soul helps its future mother overcome sterility.

Stephana and her husband worked with a gynecologist for five years trying to have a child and were unsuccessful in discovering what their infertility problem might be. "A few days before we took steps to adopt a child, I received a frantic call from my brother: 'Dad died in a fire. The house blew up and burned down. Get on a plane right away. No phone lines are working. I don't know what's happening with Mom.'

"Dad and I were very close. He was definitely someone I chose before I came into this life. He was an awesome being. When he was gone, I was reeling. After I returned from the funeral, I had a strong communication: 'Okay, I am ready for a new body. It is time to make a body, please.' I felt a one hundred percent absolute presence in the room. I did not expect this message. It was ten days after Dad's death. I was doing a chore in the middle of the day. It was the purest communication I have known. I felt a tremendous calmness and strength—it was definitely not of this world. Also there was a sense of humor or lightheartedness I recognized as Dad's essence. 'Okay, I am ready for a new body now' were the words, but the concept came more from a spirit of playfulness, like he was ready to create again, and the loss or trouble and trauma of his previous life was no longer there. It gave me a reprieve from my intense grief. Very matter-of-factly I shared the communication with my husband.

"We conceived ten days after my father's transition. It was not a typical sexual interchange—it was a purposeful cocreating, and there was no question of a divine presence. I was not in any place, interest-wise, to have sex prior to receiving this message. I was not aware of ovulation or any of this to know if I could conceive—it was all divinely led and cocreated from a higher source."

At the end of her first successful pregnancy, Stephana noticed a shift in awareness when she reached ten centimeters during labor and was ready to push. "I went into pure bliss and joy and started laughing because I got this intense telepathic communication, a higher vibrational wave length: 'All right, it's time.' It was a message from this being saying he was so excited: 'This is going to be cool. This will be fun.' It was playful, kind, compassionate energy of my father, but not as Dad. It was the same energy, the same being as the first message.

"I did not project anything on my son, yet for the first twenty-four hours, Randall looked like Dad, the same face and mouth. We were looking at each other and smiling. When Randall was two years old, he told me, 'Do you remember when I was your Dad and I died in a fire?' He said it very matter-of-factly, out of the blue, and then went back to his toys. He was not obsessed with it, nor upset." Today Stephana and her husband also have a little girl as evidence that their sterility was mysteriously overcome.

What Sort of Rebirth Do You Want?

Raghavan recalls the passage into his current life.

Raghavan, a forty-four-year-old businessman from India and a happily married man with three children, recalls: "I remember my untimely death at a young age in my previous life. I was stabbed, and life ended in pain. While dying, I tried to remember details about that life. Some external force purposefully erased my memory. I only recollect the dying process. After death, I flew with God's messenger. The divine escort telepathically informed me that I was going for judgment. The messenger asked me to wait in a dimension of total emptiness. I stood on a platform structure, floating in space. My Soul felt liberated from all burdens. I discerned that it was not my time to go to Heaven permanently for final liberation. Instead, if I do good deeds in my next birth, these merits will count toward final salvation.

"Finally the Supreme One entered my thoughts: 'What sort of a rebirth do you want? Do you want luck? Or do you want a good family with secure finances, but you will not have any luck?' I opted for the good family without luck. Next I found myself nestled in Mom's womb. I recall waking up once and seeing one of my mother's organs and trying to figure out where I was. Somehow it came to me that it was her liver. I thought of how to spell the word *liver*. Then I realized, 'I don't know the letters of the alphabet yet. I have to grow up first.' Afterward, I dozed off again. I woke up right before delivery. I was suffocated due to a gush of air. I felt trapped, claustrophobic, as if I were in a cave and wanted to rush out. I started kicking, not knowing that I was causing discomfort to my mother. I mentioned my memory to my mother when I was twenty-seven."

His mother, Vimala, confirms Raghavan's birth memories. "First, I wish to point out that it was my only delivery, Raghavan being my only child. Second, I do remember the kicking and felt as if my lungs would burst. He kicked again and again in the womb before starting down the birth canal. I didn't feel any pain in the womb, but I suffered great pain during childbirth. Since my son is a very truthful person and he told me that he has vague memories of pre-birth, I was forced to believe that what he said was true. I am baffled how a baby in the womb could remember that."

How does Raghavan's pre-birth choice measure up to his life? "I essentially have good parents, an understanding wife, good children, and I am satisfied with whatever God has given me monetarily. Even so, right from childhood, I have encountered obstacles. Normally a person has financial or relationship problems; however, despite having all the things to lead a good life, I have not had a smooth ride. My wife often says, 'Everyone has problems, yet I haven't seen anyone have such unique problems, and that too at each and every step.' The obstacles I have faced are ridiculous and out of the ordinary. Once my wife and I went on vacation. People will not believe this: I sneezed and dislocated my hand. It simply popped out of its socket. After major surgery, including a bone graft from my hip, I was bedridden six months."

Soul Reborn from Tibet

Floyd knew before birth that his spiritual journey would not be easy in this life.

Compared to his select past life in Tibet, Floyd's birth into a Mormon family in the United States has been filled with turmoil as a test of his spiritual nature. People often misunderstand how Souls evolve. They assume that with each successive lifetime, our position becomes more elevated: first a student, then a teacher; next an advanced teacher, and so on. In reality, it is not that simple. Even the most advanced Souls accept a lower position to help fill in the gaps of what they need to learn.

Floyd recalls his past life as a young Tibetan monk and spiritual leader who died in 1960 after fleeing Tibet to India due to China's invasion: "Following death, I floated above the planet within a blue sphere representing the boundaries of my consciousness. I observed thousands of exiles fleeing from one country to another. I could feel the minds of thousands of people praying for me and wishing for my rebirth. I realized that the world's problems were great. I was aware of atrocities of history such as the holocaust in Nazi Germany. I felt I needed more experience from the Source in order to help others. If I were to be born as a Tibetan teacher again and merely held that position, I would not make a significant difference. I chose to learn from a different perspective, to bring something new to Earth, beyond what I had known in my previous life."

Unification and Birth within the Great Mother

"When I sensed conditions getting better on Earth and the storm passed, or at least stabilized, I looked within my being at a tiny spark of reddish-orange light. During this contemplation I broke beyond the veil of the blue sphere, beyond what was taught to me as a Tibetan Buddhist, and beyond my limited perception. I began traveling toward the southwest. My consciousness seemed so vast. I became aware of a state in my evolution never experienced before in past lives.

"I then traveled into the center of the galaxy, approaching a great black Void, where I became aware of a vastly primordial motherly presence. While communing with this presence, I felt the life force emanating from every living being on every star through me, as if I were a conduit. I resolved, 'This is too much of a gift for me alone. I need to share it. I want every being in the universe to experience this.' I vowed to forever work for this purpose."

Ultimate Bliss of the Center of the Galaxy

Floyd looked at the heavens before entering the Void—reflecting on where he had been, his past lives of working to help others, and the infinite possibilities of where he was going. "It was so beautiful looking across the vastness of space: I was only a speck, yet a part of that whole organism envisioning the infinite possibilities of evolution." Floyd entered the Void knowing that he was going to give up prior positions as a teacher for the unknown. "I perceived an odd sensation of a dual consciousness—a sense of individual identity along with awareness of everything. Every being was linked with every other being. Every being was also linked with the entire megaverse, with infinite growth potential. It was as though no one had ever thought of this place; it was a secret entrance into another dimension. I felt a profound connectedness and love."

Floyd felt fulfilled with a great mystery: "The Void was a holy place. There was only Light. Evil could not touch this realm. I pondered what my new awareness meant. The Light was a part of me, and I was a part of the Light; the Light had an intelligence and identity. I had been reborn into nonduality, a community of spiritual beings who were Pure Consciousness beyond the confines of ordinary perception, where everything is filtered through our five senses. They had neither masculine nor feminine presence. Identity was distinguished by character, telepathically radiated through the Light."

Supreme Initiation by a Being of White Light

Floyd caught a glimpse of one great Being of White Light. "This being had served the Light for many cyclical existences of a multitude of universes. I was amazed at what could be accomplished by dedication to others. This immense being no longer needed to incarnate in physical form, was still in service by teaching others, and could pass into other dimensions of consciousness far beyond my comprehension. I aspired to reach this infinite consciousness someday.

"The Light Being guided me into another Universe via a sphere of Light. I was overwhelmed with tremendous power and knowledge. An uncontrollable emotion of gratitude swept through my being as I recalled my past life. I felt honored to have this experience. All was perfect Unity. The mysteries of life were revealed, yet it was too much to contain, as if it were a storehouse of knowledge and power encompassing all points of time, space, knowledge, and a profound plan. I looked back at past lives. All my worries and complexes were nothing in comparison to this sense of belonging."

Floyd had been given the choice to stay in the higher worlds for a while; instead he chose to be reborn: "The immense Light Being counseled me, 'Your next life will be difficult, yet you have an opportunity to grow more. Many atrocities will be committed in the world. You will not have the same opportunities as in your prior life. You may not be recognized; circumstances will be more challenging. The vast consciousness of this Light Being inspired me to continue my evolution, and I desired further growth."

Floyd recalls being in a group of Souls getting ready to incarnate. A voice spoke to each of them about their upcoming life and what to expect. The voice asked for a volunteer to be the next messenger. Floyd accepted. "Soon after this, I was told, 'It's your time to go.' I proceeded onto a cloud bank and entered the sixth red elevator box. I fell into a precipice. The universe seemed to turn upside down. When I got my bearings, I stood at a doorway illuminated by the light of two universes. The light particles within this barrier were interacting intelligently. I started toward a point of light in the heavens thinking, 'I want to remember what I had learned and share it. I want to forever work for this purpose.'"

Entering the Fetus: A Huge Leap in Space Exploration

"I was traveling toward our star and was drawing lines between the planets as they orbited the sun. As I approached Earth, I saw a space capsule orbiting. I was excited to be born when humans were making such technological strides. I looked in the window and a guy at the control panel looked back at me." As strange as it appears, February 20, 1962, seven and a half months before Floyd's birth, was the day John Glenn orbited Earth on *Friendship 7*, a NASA spacecraft. The flight log records Glenn's excitement at seeing a mass of tiny luminescent particles—a shower of brilliantly lit sparks swirling around the capsule, traveling at eighteen thousand miles per hour. Floyd was unaware of other beings when he looked into the spacecraft. Could the "fireflies" be a stream of Souls coming to be born, with Floyd being one of them? Floyd followed the spacecraft, looking into the window until it started going on the lighted side of the planet. He observed the flickering lights on Earth, embracing it in contemplation: "We were all going to work together. I felt that I had something to share."

On entering the womb, Floyd saw the faces of his father and uncle when they were young. "I also got the impression of a boxing ring. That makes sense because my grandfather was a boxer. While in this dark womb, a blue light appeared; the instant I entered it, I was aware I had lost these memories." At first, Floyd felt betrayed because he was "supposed to remember" and share his memories. However, many of his memories were later "rerouted" in his brain via dreams during fetal development. Floyd recalls birth: "I felt vulnerable and shocked to suddenly be in a wide open space. I thought about what I came here for. I could hardly wait to communicate with people."

Baby Recalls Past Life as a Tibetan Lama

When Floyd was six months old, his mother was carrying him past a Catholic monastery. Three nuns passed by and said, "What a pretty baby. What is his name?" Floyd's mother replied, "His name is Floyd." Floyd thought, "Wow, that's who I'll be known as, but that's not really who I am. The essence of who I am can't be defined by a name or a title. No one can be known by a name. Everyone's core is infinite and indefinable."

At the same time, baby Floyd was aware of his prior life as a Tibetan lama: "I knew people in another part of the world were looking for my rebirth. I thought, 'These people are wearing robes, though different from Tibetan monks. Maybe they can help me.'" He attempted to telepathically communicate with the nuns, searching their eyes for a glimmer of remembrance. Then he tried to say, "Do you know who I was?" All that came out was gibberish. The nuns asked, "How old is he?" Floyd's mom said, "Six months," and went on to share details. Baby Floyd thought, "I will have to be veiled in this form with an identity set by the standards of others.

Even if this group finds me, my parents will not allow me to go with them."

Walter Cronkite and the Evening News

Floyd was less than one year old when he saw the Dalai Lama on TV: "I was excited. I wondered, 'How am I going to contact him? I cannot even communicate.'" Later, thirteen-month-old Floyd was shocked watching the news of the tragic fate of JFK. "President Kennedy's death was a great shock. I cried my eyes out. Dad yelled, 'Shut that f-ing kid up.'" By becoming aware of the injustices in the world, the toddler decided, "My quest will not be easy." Because he was highly evolved, Floyd was shocked by the JFK violence and already understood the dangers of life: "I realized that most people do not remember their past and are ignorant of their spiritual nature. I concluded, 'I am in danger. I must forget.' I consciously chose to forget as a protective mechanism." Then, as a teenager, Floyd awoke one morning with full recall of his pre-birth memories: "Where did this come from? I had forgotten this part of myself. Afterward, I thought about it all the time. My family thought it was a joke because it did not go along with their belief system."

Learning Humility

Long gone are Floyd's glory days in Tibet after birth as a Mormon, where his ultrazealous family harped about the Mormon faith, while he felt disconnected from it: "I was told to give up my memories and experiences for beliefs I knew were fiction. My family did not listen. It's no wonder, being related to Brigham Young and the Mormon pioneers."

Floyd's life is not as centered around religion as his previous Tibetan life was. Floyd has been blessed with transformative awakenings of Oneness and mystical dreams. Juxtaposed to his inner life is growing up within a chaotic family. Floyd's father was abusive, and his parents divorced when Floyd was twelve. Floyd lived with his dysfunctional father, who remarried an alcoholic blind woman.

Then, as if life could not become crueler, his father padlocked young Floyd out of the home with a note saying, "Go live with your mother." Later, Floyd's college education "went out the window" due to further family turbulence. Life settled down once he separated from his family.

Floyd now realizes that the high Tibetan Buddhist position in his prior life was an attachment or a hindrance to spiritual growth: "I needed to learn humility. I also needed to see things from a different perspective and to be born in a different culture." Floyd feels the interlife experience prior to his current life is a milestone in his evolutionary development and a literal rebirth into something else. Breaking free of the blue orb and traveling into the galactic center, his consciousness sensed that this was different from anything he had ever encountered before. Today, Floyd is finishing a college degree in computer technology.

The Human Body Is an Ultimate Gift

A spiritual healer recalls her journey from Source.

Diane was born with a gift to heal, guide, and connect. Trained from an early age, she has dedicated her life to alleviating suffering. She has assisted in over 160 successful surgeries and taught health and wellness curricula to large companies.

Diane's Soul entered this life after a long course of previous existences on Earth and in other dimensions where she acquired her gifts as a healer: "Our Soul seeks wholeness. Our Soul is designed to grow. We take journeys into a diverse array of forms to enhance our awareness. When I came out of flesh as Spirit after my last life, I went through eleven substations before resting in an inner realm of Light. I reviewed my life's lessons and my awakenings to the truth: 'What was that about for me?' 'What did I learn?' 'What is it in the life that I kept out because I was afraid?' 'What did I not allow to happen because I didn't see the whole picture?' Sometimes I was not as open to the love and opportunities because my upbringing shadowed over the truth of my Soul.

"I reflected on what I wanted to learn and take forward. I remembered all the times I had been a light healer. Some were grand lifetimes; lives in the dark ages were filled with heartbreak. I was a very excited spark: 'I want to try again,' 'I want to do it better than the last time,' 'I will remember who I am once I am in the flesh.'

"My Soul likes the challenge of bringing the truth down to Earth. I wanted my grandmother's gift of healing, to carry that lineage of spiritual healing forward. I was way up 'there,' back at Source, and felt invincible: 'Oh, it will be easy to remember who I am and do my divine work. I'll sign up for that.' We think it will be easy because it is easy 'there,' where you think 'it' and 'it is.' I disregarded the earthly discomfort that was to come about in my upbringing."

Diane's Descent into the Amniotic World

"Conception and the physical piercing of my father's sperm into my mother's egg created a Fourth of July celebration and reverberated Source. My signature started flashing sharply, like an explosion. It triggered: 'You are on. You made it.' I descended down the tunnel of light. I was showered with huge gifts, like a wedding. Higher beings were throwing flower petals and the best of everything. As I approached Earth, I encountered duality, light and dark. Time and space create spin, distortion, and confusion. I thought, 'It's getting turbulent.' I felt disoriented, yet I kept an intense focus and did not get lost.

"A woman's emotional, mental, and electromagnetic makeup are in the egg. My mother was anxious. I sensed the frequency of her egg, the vulnerability. The egg was not warm and nourishing. I thought, 'Oh, no. It's not a soft place to land. This is going to be rough. Is there any place that's comfortable here? I do not fit.' Love was missing. My parents had been headed toward divorce before I was conceived. They stayed together and continued to argue about their opposing religious beliefs. During womb-time, I flitted in and out of the disturbed womb. I returned to the Soul place and kept affirming: 'This discomfort is temporary and unimportant. I am determined to have my grandmother's gift.'

"I couldn't wait to be born because of frequency differences between me and my mother. As my head crowned, Mom had an NDE. I got jolted back to the spark. I thought, 'Wait a minute. I thought I was going to be born.' I decided not to return to Source, and the doctor yanked me out with forceps, a brutal beginning. I tried to say, 'You're much too harsh. Does it have to be this painful? You're destroying my neck.' I was angry. I thought I could bring wholeness down into the physical plane. However, this plane has its own laws, constructs, and structure. Even though I turned out blue and they barely got my airways open, I was three-fourths connected to Source. Most babies are one-fourth to one-eighth connected.

"Even as a newborn, I thought: 'I came to do this job with my grandmother's gift in addition to my other healing gifts.' I just had no idea that earthly life was going to be so dense, constrictive, and heavy. I took twenty-five years to make peace with being in human form and to be in service to others with memory of Source, inner dimensions, and past lives. Because my Soul is so bright and expansive, I found the flesh restrictive. I prayed, 'Make peace with this confinement, that we call flesh.'

"I never bonded with Mom. I did not receive any nurturing, love, or support. She had a breakdown and did not hold me for my first eight months. I could not find comfort in this harsh place. Why do people yell? I did not understand the nonloving part. Memories of Source were my comfort. I kept going back to that place where I came from, where it was safe and I remembered why I was here. Going back to Source was a blessing and a reminder: 'Oh, that's right. Keep the enthusiasm up; keep it going.' At ten months, I had contagious diarrhea and a second NDE. I was in an incubator. No one touched me. For seven weeks, a priest did my Last Rites every day. It was not a pretty picture. I had a choice to return to Source. I decided, 'No, I can do it.' When I was two, I told Mom, 'I am an orphan. I did not come from you. I came from the Light. It's much happier there.' I also saw light beings and asked, 'Mom, did you see the beautiful light?' My parents said, 'Be quiet.' My family wanted a normal child. They didn't have the capacity to see who I was. Mom was afraid because I was so willful and powerful at the age of two. I moved objects at the dining table with my mind. The TV channel changed when I walked by. The more I did these things, the angrier Dad became, and the worse the energy became in the house. I realized I was creating problems and started suppressing it by the time I was six.

"My parents dropped me off at Grandma's farm for the summer when I was three. Grandmother was the love and light that made sense to me. She taught me hands-on healing. People came to her after church. She put my hand underneath hers on someone who needed healing, and asked, 'Do you feel it?' I would say, 'No, I don't feel that, Grandma.' A few years later, I started to feel it. She said, 'That's it. Now put your hand here.' She taught me about the lights that came into the room: Archangels Raphael, Michael, Gabriel, Uriel, and the Holy Spirit. Grandma taught me how to be the connector, the arc, from the celestial realm down through the Earth to the crown chakra.

"To be in human form is the best gift we can receive. Each body is a unique genetic blueprint. Compared to all the angelic realms, Source included, human existence with all its diversity, coexisting opposites, and all its learning and sensory input is the grandest of the grand. Source is easy. It only knows Source. Human life is the beauty.

"I love being on Earth. I did get what I came for. I just didn't know what I would have to unwind and to make peace with. I am happy to serve. I want to get my message out and for people to receive my gifts of healing. I didn't do all this work for all these lives and go through all the discomfort for nothing. I did it for all of those who were to develop. I am so honored to be in this body and to have made the choices I have made, and to be moving forward. Despite all the sadness and suffering of life, Source triumphs. What an honor to bring the knowledge to the people."

Awareness of First Individuation from Source

"I remember Source. It was the most amazing bright light. Source has a definition, but it does not have the same edges as we do when we are in a human body. I remember the immense radiance and specific colors. The love at Source is so pure and strong. We think it will be the same when we get down here. I go back to that memory of All That Is, All That Is One, and the Source of all of us when I do my healing work. Source is a place where there is no resistance, no contrast, only light, love, and purity. It is so broad and full; you don't see the parts. All feelings are there—not delineated feeling.

"When I was that flame, that undefined, unformed energy, I only felt expansion and the truth of that. I also remember the first time I dropped off from Source and chose to go down a separate path. I felt a gravitational pull to go and a force to stay. To stay in this place was perfect: 'Oh, my God. How glorious is that.' Yet the force to go was more important. My Soul's enthusiasm wanted to explore and won over the safety and comfort of staying at Source. But I wanted the experience, it was like saying good-bye to your best friend: 'Why would I ever leave here? What was I thinking?' It was 'hello–good-bye' all at the same time.

"To know 'thyself,' you have to separate and come back. How do you know yourself if you are all Oneness, all things? You cannot recognize something in Oneness, you have to go out of Oneness and experience the contrast. How can you recognize 'that' if you don't move into duality so that you can see that there is 'this' and 'that'? How do you 'know thyself' if you are all things and you do not have any contrast? That force was drawing me out. How can I know myself as a Soul signature that is eternal if I do not move out of Oneness? Most Souls think they will remember when they leave Source; paradoxically, one-eighth of their memory is left at best.

"We emerge from Source as a specific signature, an individual spark. A Signature defines our Soul with a significant tone, colors, configuration, and visual placement. No matter how many billions

of people there are, there will never be anyone else with your signature. I love that. This eternal energy will move forward forever and
always be that exact pure divine Truth."

Cultural Parallels: Humanity, Crowning Masterpiece of Creation

Diane's memories line up with wisdom asserting that human life is
the greatest gift.

- ✿ Judeo-Christian: God said, "Let us make man in our image, after
  our likeness. And let him have dominion over the fish of the sea
  and over the birds of the heavens and over the livestock and over
  all the earth and over every creeping thing."[7]

- ✿ Ancient India: minerals exist, plants feel, and animals know;
  at the same time, they do not know that they exist, feel, and
  know. Man, on the other hand, exists, feels, knows, and knows
  that he exists, feels, and knows. Self-consciousness manifests
  and for the first time, it is possible to know the Great Self.[8]

- ✿ Buddhism: suppose Earth was covered with an ocean and
  a yoke with a single hole floated on the water. A blind turtle
  surfaced from the ocean depths once every hundred years. It
  would be sheer coincidence for the turtle to stick his neck into
  the yoke. A similar coincidence occurs when we obtain this
  precious human birth.[9]

- ✿ Dr. Bhagavan Das (India, 1869–1958): only the human Soul can
  bridge the finite and Infinite. This is liberation or enlightenment
  (Vedas); union with God with ecstasy of joy (Islam, Sufism);
  Kingdom of Heaven (Christianity); Nirvana (Buddhism); Palace of Love (Kabbalah); Pleroma of Eternal Light (Gnosticism);
  freedom from doubt, error, and matter (Vedanta); and Oneness
  (Yoga).[10]

Parallels: Memories of Source

Two near-death experiences portray awareness of Source similar to Diane's memory of something larger than or transcendent to herself.

❁ P. M. H. Atwater (United States, born 1937): "I could hear, feel, move around, think, remember, reason, and experience emotion, only all this was different because I no longer had a physical body to filter and amplify sensations. I did not need that body any more. I was free! I was free! So great was my joy in my newfound freedom that I danced and whirled around and around the light bulb as if it were a May Pole, and chanted with unbridled glee, 'I'm free, I'm free, I'm free.' Everything was bright and there was no fear. I was my true self at last. I was me and nothing else mattered. All my obligations, responsibilities, and duties were over. It was all over."[11]

❁ Reverend Howard Storm (United States, born 1946): The divine Light is "a concentrated field of energy, radiant in splendor, indescribable goodness and love. This was more loving than one can imagine."[12]

CHAPTER 8

I Saw All My Costumes

~

BEVERLY'S EVOLUTIONARY REBIRTH JOURNEY

> The time that my journey takes is long and the
> way of it long. I came out on the chariot of the first
> gleam of light, and pursued my voyage through the
> wildernesses of worlds leaving my track on many a
> star and planet.
> —RABINDRANATH TAGORE, *GITANJALI*

*Beverly recalls thirty past lives on Earth and how and
why she planned each life.*

EVERLY, A MODERN MYSTIC, CLAIRAUDIENT, clairvoyant, and
spiritual healer, takes us on a journey of her Soul through
eleven lifetimes: "Where do I start? My collective consciousness is an unbroken line now. There is no delineation except that my
Soul became encapsulated in different human forms, cultures, and
times in order to learn different lessons of perception and awareness. I have always been the same person with the same consciousness, personality, insecurities, and confidences who has simply matured like a child growing up.

"I remember the in-betweens [Heaven]. They are another form
of being that is not squashed together in such a small package.
When you are 'there' and not currently occupying a shell [a human
body], we do not change anything except our fear. Fear is a function
of survival incorporated in the humanness of our bodies. I am more
than any or all of the faces I have worn. Our essence is eternal and

the only part of us that is real. The different faces we put on and how we express ourselves changes for the lessons we wish to learn. Otherwise, if we don't change our costume and the setting, the play will be the same over and over again."

Awakening in Childhood

"As a two- and three-year-old child, I had all kinds of 'dreams' of falling into my body. I woke up crying and screaming. My mother would run into my bedroom. I told her, 'I just fell from the sky.' I literally remember waking up in my body with a thud. I had this dream of falling down through a tornado hole over and over again. It terrified me. When I was about five years old, I realized this experience had really happened. I did fall down through the hole, backward. My superconscious mind had been replaying this experience for me. As a child, I interpreted my memory as a falling, but it is not a falling. It is a shift. It is a tornado hole and then you are here.

"I was also born with past-life memories. My feelings and remembrances made no sense. They were in my superconscious mind, nagging and poking at me. I dreamed I was a Persian girl and woke up feeling stunned that I was a little girl in a light-skinned body. I thought, 'Damn, this is weird! Why am I female and Anglo? I have always been dark. Why am I in this life and in this white body? It doesn't make any sense.' I can tell countless stories of lying in bed and feeling frustrated that I had no servants. 'Don't they know I am the queen? They're supposed to bring me what I want.' I thought, 'Why do I feel that way?' I was aggravated that nobody knew who I was.

"Memories were brewing in my superconscious until the Universe arranged an NDE to download more information. I was nine years old and flew off a galloping horse and almost cracked the back of my skull. I was literally sucked, like a magnet, through what I call a vortex. It felt big, then it was little, and then it got big really fast. The middle part, what I now call 'the veil,' is that last little bit of consciousness of being in this earthly dimensionality. On the other side of the opening, it was a beautiful place of bluish golden Light. The Light was incredibly tender, gentle, nurturing, and satisfying. When that Light touched me, I did not have a care in the world. I remember meeting a group of three luminous beings that had coalesced into human form for my benefit. We floated in open space and had a conversation. They asked, 'Well, Beverly, what do you want to do here? Do you want to stay or go?' I said, 'This place is beautiful, and you are all very wonderful, but my mother is awfully upset, and she sure would miss me.' The instant I had that thought, I got sucked back through the opening. It was not pleasant coming back. I landed abruptly in my body and woke up in the hospital. Later on, I learned that I had been in a coma for three days with no brain activity. Time is not what we think it is. Our version is just an illusion.

"When I had walked back through the veil, I had seen all my costumes. They looked like different clothes that I had put on. I have the most memory of lives when I practiced mysticism or a healing art. I saw how I affected other people's growth and learned what not to do with my abilities. When I walked back through the veil into this molecular vibration, I brought back memory of all of me: memories of all the in-between times and all of the times here. Divine Grace allowed my brain to access more of my memory of the All and to access other people's memories of the All. My NDE gave me a perspective of who I really am.

"Psychic skills run in my family, but reincarnation was one subject I could not broach with my Southern Baptist mother. Fortunately, by the time I tried to get a grip on who I was and why I was here, I was given a teacher: my brother, a Zen Buddhist studying martial arts. So by the time this stuff starting driving me nuts, the universe, or he and I, arranged for him to be in my life and help me. He is very precious. He is the most Zen person I have ever met. I get the feeling that he used to be one of my teachers."

Movies in Heaven

Beverly recalls the step-by-step events between one
earthly life and the next.

"When I die, I am liberated from up and down, forward and back, left and right, beginning and end. I become a free entity unencumbered by time and space. Within a short time, my angel encases me in her protectiveness—she wraps herself around me to give me a cocoon. She floats me for a while until I adjust, so it does not take long. I know her well. She is always with me.

"Some people are so frightened by that event that they do not allow the cocooning to happen. They are afraid of the limitlessness of themselves. They assume they are not worthy to simultaneously face their god-self and God. They panic and are quickly reborn in order to feel safe again. My angel takes me through the Light into Heaven. Heaven is you being all that you can be. It is the limitlessness of yourself in an energy platform, spatial dimensionality unencumbered by physical form, hunger, cold, or fear.

"The in-between zones are instantaneous and responsive. We breathe a thought or a desire, and it manifests. I instantly receive any knowledge, information, and resources. We are angels at whatever level of expression we allow that to be. Heaven is magnificent, although it does not give the satisfaction of earthly life. In Heaven we do not need to try hard. No furnace tests the mettle of our being. There is little satisfaction in accomplishing something effortless. We do not learn when things are so easy. We simply hang out. So even though Earth is slow, dense, and sticky, human life is important, or we would not bother with it. Heaven is a marvelous place, and so is Earth. We cannot exist without either of them. Balance exists in the universe: yin and yang, dark and light. Some people say, 'When I die, I'm going to Heaven and never coming back.' I challenge that. Heaven gets boring after a while. God gave birth to this Earth plane in order to add a base note to His reality, a slower dynamic to the parameter of the universe. The problem is, people don't slow down and listen to the tone and experience how delicious this tone is. Even angels are occasionally jealous because there are unique aspects to this level of reality. This place is Heaven if we live it like that.

"Heaven is where I set the stage for my next life on Earth. I see how I'm doing. I have an overview and know what I am lacking in my overall lesson plan. Nothing is forbidden for me to know. I scan past lives. I look at what I need to do nine lives ahead. I can experiment to realize what I need to figure out about myself next, so I can grow more. I can go anywhere, learn anything, and hang with anyone I want to be with, including myself. A discussion, a powwow, takes place with my angel or Soul group. I tend to be hypercritical: 'I didn't get that right. Boy, I wish I had done that differently.' My angels encourage me to be gentle: 'No, you did fine. Your life was lovely, incredible. You learned this, and you learned that.' I always pick the one thing I didn't hit. They say, 'Don't be upset. Look at the big picture, not that tiny speck that didn't turn out perfect.'

"My overriding lesson plan is to understand my function as a catalyst. I am like the oxygen molecule that has a molecular structure, tone of being, or energy dynamics that can interact with lots of elements and make things change. My lesson plan has been to understand that there is no power other than the All That Is, and I am a piece of that. Each Soul is a different tone. I am a screamingly high-pitched tone. I want the most out of everything because I know it's available. My angels ask, 'What do you want to do to get it better?' I answer, 'Do you have any suggestions?' So they show me movies, spectrums of potentialities—like looking at a movie screen and picking the movie we want to be in, out of five movies in the future.

"I can pick time zone, culture, economic situation, topography, climate, a comedy or a drama, and I can mix and match the characters. I think, 'That movie looks interesting. I could do that. That might work.' I have a selection of actors to be on my stage. I correlate my productions with those with whom I am most tightly bonded. If we are paying attention, we can cook up a really good movie. Selections are agonizing if I have regretted some previous actions. If I did not do a good job on a previous lesson, I can get between a rock and a hard place and select unfortunate experiences in order to get the point. The angels urge me: 'Be more gentle. You do not need to be that harsh with yourself,' or 'You don't need the lesson that strong, do you?' However, I am strong-willed, and they can't talk me out of it."

Eleven Past Lives and the Interlives

Eleven dramatic lives affected Beverly the most and carried karmic lessons.

"My first life on Earth was in the Garden of Eden, a place of total balance in the ecosystem and abundance. Because we were very awake, everything was easy, and everything we thought manifested. We communicated with animals and plants because our consciousness connected to the life force within everything. We were telekinetic—we moved things with our minds. We felt weather patterns change and predicted what crops would grow best. No fear, violence, or aggression arose. People shared freely. We were a people of Oneness, instead of separate individuals full of fear. There was no selfishness, greed, coveting your neighbor's property, or lust. All the Commandments were unspoken; there was no need for rules. My life in Eden was one of balance, bliss, and peace. I am at peace because I remember it. I know humans can live in balance with the ecosystem. As soon as we find balance within and open up to the superconscious mind, there is no fear because we know we are not alone and feel eternity. I pray for people to know that."

Beverly highlights ten more past lifetimes and the preplanning phases:

❀ Shaman hunter-gatherer (3060 BCE): "My present karma cycle started in Tibet. That was a natural life, tied to the land, mountains, and holy places. It was effortless. I got a focus of balance, of the power of Earth within my resonance."

❀ Egyptian priestess (2380 BCE): "I jumped into an arrogant, overly bureaucratic society to see whether I was mature enough to bring balance to that sophistication. I was a beautiful, tall, imposing royal priestess, the living god, an arrogant blue blood. I became wrapped up in my lovely brain and its curiosities and turned out to be a terror. I did stupid, childish things and was disrespectful of my station and responsibilities. That was the least positive manifestation of my skills and gifts. Melding church and state did not work because I did not appreciate who I was."

❀ Persian princess (1812 BCE): "I chose sensuality and hedonism, to roll around in humanness and have fun as a princess in the true Sumerian Persian culture. I learned the art of sexuality, pleasures of the body and senses, and how delicious it was to be human; unfortunately I did some of that at other people's expense. I was voluptuous, loud, and outrageous in my femininity. I used it like a sword. I was spoiled and did not appreciate my station in life and the responsibilities attached to it. On the other hand, I had learned enough about love, and I appreciated compassion and my healing gifts, so I had love in that life."

❀ Persian warrior-prince (1336 BCE): "I gained maturity and learned to relax with my authority. So, in the next life, I protected the kingdom and my duties and honor with greater responsibility. I was warlike, yet had a mystical side and healing powers. I was torn between duty and responsibility and my aggressive desire to lead. My mysticism made me an effective general-warrior. I could outthink the enemy. That life taught me that I can be in charge and make decisions: 'I am right. Don't argue with me. Get after it. Do it now.' That was a good life, except I had macho stuff going on. I was a bit of a chauvinist. I picked being male so I could have all the women

I wanted. I enjoyed a voluptuous, sexually oriented life style. I enjoyed my maleness so much that I took the feminine expression for granted."

❀ Celtic shaman-chieftain (1173–1118 BCE): "I spent seven hundred years settling on my next life. I picked a tall, strong shaman. I was female yin, with yang in my leadership abilities. I was like the living God, even while I knew the living God was all of us; it was to be respected, honored, and to be used to heal and not harm. My lustiness also stayed with me. I had learned a lot in Persia."

Wise Women (Middle Ages)

"People lived in the deepest, darkest fear during the Dark Ages. And when people are in fear, they react violently and aggressively. I am clairvoyant and clairaudient. I try to help people. When I operated on this level, it cost me my life four times. Prior to each of those lifetimes, my angels advised me it was an Age when fear was in control and I was beating my head against the wall trying to make a difference. I was persistent and stubborn and refused to surrender to 'deceleration'. These lives were an exercise in futility. I should have skipped that time zone; then again, I meet kindred brothers and sisters from those lives and understand their phobias. So it was beneficial even though I probably did not have to do it four times. My current phobias originate from being branded as a witch:

1. Fear of fire: burned alive at seventeen.
2. Fear of standing in an elevator with the door closed: buried alive, and tried to claw out of the box. People were laughing and clapping as they dropped dirt on the box.
3. Fear of the sea and drowning: dropped off a boat with my mouth bound, hands tied, and a rock tied around my ankles.
4. Fear of heights: dropped off a parapet of a castle to rocks below."

Appalachian Woman (1860–1902)

"We carry judgments about ourselves beyond this dimensionality. We do not let go of the feelings of 'could have,' 'would have,' 'should have,' when we touch the All-encompassing Love Source of ourselves and God. I carried perceptions of debt, shame, and self-judgment as reflected by my thoughts in the interlife period prior to my next life: 'I have had it easy. I have been a blue blood so many lives. I have been arrogant in my assumptions that I understand where people are coming from that have not been born with so much abundance. I have had attractive, powerful, dominant, charismatic bodies. Perhaps I should say 'thank you' and appreciate and acknowledge from whence it comes, instead of thinking I am the biggest, baddest thing walking around.

"So I got after it with gusto. I selected an illiterate woman born during the Civil War. I was born into abject poverty. We lived in a shanty cabin with a dirt floor. My husband left me with a bunch of children. I was frightened. I had no resources for food and clothing. Sickness was everywhere. Some of my children starved to death in the cold winters. I was born with a fragile body. I died at forty-two. I did not need to do that life for God; I needed to do it for me. Boy, did I come out with appreciation. I learned the preciousness of the vitality that I had previously been given. I only needed to do that once. I got the point."

Modern Mystic

"I was in a hurry to return in 1954; there was a lot happening down here."

"There were fifty-two years between the Appalachian life and my rebirth. My Soul development did not need this life; God needed me for His overall scheme on Earth, and I am aware of who I work for. Actually I was jumping up and down and saying, 'The party looks cool over here in this movie. Can I do that? It looks interesting, but give me enough tools. I am not going unless you arm me up. Remember my frustration during the Middle Ages when I didn't make a difference.' So they gave me tools when I walked back through the veil after my NDE. What I do with my tools is up to me. The angels had explained that I would go through trials to make me a more sophisticated operator of the tools, to get me up to speed for what I needed to do. A variety of profound experiences have kept me continuously growing.

"Through this series of human births, I have learned that there is no need to beat myself up to get the point. Eternity is all there is. This is not a hurry-up program. So there is no budget in this flick. God's love and ability to create this format for us is limitless. The more I enjoy each lesson plan, the more abundant and effortless is my journey. I will still get all the lessons, both the high and low notes. So I am no longer the headstrong, impetuous child that I was millennia ago. And that is why they let me bring back so much of my collective memory. I respect it more.

"Looking back, I have been the same being, like a child who grows up. I still look in the mirror, and I am stunned. Is that my face? I often wake up and feel I am a man or have a large body. Then I get out of bed, and I am this little bitty body. Ironically, my Soul has not changed. I can be the smallest person in a group, and I get everybody to do what I want because I remember being in charge."

Soul Witnesses Conception, Pregnancy, and Birth

"Before conception, I picked a small female body. So often I have been big, strong, and bold. This is my least imposing physical form. I consciously did that so I would not threaten people. I witnessed my conception. I was perturbed about how my parents conceived me, because it happened in less than favorable circumstances and I was a big surprise. Yet I was insistent on being born, so I take responsibility for my part of the deal. My mother nearly miscarried in the third month because I was being pouty about the circumstances of conception. So for a while I was being stubborn, but my mother's body did not reject the fetus. Then I thought, 'Oh, what the hell.' I landed in the fourth month. I remained fully conscious throughout the pregnancy.

"My mother was in labor twenty-six hours. I remember panic, commotion, a horrendous noise of machines, and agitated doctors yelling and running around. I felt cold. My mother 'died' and had an NDE during delivery and later explained, 'You were too much for my body to handle.' The doctors zapped her heart to get it beating. I saw the doctor in surgical garb and was shocked by brilliant light. After birth, I recognized people, things, and places I had become familiar with during my womb time."

A Projectile of Light

Beverly remembers when God initially spun her on her merry way and said: "Have a good time. Come back when you're all done."

"My continuous conscious memory extends back to when I was created as an individual spark of God. My Soul journey began at Source. I remember coming from the All That Is as a projectile of light. I remember being spat out, pushed out like a projectile, and I was screaming through the universe as a spark of light, a little star. I felt sheer exhilaration and knew I was going somewhere, yet I did not know where. Stars whizzed by, although there was no sensation of movement: no density, no up or down, no left or right, no time, no sensations of colors, sound, or heat. I existed as pure energy surrounded by comfort and ease. I remember my spark and Him. And the profound limitless power of that makes me a little nervous. He is in the major leagues, and we are in the minor leagues. Yet talent grows, evolves, and matures, and we will get there too. I will be fine doing the minor leagues for a while. I am not ready to do that format. I do not respect it enough. I will, with time, as we all will."

Cultural Parallels: Soul as a Projectile of Light

Beverly's memory of being a projectile of light falls into a pattern with memories and spiritual teachings on our journey from Oneness to separation as a Cosmic Spark.

❀ Thakur Anukulchandra (India, 1888–1969): Thakur saw how the Cosmic Soul created everything out of itself by exploding into millions of hyper-atoms. Each hyper-atom then burst into millions of supra-hyper-atoms. That ultimate point created an infinity of beings out of itself like thousands of sparks coming from a fire. Souls were destined to live a series of lives so long as they remained subject to the illusion of personal individuality. Thakur recalled his unbroken chain of births. En route to his mother's womb from a higher region, Thakur traversed through forty-four thousand planets. Thakur arrived in our solar system by coming through a ray of light and descending into the sun.[1]

❀ Christianity: "In the beginning was the Word, and the Word was with God, and the Word was God. All things came to be through Him, and without Him nothing came to be."[2]

❀ Ancient India: "In the beginning there was Existence alone— One only, without a second. He, the One, thought: 'Let me be many, let me grow forth.' Thus out of himself He projected the universe and entered into every being. He is the subtle essence, the truth, the Self. And you are That."[3]

❀ Ancient India: all the multitudes of beings in creation manifest from the Eternal Source like thousands of sparks arising from a blazing fire.[4]

❀ Gnosticism (second century CE): the Soul issued forth from the fountainhead of God as a divine spark. Each Soul is a spark of individualized spiritual essence dwelling within the consciousness or mind.[5]

❀ Muhammad (Islam, 570–632 CE): the Divine Voice cries: "I was a Hidden Treasure; I desired to see my Self; I therefore did create this world of forms and lives beyond all count, that I may realize my Self therein."[6]

❀ Kabbalah (Spain and France, 12–13th centuries CE): "From God knowing All, God willed the first separation so that God might behold God."[7]

❀ Rabbi Shmelke of Nikolsburg (Moravia, 1726–1778): "All Souls are one. Each is a spark from the original Soul, and this Soul is wholly inherent in all Souls."[8]

❀ Kahlil Gibran (Lebanon, 1883–1931): "The human Soul is but a part of a burning torch which God separated from himself at Creation."[9]

❀ Paramahansa Yogananda (India, 1893–1952): "When the sparks of Cosmic Creation flew from Thy bosom of flame, I sang in the chorus of singing lights, which heralded the coming of the worlds."[10]

Cultural Parallels: Memories of Source

Beverly's Soul needed to experience some separation from the Source. She needed a physical body as a vehicle to move within creation. References to this process are found in spiritual literature around the world.

❀ Judeo-Christian: King Solomon recalls being created as a Soul before the Earth was formed.[11] Job witnessed God creating the Earth's foundations.[12]

❀ Rabbi Moses ben Nachman (Spain, 1194–1270): "From the beginning, before times long past, I was stored among His hidden treasures. He had brought me forth from Nothing, but at the end of time I shall be summoned back before the King."[13]

❀ Rumi (Persia, 1207–1273): "For a million years I floated in ether, even as the atom floats uncontrolled. I often dream of my atomic travels."[14]

✤ Rabbi Jacob Yitzchak (Hasidism, Poland, 1745–1815): Jacob gazed upon the foreheads of people and "saw the origin and story of the Soul—Soul's ultimate descent and root."[15]

✤ Yaakov Yitzchak Rabinowicz of Pzysha, "the holy Yehudi" (Hasidism, Poland, 1766–1813): Yehudi could see the paths each Soul took from the beginning, and he penetrated through "the background of that row of figures" until he arrived at "the very being of the primordial."[16]

✤ Rabindranath Tagore (India, 1861–1941): "At the far end of the stage of the world's play I stand. Each moment do I see the shore beyond the darkness where in the vast consciousness of the Unmanifest I once lay merged."[17]

✤ Creation Hymn (ancient India): The nonexistent was not, the existent was not. Then the world was not, nor the firmament, nor that which is above the firmament. Death was not, nor at that time Immortality. There was no rhythm of day and night. That One unbreathed upon breathed of His own strength; other than That, there was nothing else whatsoever. There was darkness wrapped in darkness in the beginning. All this world was only undistinguishable water. That empty united world which was covered by a mere nothing, arose at last, born of the power of austerity. When did creation start? How did creation happen? Who really knows? Who in this world can truly say? The gods were subsequent to the world's creation, so who knows when it originated? He, from whom this creation arose, He may have fashioned it, or not. No one else can. He who is its superintendent in the highest Heaven, He assuredly knows, or if He knows not, no one else does.[18]

We are divine sparks. Some may be young Souls just beginning to grow; others are old Souls nearing the end of a long cycle of human births. The notion that our life may be an extension from the superphysical down to the physical is spiritually provocative and inspirational. Human life is intertwined with the divine, and why we are born here fits into that wholeness.

PART TWO

Pre-Birth Communications

THE ABILITY FOR A PARENT to interact with an unborn child is a result of an innate psychic awareness. Part Two presents summaries of our interviews with parents highlighting four categories of pre-birth experiences:

1. Communications with Souls prior to pregnancy
2. Awareness of the mystical side of conception
3. Communications with the child-to-be in the womb
4. Pre-birth communications that precede a miscarriage or stillbirth

The intuition of the majority of these parents had naturally become clearer through meditation, healthy diets, and positive lifestyles. Communicating with the incoming Soul represents one of many spiritual abilities delineated by the father of Yoga, Patanjali. This transcendent faculty is a way of knowing without using the mind or senses. Parents who use their intuition or inner third eye can tune into invisible Souls seeking birth.

When we probe more deeply, we find that these reports support how a future child is sending barely perceptible signals and interacting with potential parents because it seeks a life experience on Earth. Without such discrete dialogue, parents might be less inspired to have families.

CHAPTER 9

Souls Waiting in the Wings for Birth

❦

SPIRITUAL PREGNANCY

The baby's Soul floats in the mother's aura for three
or four months prior to conception.
— TORKOM SARAYDARIAN

*Whispers of a Soul into a mother's ear reveal more than a
desire to be born.*

A VIBRATION STIRRED DEEP WITHIN Joanna's being. The im-
pulses were persistent. Joanna intuitively knew she had
children waiting in the wings. She had tuned into a higher
power, an inner light. Through a ray of consciousness, she felt connected to the Cosmic Mother, who watches over the Souls of unborn children.

An intuitive woman, such as Joanna, often hears the Soul's messages within a more expanded wakefulness—a relaxed, ultra-aware
state of being. Due to higher sensitivity, parents can tune into the
Soul during meditation or anytime they experience being in the
now. Pre-birth communications are part of the collective databank
available to parents who naturally have attained new dimensions
of consciousness. The opening of subtle communication channels
in more and more parents signifies that the veil separating humanity from higher dimensions is becoming less dense. Soon, pre-
birth communications will be commonplace, in the same way that
increasing numbers of pregnant couples talk to a child in utero to

establish early positive contact. In fact, doctors and birth therapists already advocate initiating conversation with a child in the womb and teach parents to do so.

Chapter 9 highlights a spiritual pregnancy, where a couple senses a potential child's presence or telepathic messages from the baby via a dream, meditation, or a vision. Soul visitations cultivate the desire for a child or empower a couple to follow that path if a desire already exists. Pre-birth communications establish a new parent-child relationship long before parents and child meet in the flesh.

The way parents approach fetal life and newborns is becoming more enlightened as we come to understand pre-birth communications. We are transcending the former view that a fetus or a newborn is a passive, mindless creature. We are learning to handle pregnancy and birth with greater respect and awareness.

Hovering at Heaven's Door

A young couple faced the greatest tragedy—the death of a child.

The stage of misfortune was set for Jennie and Tony, a couple practicing daily meditation for more than ten years. Tony backed the car out of the garage without realizing that two-year-old Alan was playing in the driveway. The death of their only child was a tragic mishap defying rational explanation.

Hours after the accident, Tony needed time to be alone. Jennie: "While walking along a quiet country road, my husband encountered healing love from our son's translucent form. Our son said: 'It's all right, Dad. It's okay.' Later, Alan entered our bedroom as a rosy red light. I recognized his voice when he said, 'I'm fine. I'm free.' That night our neighbor brought over a pizza and said, 'We didn't know what else to do.' I took a bite. This whole area was so empty [heart and stomach]. Food could not fill it up. Something had been cut off from this area. My husband cried a lot.

"We continued to go through the grieving process, yet the grief wasn't dominating. The main feeling was bliss, strange as this may sound. That is because for the next six weeks, Alan continued to come as a joyful messenger between the unseen world and the seen. Our son took us on a journey that we may never have experienced in any other way, a unique opportunity. A powerful bliss and serenity grew deep within our consciousness. 'Why do we feel like this?' We almost felt guilty. Alan's death was a huge shock, along with an incredible blast of elation and freedom. His death was as powerful as his birth, if not more so. Birth and death are in the same region — from where they come, they go. The gates of Heaven opened in both cases."

A few days after the accident, Jennie prayed for a higher understanding to know why Alan died so young. "In my mind's eye, I saw our spiritual master. I asked: 'Why did Alan die so young?' He raised his hand to the left. Alan was standing at his side: a young prince, very pure, with great responsibility. Our son also appeared to my friend Summer: 'The light-hearted feeling of Alan's Soul entered our home and bounced through the house. His Soul energy was sweet and powerful. He was happy and realized his death had to happen. I feel it was a contract fulfilled and there was no way around it. And there was no other outcome but evolution. I was astonished to see that Alan had become a magnificent being who had catapulted forward through eons of evolution. The shackles of infancy had been pulled away. He evolved through four lifetimes in less than seven days.' It is hard say what the purpose of my son's short life was, except that it was his time to go on. We had a contract with him that was written before he was born. His early death was part of the contract."

Vision of Souls Seeking Birth

Jennie and Tony desired to shower love on a second child. The couple had "unified as one" and combined "into total giving." As Jennifer rested in silence after meditation, she explains: "I had a beautiful, awe-inspiring vision. The Souls of twelve children who wanted to be born faced me standing in a semicircle in an angelic, ethereal world of light. The light around them radiated toward Earth. My attention was drawn to one who had connected with me. He wanted to be ours.

"Within days, we sensed the creation of life, the moment we made a new body for a Soul. Our sexual union created a wholeness of energy, light, and bliss. I later felt a subtle physiological sensation in the uterus, like a pinprick. Intuition told me the fertilized egg reached the uterus and attached itself. My doctor pinpointed the location of the placenta with a fetal scope. The position was where I had sensed the piercing of the uterine wall."

Could the uterine wall have sensed this? Was the uterus lining like a miniature quantum mechanical telescope? Did Jennie feel the guiding hands of an angelic being attaching something to allow the fertilized egg to live? Studies have demonstrated the ability of the human eye to perceive a quantum of light, a photon—the smallest unit of light—while sitting in a dark room with eyes open. Subjects swear they do not see the photon, whereas their visual cortex registers the light when the photon strikes the retina and stimulates the optic nerve to send a message to the brain. If humans are this sensitive, a woman may sense the change in the electrical field around the egg at fertilization. The electrical polarity change in the fertilized egg's cell wall membrane when the sperm penetrates is a gross quantum physical event, sufficient to register in the consciousness of a sensitive person.

Rebirth under the Right Star Dance

The wheel of time returns the ones we love the most.

Jan: "One day during meditation, Mira appeared to me as I knew her in the lifetime we shared in India. I had been Mira's mother. In fact, Mira, my husband, and my son were all together in that life.

She told me, 'I'll be coming soon.' My husband and I weren't thinking of having a child. We had been willing and had done nothing to interfere with conception. No child had come, so we had let go of the idea and were past the point of trying.

"Astrology teaches that children come at specific times. I think Mira waited for the right stars. I conceived her one month after my vision on a full moon night. A unique radiance and light surrounded me. It was impossible not to have sex. My husband commented, 'You are radiant.' It was obviously a specific moment and the purpose was clear. Within twenty-four hours, I felt a whole life shift, a chain reaction, an intense awakening: 'I am pregnant with a child.' It had been easy to focus on my spiritual life and regular meditation, but now my life was about to be totally transformed. When I was three-and-one-half months pregnant, Mira's Soul entered my womb. I saw a vision of Mira's past life as an Indian man."

Rebirth of an Advanced Soul

Debra conceived a child at a safe time of the month.

"I was single. Having a child was the farthest thing from my mind until a transmission of knowingness came through my body: 'You will give birth to a very advanced Soul.' I was overwhelmed. I felt open to it and knew it was a given. Several months later, I felt a connection with a fellow classmate. That was it, and it went fast. Ron and I conceived our son ten months after we got married. We had no reason to use contraceptives since I was on my menstrual period. It was a deep connection that night. It felt ancient. Intercourse was so dramatic that we starting talking about having a child the next day. Ron wanted a boy and we argued about it. I thought he was sexist. A few weeks later, I discovered that I was pregnant.

"Soon after Devon's birth, I began to gain insights about who he was, when the minister began to cry and shake during his baptism. He said: 'This child is destined to be a great leader. He will bring through something tremendous for humanity. We are honored to have contact with him.' When Devon was eighteen months old, an astrologer told us, 'Your son is destined to be a spiritual leader. Most people will find his unconventional path baffling; however he will have a great following. Do not try to understand his ways. They will be different from yours.'"

Devon's life has been filled with unusual incidents. When Devon was seven, his screams woke up his mother one night. "I asked, 'Why are you screaming? What happened?' He said, 'Oh, God, it is my fault. I let in the people who sabotaged the records. They set fire to the library.' Devon described discs where information had been stored: computer chips that were holographic images." Debra believes that Devon was a custodian at the Greek library in Alexandria, Egypt. "From early childhood, Devon liked to draw geometric patterns. When he was eight he played in a children's playroom while I attended a meeting. I felt a chill when I returned. Something so holy had happened. The blackboard was filled with physics symbols. Devon said, 'I felt something inside of me that wanted me to do this.' Today, Devon seems to be a normal high school student; however he continues to have dreams and visions of other universes and dimensions."

Years later Debra received a second unexpected message from a child-to-be: "I was driving alone through a long stretch of desert and felt like the top of my head was opening up. A voice said, 'If you let me come through, I will heal you.' Some months later, I conceived a child. I was thirty-nine and knew what it meant to have a child at forty. Throughout pregnancy, I released intense sorrow and grief. I felt so frustrated about my career. That pregnancy forced everything about which I was in denial to the surface. I had a great purification. I also laughed a lot. After Jennie was born, I realized that that had been my daughter's laugh. I stopped laughing like that once she was born."

Golden Messages from an Unborn Child

Women report awareness of the incoming child more often than men.

Twenty-two-year-old Caitlin failed to conceive after trying for a year. She and her husband had become discouraged. One day Caitlin was walking in a field of flowers feeling very much in the moment: "Normally, I am thinking about the past or upcoming tasks. All of a sudden I was struck with a sense that someone was watching me from the sky: someone was choosing me to be its mother. I heard a message in my heart—a feeling or knowledge of being admired and chosen: 'There. Her. She is the one I want to be my mother.' I felt beautiful and honored (I rarely feel that way). I felt flattered, yet humbled, that someone thought so highly of me. Whoever was choosing me had been watching and considering me for a long time, possibly a few years. At first I wrote it off as wishful thinking. Three months later, we conceived. I feel so blessed to have glimpsed the spirit of my unborn child. God and my unborn baby had a plan and a time for everything."

During her pre-birth communication with the incoming Soul, Caitlin's Higher Self was looking down at her "little self." As Caitlin explains it, "When I think back on this moment, I see myself below, as if looking down from above at myself, rather than how I actually experienced it. My experience makes me confident and less fearful of facing the challenges of motherhood. I feel loved and wanted by my child, as much as I love and want him or her. This is beautiful, to know that when my husband and I were choosing to start our family, our baby was choosing us too. If God and the child chose me, they must have faith in me being a good mom. That makes me feel wonderful."

Meeting My Daughter in the Cosmic Void

Even in the case of adoption, the first step is choosing parents.

David entered a deep state during meditation. He entered the Void, a state of absolute stillness. "A feeling of great love permeated the experience. A bright light manifested and said, 'I am going to be your daughter, and my name is Zara.' I felt overwhelmed with joy and peace. At the time I had frequent meditations of the Void, and yet I had never had a similar experience before or after. I felt a deep sense of gratefulness and joy about having a child. I was single at the time, and I never knew how, where, and when Zara would come through. In 1997, a year after I had this vision, I married my first wife. She could not have children and we became foster parents for a while."

David remarried in 2007. He and his wife tried to conceive a child. They even sought medical advice and tried fertilization. "I kept telling my wife, 'We are going to have a daughter.'" After two years, David and his wife decided to adopt (August 2009). One week before finalizing plans for a European vacation, they responded with a "yes" to adopt a girl who was to be born in October. David canceled their vacation. The birth mother sent them a message that she had also chosen them to be the adoptive parents. A few weeks later, David met Zahra, fifteen-hours following her birth. David feels Zahra is the special little girl he has been waiting for all these years.

Soul Heals Marriage

Visions and dreams give advance information about the child coming to be born.

Lia and John, a newly-married couple, shared some unexpected perceptions when they did their morning meditation one day. John: "I fell asleep and had a lucid, dramatic dream. I saw a beautiful, gentle woman on the ocean beach. She was of medium height, light build, and had distinct sharp facial features. Her long auburn hair was blowing in the wind. She wore a lovely flowing white gown, unlike earthly clothes. I felt a warm feeling as if meeting someone you love after a long separation. I sensed, 'She is my unborn daughter. Our Souls are greeting each other prior to her birth.' My daughter's Soul was saying, 'Yes, I'm coming.' Our meeting really touched me."

Lia: "Meanwhile, in a meditation vision, the same woman appeared to me: fairly tall and long curly hair. I asked, 'Who are you?' She answered, 'I am the child who is coming to you.' I said, 'Do you have a message?' She explained, 'I am the one who will come and heal this family.' Considering that John and his ex-wife Sandra were involved in custody battles, John and I hoped that Molly might heal John's relationship with his children. Unfortunately, the custody battle ended up taking its toll on our relationship. We separated and were heading toward divorce. When I missed my next menstrual period, I thought, 'Well, I just split up and I'm getting divorced. It's because I'm very upset and emotional.' And then you know what it is like. Your period is late, and every day you wonder if you're pregnant. I became obsessive, checking every day. When the doctor told me the results of my pregnancy test, I said, 'Oh, no. I came here to find out that I'm not pregnant, so that I wouldn't have to worry anymore.' I cried and was furious. I had expected to conceive after my vision. Instead it happened the last time John and I had intercourse. My daughter took her chance: 'Oops! Better do it now. This is it: last time out the chute.' Despite my feeling of connectedness to this Soul, I did not want to bring in a child as a single parent. I called on the girl's Soul, trying to convince her that I would do it at a later time under better circumstances. The child would not go for that.

"I consulted an intuitive who advised, 'The Soul insists. I cannot get you off the hook. An abortion will disrupt the child's Soul agreement, and you will incur negative karma.' A friend further informed me, 'Medicaid pays medical expenses for single mothers.' That settled it. I had a heart-to-heart talk with the child in my womb: 'All right. What kind of a conception is this when I'm on my own, with little money, no insurance, on the brink of divorce? If you're that determined, you had better figure it out. I hope you have a good plan to pay for this.' After that, my business profits surpassed what they had ever been before. Plus John and I felt a strong pull to work out our differences if we were to share a child. We started marriage counseling. We got more than we bargained for. By the time of Molly's birth, her message, 'I am the one who will come and heal this family,' was clear. If I had not conceived a child, John and I would have divorced. Instead, we live and work together and have resolved the conflicts with his four other children, who had been a source of controversy.

"Our Souls make pre-birth choices and agreements. The more we honor our Soul's path, the more we walk in the light. With this child, I honored a Soul contract that needed to happen despite the circumstances. I am grateful to bring a Soul through who has a real purpose; it makes my path more meaningful. This fulfilled my Soul's desire, her Soul's agreement with me, and the Soul contracts Molly made with everyone else."

Meeting My Son's Soul over Chesapeake Bay

Cathy saw the radiant blueprint of her son's face years before birth.

Children are self-determined beings with intentions to be born to particular parents at a particular time. So once a child finds its mother, he must wait for the proper father and the proper time. Cathy, a forty-four-year-old, full-time mother recalls: "When I was sixteen, we lived in Maryland on Chesapeake Bay. One afternoon like any other afternoon, I walked out my back door and it was like the whole universe opened up. Everything was illuminated with an incredible glow. The sky was brilliant. I was filled with bliss. I began to laugh and realized, 'I know everything.' This little voice inside of me asked, 'What do I know?' Then in the sky before me, I saw the face of a five-year-old boy as clear as a bell. I knew that was my son. Looking back on it, I figured what I really wanted to know is what every teenager wonders, 'Will I get married and have children?'

"Life was different from that moment on. The little boy never left me. I sensed his presence around me, no matter where I was or what I did. In my early twenties, I looked for a partner with blond hair and green eyes to match the child's appearance. Until I was married, I told my son, 'I know you are there, but it is not time.' The night my husband and I conceived, so much bliss washed through me, I began to cry. I felt a 'knowingness.' My husband didn't know what was going on and asked, 'Why are you crying?' I did not dare say, 'Oh, by the way, Jon, we just conceived the child who has been hanging around for years.' That's because Jon had not finished college yet. I said, 'Oh, it's nothing.' A few weeks later, my pregnancy was confirmed. Somehow everything worked out perfectly. My five-year-old son Michael is a replica of the child who appeared in my vision fourteen years ago."

Radical Eggs and Miracle Pregnancies

A cosmic intelligence plays a role in overcoming obstacles to motherhood.

Skye, a thirty-five-year-old mother of three, did not expect more children until she awoke one morning recalling a message received in a vivid dream: "You have radical eggs in your body, and you will conceive another child." Skye felt elated, until she remembered: "Oh, this dream is simply wishful thinking. I have no ovaries or fallopian tubes." Skye's right ovary and fallopian tube had been surgically removed following her second child's birth in 1973. Four years later, in 1977, the left ovary and left fallopian tube were removed during her pregnancy with her third child. Four months after her dream Skye scheduled a doctor's appointment. Something did not feel right. "My doctor asked, 'What are your symptoms?' I explained, 'I feel nauseous. I'm puzzled by my pregnancy symptoms because I don't have ovaries or fallopian tubes, so I could not be pregnant.' He said, 'Let's take a pregnancy test anyway.'

"Two days later, the doctor told me, 'You are pregnant.' I confronted the obstetrician who performed the surgery in 1977. He exclaimed, 'Your pregnancy is a miracle. The fetus must be in your abdominal cavity. We must remove it. You have no fallopian tubes, and we sutured the uterus closed; it cannot be an intrauterine pregnancy.' He explained how a fetus could develop outside the uterus: 'An egg can travel from the ovary into the abdominal cavity and attach itself to the intestinal wall. You need a sonogram to determine the location of the fetus so we can remove it.' When I returned for the results, I asked the radiologist, in a pained voice, 'Is my baby in my abdomen?' He said, 'Oh, no, the baby is right here in your uterus. See that little being right there? That is your baby.' My knees buckled and I caught myself on the counter. The obstetrician who had performed my surgery was afraid of a malpractice suit and treated me without charge. My pregnancy was healthy, as if everything in my body were normal. I birthed a baby girl at home. A few years later, I gave birth to one more child. A third miracle pregnancy ended in miscarriage."

Miracle of the Radical Eggs

How did three "radical eggs" appear? The radical eggs formed and made it to the uterus. One more part of the medical paradox is, at the time, Skye was a single parent nursing her youngest son and slept with the father a few times. A cosmic intelligence operates within the egg, uterus, and body. Medical theory suggests that Skye's ovary regenerated, creating new eggs, and each migrated to the uterus. Three Souls maneuvered around the barriers to motherhood, and two children are living proof that miracles happen.

Brotherhood Takes Nine Years

A highly evolved Soul chose to be Sharon's son.

"Eight-year-old Vincent kept pleading with me, 'Mommy, I want a brother.' I said, 'Well, you are not going to get one.' I was a thirty-two-year-old single mother. Raising another child was the remotest thought in my mind. On the other hand, when I did become pregnant one year later, friends reminded me that whenever I had seen parents mistreat their children, I had said, 'I should have a baby so that one less baby gets abused,' or 'Why do couples have children if they don't know how to take care of them?'

"So I had been making innocent comments while my son Vincent had been begging for a brother. Plus John had been asking to date me for a year. Then one night, John and I made love. Afterward I rested in bed in total silence. All of a sudden, a voice that resonated with authority said, 'Sharon, you are pregnant.' I thought, 'That'll be interesting.' The next day my whole body felt full of presence, soft, and satisfied: a rich, deep, quiet, full biological satisfaction. I savored a maturity in my body.

"I missed my period. I panicked. Getting pregnant was a bad idea; my relationship with John felt temporary. My stepmother tuned in: 'Sharon, are you pregnant?' I said, 'Of course not.' She said, 'If you are, don't do anything foolish. Your father and I will help.' When my doctor confirmed, 'There is a fifty percent chance that you are pregnant,' I tasted true joy. I was ecstatic, complete and total bliss. A few weeks later, I thought, 'What am I doing? I must be out of my mind.' I made pennyroyal tea to abort the baby. As I was about to drink the tea, a loud raging voice said, 'No!' I spilled the tea. The voice explained, 'I am coming to the planet, and you are the vehicle I must come through.' I said, 'Okay, I will be the vehicle for you.'

"When the nurse brought my newborn to me, everything disappeared when he looked into my eyes. That was the most significant moment of my life. I could not hear or see anything else. All I saw was this completely conscious being looking into my eyes. My son looked all the way into my Soul. I witnessed a pure consciousness and a knowing that I had not known in myself. He knew who he was, and I did not have a clue who I was or who he was. The experience set me on a search to find that knowingness within myself. My son Jon is a young man today and continues to be my spiritual teacher."

Cherubim on Pink Clouds

Ellen's love for a child began two years before birth.

"One morning I was meditating in a huge hall with several hundred women. I sensed a sweet, peaceful, calm energy. In my mind's eye, I saw a misty, puffy cloudiness and a cluster of cherub-like babies gleefully rolling around fifteen to thirty feet overhead. They were intelligent, aware beings in baby form. My attention became interested. For a while I casually observed the cherub babies laughing and talking high up near the ceiling. Then two cherubim looked down in my direction. I thought, 'They are looking at women around me.' The more mature, girl-like cherub read my mind and said, 'I want you to be my mother.' I thought she meant someone else. Then they both said, 'No, you.' I was twenty-six and had been married one year. We were not financially ready for a child. Yet I did not feel we needed to go about this right away. A warm, secure connection to my future child made me look forward to motherhood.

"This encounter occurred two years before Ariel's birth. Once I became pregnant, I felt Ariel five feet above me. We communicated telepathically. She chose her name."

Cultural Parallels: Soul as a Cherub or Child

Ellen's vision of subtle childlike beings reminds us of representations of the Soul as a child decorating medieval Christian cathedrals, bas-reliefs on royal tombs, biographies of saints, as well as on the art of woodcuts. Ellen's vision also parallels theosophist Geoffrey Hodson's clairvoyant perceptions of the prenatal etheric blueprint of a recently conceived child: it resembles a baby body built of etheric matter and "shimmers and shines with a moonlike luminosity."[1] It stands eight to twelve inches high and is male or female. Every tissue-to-be is represented in the blueprint as flowing energy, each with a particular wavelength: bones, muscles, veins and arteries, nerves, and brain.

The Buddhist interlife being getting ready for rebirth reflects a similar notion: proportions of a five- to ten-year-old child; capability of locating future parents; with a transparent body capable of travel by mere intention that can pass unobstructedly through walls; seven times more aware than humans in terms of being clairvoyant, telepathic, and able to read minds; and possessing an intellect, emotions, will, sensory organs, and a subtle body that casts neither a shadow nor a reflection in a mirror.

Other references to the Soul as a tiny human-like form are found worldwide.

❀ Malayan Peninsula: a thin, thumb-size, vaporous human image that can fly quickly from place to place.
❀ Nakelo people (Fiji): a diminutive child.
❀ Indigenous peoples of Australia: a tiny, fully developed Spirit-child who selects parents, ethnic group, and social class.
❀ Seri people (northern Mexico): the baby's spirit descends into the mother's womb as a tiny flying winged figure.

The indigenous North American "free Soul" is an ethereal mirror image of a human:

❀ Huron: a tiny human with head, body, arms, and legs.
❀ Kwakiutl: a person's double, but like smoke or shadows.
❀ Haisla: a precise image of the person the size of a fly.
❀ Quinault and Salish: a miniature baby who looks like fog.

- ✿ Athabaskans: a two-foot-tall being who dresses and acts like a human.
- ✿ Shoshone: a person as small as a pea or ten inches high.
- ✿ Cheyenne: a mere shape, like a shadow without detail, clothing, or features.
- ✿ West Greenland: colorless, as if they were nothing—no flesh or bone.

CHAPTER 10

Soul as a Sphere of Light

Visions and Memories

Conception causes an anchor of a blue light to go
from the heart center of the incoming Soul to the
embryo in the womb.
                              —Torkom Saraydarian

The human Soul is a luminous spark or sphere of light.

T
HE SOUL OF SHANE'S CHILD entered her womb as a spiral-
ing tornado of light in the third month of pregnancy. Pregnant for the first time at twenty-seven, Shane relates: "Suddenly the room became illuminated and increasingly flooded with
brighter and brighter light. The rainbow-colored shimmering light
entered my navel. My mind passed into a mystical ecstasy. I was
filled with bliss for days afterward."

Chapter 10 focuses on psychic perceptions of Souls appearing in
the forms of tiny orbs, sparkling bubbles, and bright lights. Reports
from mothers such as Shane open a door to the Soul as an eternal,
blissful being of Light, untouched by outer change. As individual spiritual sparks, awesome possibilities await us: states of self-
realization and cosmic illuminations. Each spark embodied in the
physical realm is one with the Source, a conscious intelligence per-
vading the universe. Mystical and religious teachings point to such
possibilities. Become the Self that you truly are; transform your life
and the planet.

Thousands of Soul Bubbles of Light

Millions of Souls, flickering like stars in the night, hover around seeking parents.

Mystical experiences are often so personal that many remain confidential. Even husbands never hear about them. Perhaps that is why Elsa, a thirty-seven-year-old mother of two, felt self-conscious sharing her story. "I do not like to make my spiritual experiences more or less than they are. When I have an experience, I do not have to decide whether it is real. But, if I share it with someone, suddenly there is an outside opinion deciding whether my experience is imaginary or real. It loses its innocence."

Meditation was part of Elsa's daily routine for spiritual growth. On a meditation retreat with thousands of people, unexpected thoughts came up during meditation: "Have another baby, have another baby, have another baby." Elsa thought, "No, I have enough children." Elsa realized that these desires were coming from thousands of little bubbles of light with a pearlescent sheen floating around in the room. They were four to five inches in diameter, each having a liquid gold color. Each bubble had a faint impression of a beautiful, little round cherubic face, with pink cheeks and golden hair. These Soul bubbles were very lovely and absolutely pulling at her heart.

"The Soul bubbles were inside my consciousness when I closed my eyes and outside when I looked around the hall: 'You are such a good mother. Have another baby, have one of us. What a good mother you would make. We want you for a mother.' One golden bubble even came up and went 'ping' right on my abdomen while I was resting. I felt a sensation gently landing on my tummy. 'I'm coming. Here I come.' I thought, 'This is ridiculous. You can't make babies like that.' I remained firm: 'No, no! Childbirth is too hard on my body. I already have two. Find somebody else.' The Soul bubbles persisted: 'You are such a good mother. We want you for a mother. Come on, have a baby. Have one of us.' After five days, the

Souls began to fade out and said: 'All right, we're going away. You can't have us.' I thought, 'Oh, no! Come back. I will have one.' That was a great sales technique. The adorable bubbles had gotten to me at last. I sensed a wonderful feeling of being chosen. What an honor. I kept my visions to myself. Ironically, by the time the Soul bubbles had talked me into it, my husband, Jim, who was against more children, said, 'We should have another child.' We conceived Julian on Valentine's Day. Within twenty-four hours, I perceived a feeling in my head, like going up and down in an elevator or driving over a steep hill. Since birth, our third son has looked like those cherubim. He just needed to wait one year for us to make him."

Cultural Parallels: Millions of Souls Seeking Birth

Souls competing for Elsa as their mother dovetails with three more examples.

* ❋ Paramahansa Yogananda (India, 1893–1952): "The adventure begins with the struggle the soul goes through to enter a womb at the time of conception. In the astral world, there are millions of souls struggling to return to earth, to enter the mated sperm and ovum cells at the time of conception. Saint or sinner, unless you have attained final redemption, there is a great desire to reincarnate again on earth. At the time of conception, there is a flash in the ether, and one soul enters as the sperm and ovum cells unite. You had to fight to get into the womb. Not only you, but many souls rushed to enter, and the ones that won are you, and you, and I. It was not an easy victory."[1]
* ❋ Tibetan Buddhism: two lamas discussed what they hoped to achieve in their next birth. The first monk said, "I will be reborn in Tibet so that I can advance within the same monastic tradition." The second lama said, "I will be reborn as a minister in China." The first monk was reborn according to plan. His friend later joined the monastery and explained, "Many candidates were striving to attain that elite

position. I was outcompeted despite my knowledge and spiritual accomplishment."[2]

✻ United States: When Brett was about three years old, he was angry one day. He said, "I hate you, Mommy. You weren't even my first choice for a Mommy." His mother asked, "Who was your first choice?" Brett said, "It was a woman from the Philippines, but she had already been taken."[3]

Cultural Parallels: Soul as a Sphere of Light

Elsa's awareness of spheres of light reminds us of NDEs.

✻ Thespesius (Greece, 46–120 CE): in an NDE Thespesius saw departed Souls rise up from Earth as small fiery bubbles, ranging from pure moonlight color to mottled and dappled with livid spots like adders. When these flame-like bubbles burst open, Souls emerged in the form of men and women.[4]

✻ P. M. H. Atwater (United States, born 1937): those who experience NDEs see Souls as balls of light, spheres of light, or light beings. "But if you look past the trappings, as I did when I died, well, there is that spark, winking at you. Ah, such bliss!"[5]

✻ Reverend Howard Storm (United States, born 1946): he saw the picture of "a galaxy." Outside the center, countless millions of spheres of light were flying around, entering and leaving a great Beingness at the center.[6]

Soul as a Blue Orb

Joanie entered a state of euphoria after lovemaking.

"As I was resting in my bed, an elliptical glowing blue orb came toward me from the left. It was five feet high. As it approached, it began to shrink. I felt the energy of love and kindness. I was about to conceive a child who was an advanced being. I communicated telepathically to this light: 'Conception would be a mistake; I am young and not ready. I will welcome you back should I become ready in the future.' With that, the blue orb faded away. A few years later I found myself pregnant again. I did a mini vision quest in the country: a day of fasting and meditation. I wanted to contact this Spirit as I had before. Communication turned out to be difficult; I was five weeks pregnant. As it turned out, by the close of the day, I moved into an altered state and felt like I had reached this being. I explained that I was single and was unable and unwilling to be a mother. I preferred that the Soul move on. The next morning, my menstrual period began."

Cultural Parallels: Soul as a Blue Orb of Light

* ❋ Kunga Palmo (Tibet): Kunga had a conception dream of her son, the Second Dalai Lama (1475–1542). A blue radiant light, the size of a sesame seed, entered her womb; the light filled her, flowing through every pore.[7]
* ❋ Murshida Vera Justin Corda, PhD (United States, 1913–2002): the Soul manifests as a tiny, glowing, electric blue light over the woman's navel. The light grows in strength and size, and spins after quickening.[8]

Struck by a Beam of Light

A mystical visitation confirmed Gerry's intuition for a child.

Gerry and Ian, a newly-married couple had no immediate plans for a child. Gerry was a full-time artist while Ian completed his college degree. Gerry: "Awareness of a child popped up on the spur of the moment. I will never forget it. I came home from work one day and told my husband, 'I must have a baby now. I don't care if it disturbs our plans.' Ian said, 'How can we afford a child?' The desire felt urgent. I had no control over it. I climbed to the top bunk in the spare bedroom and cried hysterically all night long until my husband finally agreed. Three and a half months later, I was resting in our bedroom. As I put my head on the pillow, a shaft of light descended from the ceiling from the right corner of the room. A beam of nondiffused light entered my body. I could see the fetus inside my womb, as if my consciousness were looking at the womb with X-ray vision from outside. The baby's eyes were wide open. His little hands were crossed over his chest. I knew without a doubt that the fetus was a boy. I gazed into his eyes. They were so huge. I had a clear knowledge of who was being born and told my doctor, 'I'm going to have a son.' She replied, 'Don't have any expectations. You could be disappointed.'

"My son has made my life complete. That boy knows he is a divine Soul. He says, 'I am Brahmin,' meaning he is experiencing pure consciousness, the Source of All. Why did I see a beam of light? Is this how every Soul comes into the womb? I am no closer to understanding my mystical encounter today than when it happened."

Cultural Parallels: Struck by a Beam of Light

Gerry's experience during pregnancy parallels the conception experience of the mother of the famous Bengali sage Ramakrishna (1836–1886): "A flood of divine light emerged out of Sivalinga [a sacred temple image] at Kamarpukur and entered the body of Chandramani Devi, who thereafter fell unconscious when she was on the point of telling the blacksmith woman Dhani about it." When Chandramani regained consciousness, she felt that she was with child. Her son, the great sage, was born nine months later.[9]

Mother and Daughter Skydiving to Earth

Our consciousness belongs to Heaven, not Earth.

Unlike parents who witness an incoming Soul as a light form, twenty-five-year-old Kirsten recalls how she and her mother enjoyed pure existence as spheres of pure light. "As soon as I was born, I knew there was something deeper between me and Mom. To this day, we have a deep, intense connection. When I started to speak at age two, I told Mom, 'We were together, and then you went first,' or I explained, 'We were together before we were born, and then you jumped off before me.'

"Later, when I acquired the vocabulary, I told Mom that we had been together in an assembly of Light Beings, like a gathering of your best friends having a good time. Everything was pure and on the same wavelength. We interacted telepathically. A Higher Being with a motherly presence counseled each Soul in the assembly concerning their life plan. The Great Being told me: 'This is your plan, your goal. These are things you have to endure and go through. Everything will make sense in the end. So take it and go.'

"Everyone knew when it was our turn to go. We stood on a glass-like, transparent, bright platform and jumped off, like skydiving out of an airplane: imagine a piece of glass floating above a cloud with the sun shining down and white light and little balls jumping off into a beautiful, fluffy cloud. Mom jumped off the edge in one direction. I knew that she would be born before me and some day we would be together again. I jumped off the other way soon after that. Curiously, time is different there, since my mother jumped off right before me and yet she is thirty years older in Earth time."

Soul's Fiery Light

Soul sought a mother with no desire for more children.

Mary Jane: "While I was pregnant with my second child, my third child's Spirit visited me late one night. I was lying down, ready to fall asleep. His Spirit whizzed past me like a little flash of white light, the size of a lightning bug. He circled around a few times and said, 'We know each other. I love you and want to help you. I will be your son.' I said, 'I know who you are.' I recognized his essence as a powerful, fun-loving, and happy Soul who wanted to help with my spiritual work. I explained, 'Whoa! I'm not having more children.' His little Spirit laughed and said, 'Yes, you are.' I conceived three months after my second child's birth. His presence continued throughout pregnancy. The instant he was born, I looked into his eyes and recognized the little Spirit who had spoken to me months before."

Cultural Parallels: Soul as a Fiery Light

Mary Jane's vision is hardly far-fetched when we compare it to references to the Soul's light-nature. The meaning of "Soul" can be traced to the Greek *aiolos,* meaning "quick-moving, twinkling, iridescent." Greek philosophers taught that the Soul is a moving life-force of light:

- ❀ Heraclitus (535–475 BCE): a spark of starry essence.
- ❀ Parmenides (5th century BCE): a mixture of earth and fire.
- ❀ Plato's *Republic* (circa 424–347 BCE): Souls are transferred to the mother's womb like a shooting star.
- ❀ Heraclides Ponticus (390–310 BCE): light.
- ❀ Hipparchus (190–120 BCE): fire.
- ❀ Pythagoreans: the glittering particles of dust that dance ceaselessly in a sunbeam are Souls borne on the wings of light descending from the ether.

Western religion, philosophy, and poetry refer to the Soul as light:

- ❀ Judeo-Christian: man's Soul is the candle of the Lord.[10]
- ❀ Kabbalah: every Soul, or Spirit spark, is a circumscribed light, a spark of pure love.
- ❀ Gnosticism: the Soul is a divine spark that came from God.
- ❀ Shiism: before birth the Soul exists as a celestial, radiant substance, imperishable and immortal in Malakut.
- ❀ Thomas Carlyle (Scotland, 1795–1881): man is a visible garment "for that divine Me, cast hither, like a light-particle," down from Heaven.[11]

❀ Ralph Waldo Emerson (United States, 1803–1882): "The Soul is light ... a jet of pure light."[12]

❀ Dr. Julian P. M. Johnson (United States, 1873–1939): the Soul is a spark from the Infinite Light, a drop from the ocean of being.[13]

Indigenous North American peoples describe the Soul as light:[14]

❀ Eskimo: a light or fire.

❀ Iroquois: a minute spark of fire.

❀ Naskapi: a spark of illumination.

❀ Achomawi: a full light.

❀ Shawnee, Zuni, Navaho: an element of light.

Indigenous North Americans saw the Soul's exit from the body at death:[15]

❀ Quinault: a ball of fire flying through the air throwing off sparks and making a crackling sound like burning spruce twigs; like a full Moon rising.

❀ Skidi Pawnee: a miniature star.

❀ Naskapi: a lightning flash.

❀ Chinooks: a fire with sparks falling down, like a firebrand.

❀ Goshute (Western Shoshoni): the color of fire or light, both the red and light-shimmering hues, indicating the close affinity to the supernatural world.

❀ Tuscarora and Cusabo: the shape of a spark or flame.

❀ Omaha: floats, surrounded by a glimmer of light, a halo.

❀ Mandan: color of light and transparent.

❀ Cora: a white human figure or ball of fire spreading light in all directions.

Sacred texts of India define the Soul (atman) as the brightly shining one. "The soul in the heart is identified with Brahman (God), and it is the same as the light which shines higher than in heaven."[16]

Several descriptions of the Soul's exit from the body at death in the form of a light come from India. When Sage Ashtavakra passed away, a magnificent, luminous spark burst out of his body. Likewise people gazed with wonder to see a spark of fire exit Saint Auranyaka's head. Finally, we find reports of the Soul as light in NDEs and otherworldly journeys.

❃ Christian medieval visionaries: the soul is a glassy spherical vessel, with eyes before and behind, all knowing and seeing everything at once; a luminous sphere whose gaze extends in all directions.

❃ Zosimus (medieval Christian monk): the Soul exits the body as a light.

❃ P. M. H. Atwater's NDE (United States, born 1946): "For the first time I looked upon myself to see what possible form or shape I might have, and to my surprise and joy I had no shape or form at all. I was naught but a sparkle of consciousness, the most minuscule spark of light imaginable. And that is all I was. I was content that way, without ego or identity, pure, whole, and uncomplicated. Within that nothingness I had become, I simply existed, ecstatic in perfect bliss and peace, perfection itself and perfect love. Everywhere around me were sparkles like myself, billions and trillions of them, winking and blinking like on/off lights, pulsating from some unknown source."[17]

CHAPTER 11

Cosmic Conception

~

MYSTICAL SIDE OF SOULS SEEKING BIRTH

> Each Soul preexists as an electric current, an energy
> force beyond space and time in a sanctified mental
> world where love and unity pervade. The Soul is
> entranced into a body by the love experience of its
> parents.
>
> —HAZRAT INAYAT KHAN

*The beginning of embryonic life effervesces with mystery
and intrigue—as unknown as the beginning of time and
the universe itself.*

THE SOUL ENTERS THE PARENTS' intimate love atmosphere
at the time of intercourse—"flashing with lightning speed
through their breaths and blood and along all the nerves."
The bonding of Soul, egg, and sperm is like a "gong or trumpet blast."
The summons brings in angels to build the body. This mystical description by Harold Percival[1] affirms that conception is more than
the union of egg and sperm. Without the Soul's participation in this
life-creating process, the fertilized egg might not survive on its own.

The Soul's connection creates a cosmic fertilization event that is
still not understood by science. Biological fertilization is the union of
sperm and egg so that the human complement of forty-six chromo-
somes of DNA is restored. This is only the physical side of embryonic life. Without the vigilance of the life-giving spark of the Soul to

catalyze and energize the fertilized egg's step-by-step, molecule-by-molecule, and cell-by-cell growth into an embryo, the life within the fertilized egg would be unable to sustain itself solely from an egg and sperm. Naturally, every baby born has been divinely sparked from the moment of conception. And so life is no accident.

Sensitive couples report subtle awareness of the incoming Soul during lovemaking when a child is conceived. The Kabbalah explains conception: God sends an image engraved with the Divine Seal, and the incoming Soul unites with its body. "A clear-sighted eye may see it standing at their heads. It bears a human face; and this face will be borne by the man who is about to appear."[2] An additional source echoed here comes from the western Tungusic people of Siberia: the vital Soul, *omi*, descends to Earth and drops into a smoke hole of his mother's tent. After falling into the fire, the Soul penetrates its mother's womb.

A parent's out-of-the ordinary awareness of the Soul seeking birth reminds us of the mythical Cupid, who fired golden-tipped arrows into the hearts of potential parents to trigger their falling in love. Perhaps the Cupid factor is responsible for mysterious accidental pregnancies due to condoms breaking, diaphragms slipping, out-of-body sexual experiences, sudden intense Viagra-like urges, and conception during menstruation. Kiki, for example, had passed forty and she and her husband did not intend to have another child. They were always cautious to use contraceptives. Kiki recalls, "Despite our efforts, one morning when I sensed the Soul hovering around us, I warned, 'John, I need to put on my diaphragm. If I get pregnant, it is your fault.' He said, 'Oh, once won't hurt.' Our third child was born nine months later."

At the same time that Souls are observed hanging around couples during periods of high fertility, they report phenomena such as:[3]

- ❀ Sight: "Tiny lights with rotating wings or vibratory presences."
- ❀ Hearing: the subtle atmosphere becomes "charged with an unmistakable current."

❈ Smell: odors of perfume too delicate to come from a bottle.
❈ Touch: soft breezes never felt before.

Pre-birth communications inspire parents to conceive a child. Included here are also reports from couples who conceived without any inkling. Even so, they too recalled, in retrospect, unusual events surrounding conception. Altogether, these reports transform our view of pregnancy. Only on the surface is there an accidental pregnancy.

Ecstatic Explosions during Conception

Thirty-one-year-old Lisa and her husband had been separated for three months.

Lisa was uncertain about her life until she had an announcing dream foretelling a turn of events looming in her future. "I had a dream of being on an ocean cruise in the Arctic Ocean. I stood at the railing looking out to sea at the icebergs. My arm was around the legs of a pretty six-year-old girl who stood on top of the railing beside me. She had red hair and wore red overalls. The girl made a perfect swan dive into the ocean and disappeared. I reached into the cold water. She had become a baby. I grabbed her and put her to my breast. The baby started suckling. I felt so happy. Then she dove back into the water and said, 'I will be seeing you in a little while, Mother.'

"My husband and I reconciled our differences with intense lovemaking the next week. Ecstatic explosions went off all over our bodies, like boutonnieres at the grand finale of a fireworks display. We felt a big blossoming throughout our bodies for ninety minutes. When we finished, Jon said, 'That was the best sex we ever had.' Nine months later, I bore a healthy red-haired baby girl. The ecstasy on her conception night is related to my daughter's consciousness. She is a high-level child, extremely intelligent. She has the vocabulary of a six-year-old at age two."

Parallels: Mystical Visions and Conception of a Child

Conception triggers a cascade of mystical visions, according to pre-birth research:

- ❀ I saw a sperm penetrating an egg, a blinding flash of light, and felt incredible awe.[4]
- ❀ My heart opened and I loved everybody. That energy of love opened every cell in my body and a white light entered me.[5]
- ❀ I felt a big pop inside of my consciousness, a shifting of energy, and a subtle kaleidoscope of color.[6]

Pillar of White Light during Lovemaking

Jan and Scott witnessed the conception of two children as a mystical event.

"Scott and I were married twelve years before we had children. We always wanted children, but we didn't make a conscious decision to have our first child. She came to us. Luckily it happened when it did. I would not have wanted it to have happened much later. I was already thirty-eight.

"One night during lovemaking, we both saw a shaft of pure white light descend over us from the ceiling. The light was two feet in diameter. Two weeks later, a pregnancy test showed positive. We immediately knew, 'Oh, that must have been what we were experiencing.' That was the only day I could have conceived my daughter." Several years later, Jan and her husband desired another child. One night Jan knew she was conceiving when she saw a similar pillar of white light during lovemaking. She immediately felt pregnant. Jan's second daughter was born nine months later.

Cultural Parallels: Soul as a Pillar of Light

Jan's pillar-of-light experience conforms with visions seen by others.

❈ Torkom Saraydarian (Turkey, 1917–1997): when love, respect, and admiration exist between a couple, their auras and etheric centers fuse at the time of sexual orgasm. A colorful electromagnetic funnel is thus created to receive the child's Soul. The funnel extends upward from their sex organs, etheric, astral, and mental bodies.[7]

❈ Elisabeth Hallett (Pre-birth researcher): a bolt of multicolored light came down through the ceiling and through the bed under us.[8]

Celestial Visitors in the Bedroom

Teresa witnessed the spiritual blueprint of her son's body before birth.

Teresa entered a heightened awareness during the quiet moments after intercourse: "I felt relaxed and wide awake. I became aware of the divine planners who assist me while I am on the planet. The first was a lean man with black hair in saffron robes. The other divine planner wore a neutral-colored flowing robe. They were having a board meeting on the other side—discussing whether I was going to have a child.

"A major decision in my life plan was made. I elected to have a child, and the divine planners granted permission. The two figures walked away into the mist. Next I heard footsteps and a door opening. The celestial light outline of three figures walked through the bedroom wall and approached me. The arms of the unconscious or asleep figure in the center were wrapped around the shoulders of the other two, who carried him into our bedroom. I whispered to Tom, 'Someone is here with us.' He replied, 'What?' Tom did not see anyone and went back to rest. The figures walked up to me. I felt this strange tugging at my abdominal area. I saw the perimeter outline of a face with a shadow of light around it. A beautiful energy, much larger than my form, lay down over the top of me.

"Then I heard footsteps and a door closing. Two figures had walked away. One stayed with me. Within minutes after intercourse, I had conceived our son. Once the divine planners made the decision, God's helpers arrived and attached my child's Soul to my womb. I took four blood tests before it showed positive. I went back to my doctor each week. I knew I was pregnant before it registered."

Cultural Parallels: The Sleeping Soul

Teresa's vision of her son's subtle body as a sleeping being is in accord with Greek and Roman philosophers' depictions of the incarnation process represented as the Soul waking up in a physical body and wondering who it is and where it is. Details of these parallels are presented in chapter 18, including examples from Plato's *Republic,* Virgil's *Aeneid,* and Plutarch's *Divine Vengeance.*

London Odyssey: "Let's Make Love"

Alicia's surprise pregnancy occurred when she lost track of her menstrual cycle.

Alicia: "Due to trauma in my childhood and difficulties I had faced in raising my first son, I was terrified of motherhood. My fears were so great that I needed a child to overcome them. My second husband, Tom, and I felt we might start a family 'sometime later.' Tom would not talk about it in deference to my fear. So there could be no planning to have a child. As Tom says, 'It had to just happen.' On the other hand, I had been attracted to newborns for two years. A friend pointed it out to me. I said, 'So what? Babies are cute; doesn't everybody notice them?' My fear blocked me from seeing it.

"A clearer perception came during a bout with terror. I was descending an escalator into the London subway. I spotted a poster on the wall: 'If you are pregnant and happy about it, that's fine. If not, call this number.' I thought, 'I should call because I'm afraid I may be pregnant.' I put a plea out into the air, 'Look, little kid, later; not now. Later.' That's me: procrastinate. A distinct impression of a female Soul agreed to my request. She was sweet and, while I enjoyed her energy, I was aghast that I had more or less promised to let her in."

Tom: "Alicia and I were not planning to start a family. We were using the rhythm method of contraception and had gone through some tense times when Alicia thought she was pregnant. So when did Mara arrive on the planet? Hey, I was asleep at the time of conception. Well, no, it wasn't an immaculate conception. We had gone to bed after 10 p.m. I was in bed first and had fallen asleep. I was in a twilight zone of sleep where the body rests. Awareness remains on the surface.

"I woke up when Alicia came to bed. I kissed her, a cursory sort of kiss and cuddle as if I had been neglecting her. I thought, 'I need to make contact.' I was not fully awake at first. My body awareness became lively and I started kissing and cuddling. Then it was not long before I was on top. Some force coaxed me on, and I thought, 'Let's make love.' My intuition told me, 'It's the middle of Alicia's menstrual cycle and could be risky.' Ironically Alicia did not protest. With a blasé air, I thought, 'If it is meant to be now, so what? If it's left up to me to make the decision, I might die without having any children.' That night we created a body for a Soul to enter. Mara and her angels had decided now was the time to get on the planet, and she pushed for life."

Alicia: "I had lost track of my menstrual cycle. Several months later, I was gripped with fears. Tom sensed our child was a girl. That calmed me down. When I tuned in, the child seemed like a simpatico spirit—a fun-loving friend. More than any relationship, the bond with my twenty-year-old daughter is most fulfilling. Mara continues to radiate the sweet energy I felt when she first communicated with me months before her birth."

Serendipitous Mystical Conception

One couple experienced instantaneous conception while
they were out-of-body.

Amanda: "Everything was pristine. As a child, I walked along
Hawaii's beaches at sunrise. I sat on lava rocks splashing my feet
in the tide pools and remembered my secret dream of meeting a
princely man and having a special son who would be dear and close
to me. That's the way my childhood was. I lived in a state of wonder. So even at the age of five, I already sensed a son was part of my
life plan. By the time I reached thirty-two, I had only gone through
years of celibacy and relationships having zero substance. Yet I had
been happy to put it off because I had intuited that childbirth will
be a major challenge ever since I became physically mature. My
intuition told me I would deliver in a hospital whenever my friends
discussed natural childbirth.

"My fears of childbirth begin to diminish when Michael and I fell
in love. We were like two wizards, who would stand on a log in a river
and try to blast the other one off. We'd send beams of energy back and
forth to each other. There were so many sparkling stars around us. We
played and worked well together. We had visions and knowledge from
the inner planes from past times. We were spiritual think-tank consul-
tants in an investment company. We had highly developed intuition
and could see how to make large properties saleable, bringing more
vitality to the environment.

"I began to feel secure and willing to go through childbirth with
Michael as the father. So it's no surprise that a child began to stir
my heart even more. I was having preconception experiences of an
unborn Soul. Visions and dreams were coming in at any time. I saw
a cameo of a baby boy. I'm getting goose bumps now when I talk
about it. I usually had visions in the morning between the dream
and waking state. Sometimes when I was deep in meditation, I suddenly saw a child in my mind's eye. One time I had a vision of a

baby boy in a cradle when we were driving to Mt. Shasta. These were gentle introductions, preparing my psyche for motherhood. They acquainted me with this incoming human being, this friend, this delight who was destined to change my life.

"I also noticed a shift in my body. I was feeling ripe, so full and fertile—a sensual flavor of womanhood I had never known. I felt like the sweetest, ripest fruit. I thought, "God, if I get any riper, I'm going to fall off my own tree." I kept saying to Michael, 'A child is imminent in our lives.' These feelings dominated my psychology for four months before conception. I was also aware that it was getting to be the right time. I was thirty-four years old.

"I physically sensed ovulation on the day I conceived. I always feel an ovum snip or pop away, a sharp little sting. I joked with Michael, 'Stay away from me, or get some protection.' And just in case, I purchased more diaphragm jelly. I was so tired that night. I guess it was about 10 p.m. We're both tiny people and we were in this massive, king-sized bed. One at either end, with our backs to each other. I humored Michael, 'Now, you stay away from me.' We had a little laugh over that and fell asleep."

Michael: "Three hours later, I woke up feeling that I was in the middle of doing something. My awareness lifted up to the ceiling and I observed our two bodies down below in the bed making love."

Amanda: "All I know is that in the middle of the night, I woke up and it seemed that Michael was on the ceiling above me. I didn't have a physical sensation of his body weight on me or even his body having penetrated my body. There was no foreplay. I wasn't consciously aware of any of that sort of leading into lovemaking. I just woke up and I was totally expanded. My awareness filled the ethereally charged room. I knew there was this interaction going on. I was on my back and Michael was on top and he seemed to be several feet above me. I was not having a physical experience. It was so bizarre. I was outside my body. Suddenly, I thought, 'Oh, boy. I ovulated today and this is happening. Here we are. Here we go.' I felt the click like an inner ear sound. Then all of a sudden, this soft electrical current flashed through my whole nervous system. This fluid, soothing energy gently tingled. A subtle, bright light originating in my head and heart flashed through me. I had been charged with something extra and beyond my own experience. My intuitive grasp was that I had conceived and had experienced this other Soul or spirit of this Soul. I just rushed. I was profoundly affected by the initiation of this incoming Soul. I was quietly delighted. Conception was like a marriage, a communion of two beings that expanded beyond the body and emotions. The young boy was pure spirit and fused through me. Ever since I was a small child, I had been waiting for this special son."

Michael: "I sensed the child's Soul witnessing the beginning of his biological life as a fertilized egg. The whole thing was clear. A lot of wakefulness was present in the experience, more real than real. We were three separate beings or energies, floating next to each other, meeting above on the ceiling. A hole in the fabric of reality allowed us to be in two separate time-space dimensions. One perception was normal: it was the middle of the night. The other reality was bright, like standing in light. This was a dual experience. Part of me sensed it as a brief moment. Another part felt it continued for hours. I sensed some detail and clarity in forms. I recognized Amanda and me and the third presence who wanted to join the party. This Soul explained, 'I am coming in to be born.' We talked about what was going on matter-of-factly. A power welled up in my heart. Light and energy streaked through my body. Then I fell asleep and awoke the next morning realizing something major had happened."

Amanda: "Neither of us recall physical contact leading up to this event or the sexual act being physical. There are at least three reasons why conception happened like this. First, I have a need for emotional bonding. My nature is not to start out prone and primed and ready to make love. Because I had been raped years ago, I need emotional safety, security, and trust in the man before my body is prepared for sexual union. I was not aware of any of that leading into lovemaking. I don't know how my body got primed. A second reason is that

Michael was usually sexually ready before me. And the third reason involved my reservations, fears, and doubts about birthing a child.

"My prime sexual union with the father of my child was not physically satisfying. I have no physical recollection of an orgasm, since it was charged in other dimensions. Our mating had an ethereal sensuality. The sexual interaction must have been structured and instigated by another entity or our Higher Selves. This sexual act was real, and yet we had both been sound asleep and had fallen asleep several feet away from each other. As the following weeks passed by, my breasts became swollen and sore. Garlic, coffee, strong spices, perfumes, and deodorants nauseated me. A pregnancy test confirmed it. I felt ecstatic.

"Spiritual experiences are grace, gifts from the divine. To perceive conception was a profound initiation. I was aware of conception on the most vital, subtle level rather than on a mundane level, where a woman misses her period. The experience taught me what procreation is and the magnificence of the divine manifesting His creation. That inner vision of being consciously involved in the ritual of procreation, this ceremony of birth in its initial spark form, healed old scars and removed fear."

Mystical Conceptions

Amanda's conception awareness sheds light on two theoretical aspects of conceptions. First is the potential for the Soul to be aware of the ovulation period. The Soul of the unborn child, or some higher intelligence guiding the process, has knowledge of ovulation's timing. If pregnancy is to occur, the potential will be lost if sexual union waits twenty-four hours. The windows of opportunity spur serendipitous sexual intercourse.

Even more fascinating is Amanda's perception of an electrical change within her body, perceived as a click, at the moment a spark of intelligence is magnetically attached to the egg at fertilization. One can speculate as to the unseen intelligent forces involved in attaching the spark of life to the fertilized egg.

Cosmic Conception in the South Pacific

A spark-like tickle emanated from deep within Cata-
rina's reproductive organs.

"I have endured the full range of childbirth. As a teenage mother in Australia, I bore two children through arduous, traumatic hospital deliveries filled with pain and fear. The first labor became so stressful that I absolutely gassed myself out in order to get through it. After that, I decided having more children would be no picnic.

"By the time of my third pregnancy, I had become physically, mentally, and spiritually invincible due to twelve years of daily meditation. My greatest transformation took place following a two-year, full-time retreat where I withdrew completely from the world and entered the meditation state on a much deeper scale. I released deep-seated stresses and had a major consciousness shift. Afterward, I stopped using the crutches of tea, coffee, alcohol, and marijuana. I began going to bed on time, enjoying the simple things in life and less fast living. My inner reality was unbounded bliss.

"I entered a second marriage at thirty-five. I didn't want more children. Yet I was suddenly thrown into the motherhood role all over again. Sean and I honeymooned in Hawaii. During sexual intimacy, the condom broke. Did the condom break by accident? I do not believe in accidents or even that pregnancies are accidental. From the moment we had intercourse, a sweet feeling of peace welled up inside. I was content, totally full, and quiet as if my body was surrendering to cosmic forces. A few days later, Sean and I were caught by the Pacific Ocean along a desolate wild stretch of coastline. We sat on the beach to meditate. As I closed my eyes, I became the Ocean of Life: Pure Consciousness. Within this infinite, shimmering sea of Light, I witnessed cell division manifesting from its first sprouting. At the same time, I became the process of cell division, a wave growing at a phenomenal rate and dividing from within itself. This stirring or activity caused ripples in the effervescence of the Light. The Ocean of Consciousness was growing. Life was becoming more. Bliss was becoming blissful.

"I absorbed the Ocean within my Self. I became the Ocean of Consciousness. I was the life force within the cell division: what the cell division was made of, the self-effulgent state of the unbounded Self. It was a refined experience taking place where life comes from. Established in the Ocean of the Self, I was totally in the Light where there are no boundaries. I realized that this Ocean of Consciousness as well as the transformations taking place deep within it was my true nature.

"This innocent perception confirmed pregnancy. Normally when I meditated, I became the Ocean of Being: shimmering, effervescent, full. There had never been a multiplication from within it. I opened my eyes afterward and said to Sean, 'I'm absolutely sure I'm pregnant.' At first, I felt that I had screwed up my life because the pregnancy had nothing to do with our desire to have a child. Given a choice, we would have set ourselves up financially and started a family in a year or so. The fullness of life was aching and desiring to expand. It was beyond me. Mother Nature's will became my will. I did not entertain thoughts of abortion or adoption. I simply surrendered. That opened the floodgates for more positivity, light, and joy to enter my life. Throughout pregnancy, during quiet moments, my awareness was totally pulled into the Self. A sprouting of a new wholeness inside me became a bigger fullness day by day."

Love, the Only Thing That's Real

"The reason another child came along was that it was one of my deepest fulfillments. Nothing else I had ever done or could ever do appealed to me as much as bringing up children. What is important is a mother's spontaneous giving and surrender. She gives up her life to culture the life of her child. That innocent, simple, surrendered state of life is the most important activity we can do.

"Love is the only thing that is real. None of the rest of it is real. Learning to love is what life is all about. You may get all the degrees, you may have all the experiences, yet it is how much you have loved, how much you have cultured your capacity to give, that indicates how evolved you are. Evolved people are not so much concerned about themselves. Their hearts have grown so big that they contain everyone else. My children are God to me. I look into their eyes and I see God. My children are evolved Souls and the most powerful tools, the impetus, the drive for my spiritual growth. They are pulling me along. In that deep surrender of allowing myself to be used to bring children into the world, I have been swept along with them."

Lovers Struck by Cupid's Arrow

An irresistible attraction drew Judy and Ken together.

The Soul has to find a way to spark the sexual interests of a fertile couple. In one case, it seems that a Soul with a strong determination enticed two graduate students in their early thirties to get married. Ken: "I felt a click inside as soon as I met Judy. On our first date, the theater became pitch black for a few minutes before the movie started. I thought, 'Someday we'll tell our grandchildren that this is how we met.' My next thought was, 'What's this? I only asked Judy to a movie. I don't want to get married.' I had forgotten my recent prayer: 'If I am destined to marry, bring me the right woman.' In a matter of days, Judy came to discuss a research project, and our lives changed direction. No matter how much we desired to move at a normal pace, the relationship moved on its own timetable. If I resisted getting closer, I felt strained and unnatural. Then, as soon as I relaxed, the idea of marriage popped up. The thought was driving me nuts until I proposed. We were married three months after we met."

Judy: "Nine months after we got married, we consciously chose to conceive our first child. We prayed to be blessed with a highly evolved Soul. After our first son, Tim, was born, I had an 'aha' experience: 'This is why Ken and I got together.' Our son astonished us over and over again. When he was a few months old, Tim had visions of angels and divine beings and received inner guidance. As he matured, I explained the scriptures, and he understood his visions. Tim is totally charming and has been a teacher not only by his example and wisdom but also by being in situations with him where life is a teacher. He has been a challenge and taught me lots of lessons. Ever since Tim began to talk, his statements have pierced through the illusions. His deep insights are shocking and catch me at what I am doing.

"Parents do not properly welcome their child if they do not practice conscious conception. The door is closed on one side. There is more support for the incoming Soul if parents are welcoming, anticipating, and desiring. It's a more nourishing reception. The child gets off to a better start. The Soul is surrounded by wonderful nourishment instead of having to intrude and say, 'Here, I am. Don't you want me?'"

Ken: "When we looked back, we saw a plan that went beyond personal desires for a child. Our son's desire to be born, or a cosmic desire for him to be our child, was so great that God was working in all this. With the birth of each of our children, I felt their Souls were more evolved than mine. They were perfected beings from the beginning."

Alchemy of Conscious Conception

Judy: "Before my pregnancy with our second child, I found a picture of a little girl that matched the image in my mind. I said, 'Yes, I want a beautiful, glowing daughter who looks like this.' I pinned the picture on the kitchen bulletin board. My daughter Mia displays softness, physical beauty, and spiritual radiance, everything I had aspired for. I believe that this is more than parents choosing a particular child. It is a three-way conception. The child seemed to be conceiving us as parents and triggered us to want parenthood. So we are talking about the baby's conception of a woman into motherhood and a man into fatherhood. Conscious conception sounds as if it is under the parents' control, but nothing is. There were outside influences. Conscious conception is a receptive as well as an assertive process. It is a totality working in symphony—like one organism."

Spiritual Sex to Conceive Children

Conscious conception involves being a vehicle of Divine Love.

Signe: "A spiritual teacher once advised me, 'Whatever thoughts you have at the time of conception are important.' I felt, 'God, life is so difficult. Wouldn't it make life simpler and easier if God would incarnate and help create Heaven on Earth?' So each time my husband and I conceived a child, I prayed for God to come to Earth.

"During conception, everything in my body came to a complete stop. Everything shut down. I felt the deepest ecstatic state of transcendence in body as well as my mind. A heightened awareness continued to be a constant feature throughout my pregnancies. I had my best spiritual awakenings. I was on Earth, and at the same time, I was standing at the doorway to Heaven. I perceived both sides simultaneously. Heaven was constantly flowing through me.

"When my son was born, I took one look at him and told the doctor, 'Give me that baby.' He was absolutely born for me. Nine hours later, he laughed, and he has been laughing ever since. Five-year-old Michael is brilliant, powerful, and ambitious. He is living proof that my prayer bore the desired fruit."

When Does the Soul Enter the Fetus?

Pre-birth experiences offer new insights into this age-old question.

A Soul's timing to take up residence in the fetus is related to pre-birth agreements with the parents and the interest in its growing body. Mothers appear to be spiritually linked to their child long before birth. In two pre-birth contact cases cited earlier involving pre-birth agreements, Beverly recalled Taylor's Soul hanging around for thirty years prior to the pregnancy and Cathy's son hovered around for fifteen years prior to conception.[9]

Summer believes her fourth child visited periodically for twelve years waiting for her to find her second husband. Summer: "I have no doubt that Jason was waiting for my marriage to Stephen. Jason's Soul spontaneously appeared to us during a meditation two months before we conceived him. Our son told us he was coming. We had a clear vision of him as an adult. His Soul communicated that certain children were being born at this time because of what was happening in the changing world. He told us what he planned to do in this life. He predicted global events, which surprised us. One of these events has already happened. Today Jason looks exactly like he did in the vision, although he is still a baby and does not have the same mature essence."

Different religions offer theories with a range of time frames — from conception to birth — as to when a Soul first enters the fetus. No set time applies to every Soul. A Soul may have dibs on one of the woman's eggs and after conception, the Soul hovers around its pregnant mother before locking into the fetus. Souls may use a Cosmic GPS tracking system to find and follow their mothers. After the initial visit, mothers sense the Soul's entry as a gradual process correlating with fetal growth. Early in pregnancy the Soul may be thirty percent in the fetal body. When the baby is mature enough to be born, it houses a higher percentage of the Soul's dimensions. Nine mothers share their first interaction with their child's Soul.

❀ Jennie: "The Souls of my children came in during the first four months. I communicated with them: 'If you hear me, give me a kick.' They always did. The Soul visits for a week or two. Then it's gone for a while."

❀ Marilyn: "I sensed the Soul from the earliest days of pregnancy. One minute I was alone; the next moment I was not.

The Souls did not come and go, yet the fixity, the solidity of experience, changed from abstract to concrete. In the beginning it was formless energy, big and diffuse. After three to four months, I felt a localization of energy and interactions started between me and the baby."

❧ Summer: "I felt the Souls come and go. A stabilization took place at two months, a pleasant sensation of them being with me. Greater stabilization took place at eight months. They were extremely solid and never left. They jumped when noises occurred in the environment. When I pressed my hand against my belly, they pushed out toward it. The pregnancy with my fourth child was different. My daughter's Soul did not come in until the seventh month. Her entry coincided with a vivid dream of receiving a phone call from a friend who had passed away. When I heard Janet's voice, her loving presence surrounded me and has never left. And it's still here." Summer nodded to her one-month-old daughter.

❧ Tamara: "I noticed a distinct shift near the end of my first trimester, as if I had a second brain in my womb. There was some thinking, some awareness in the womb. Afterward, this experience would come and go."

❧ Jan: "I had a vision of Tom's spirit in the light: white, gold, and then red as he entered the womb. Spiritual beings brought him in the fourth month."

❧ Mary: "My son's Soul entered at three and a half months; my daughter's Soul came in at four months. I had so much energy after that."

❧ Cathy: "Rick's Soul was in and out of the womb. When he was gone, I felt a distance between us. I felt him come and go even after birth. He was off somewhere else when he was sleeping."

❧ Judy Rose: "I was meditating in the fourth month when ecstatic energy and light came in through the top of my head and flowed throughout my body. I thought, 'What should I do

with this energy?' An answer came: 'Give it out to the world
and to the child within you.'"

❀ Beverly: "When Taylor's Soul entered my womb in the eleventh week, he rocked my body down to my toes."

Pre-birth memories cited earlier yield more insights on when the
Soul enters the fetus. Beverly's Soul entered in the fourth month of
her mother's pregnancy.[10] Elizabeth's Soul entered at conception.[11]
Summer's Soul entered at eleven weeks.[12] The pre-birth memory
of a Buddhist monk researched by Dr. Ian Stevenson exemplifies
that the Soul can even enter after birth. Venerable Phra Rajsuthajarn
recalls his previous life as a farmer named Leng who entered the
body of a newborn nephew one day after Leng died on October 14,
1908. After death, Leng's Soul entered a new existence and could
see in all directions. He witnessed his funeral and monks chanting
at his last rites. A thought about his nephew, who was born the day
before, instantly triggered the fulfillment of his desire. He found
himself in the sleeping baby's room. A surge of affection welled up.
Suddenly Leng's spirit perceived "a sense of falling." He became
aware of himself inside the baby and recalled his past-life memories
as Leng even though he was a helpless infant who could not talk
yet. As a toddler, he astounded everyone with his valid memories of
Leng's life.[13]

CHAPTER 12

Miscarriages and Stillbirths in the Light of Pre-Birth Plans

∽

It was assumed that the burden of physiologically
sustaining pregnancy fell solely on the mother.
New evidence indicates that the fetus guarantees
the endocrine success of the pregnancy and triggers
many physical changes his mother's body must
undergo to sustain and nourish him prenatally.
—DR. THOMAS VERNY

*Death of a child is a parent's deepest trauma, including a
miscarriage or stillbirth.*

SOULS ARE LIKE SEEDS LYING dormant in Earth's garden waiting
for the right opportunity to find parents. Some are blessed with
long lives; others are blessed with shorter ones. Chapter 12 focuses on Souls who fulfill their life plan in the womb or soon after
birth. People often feel that a miscarried baby or a stillborn has "lost
out" since he or she had no opportunity to achieve anything in the
world. Three mothers and one father blessed with pre-birth communications realized that this is not the case. Parents in chapter 12 share
messages that a baby is a conscious being before birth and beyond
death. The Soul's in utero passage may end early when it returns to
Spirit for various reasons. This chapter illustrates some spiritual dynamics involved in miscarriages and stillbirths. Each case is unique,
and no single explanation accounts for every failed pregnancy.

194

Pregnancy as a Roller Coaster

An unborn child became Stacy's greatest comfort in a
time of need.

"I felt the presence of a Soul who wanted to come in for eight months. I felt a feminine energy: a beautiful, youthful, mature child, twelve to fourteen years old. Since I had three children, I kept saying, 'Please go somewhere else. I know couples who desire a child.' Then, like it or not, I conceived the child the morning my husband left on a business trip. I didn't realize that Bill had left for good for a few days. Our divorce was finalized later."

The unforeseen abandonment was a bitter pill to swallow and made it harder for Stacy to face pregnancy. "As soon as I sensed the pregnancy, I thought, 'I cannot believe this. You have been hanging around for eight months. Why now?' Even though the pregnancy alarmed me, I did not have the wits to attend to it right away. Coming to grips with a divorce was all I could handle. Two weeks later, I looked at the whole picture. I thought, 'A pregnancy on top of a divorce is crazy.' Ellen, my best friend, said, 'Well, of course.' And I said, 'I guess it makes sense, doesn't it? It sort of tops the cake.'

"An herbalist discouraged me from an abortion: 'Be certain this is not a karmic trap and that this Soul has not been your dearest, closest sister who has come now when you need her most.' The advice woke me up. I no longer saw the pearl in the oyster as a bother. I suddenly let go. I felt safe and protected, connected to a greater wholeness. The Soul had held my hand for several months when I encountered rough times. She had been my best friend. She was support and strength, an act of compassion. I apologized, 'So this is why you've been hanging around. You knew what I was in for, and you waited patiently, knowing that at any moment I would need you.'

"I felt a burst of faith and took a huge leap toward enlightenment, self-knowledge, and self-empowerment. My life was happening the way it was supposed to. Everything is in perfect order. I will raise three children on my own, and if need be, I will raise four. I was sitting in a huge hand. I had mistaken the hand for a vast, barren desert, thinking, 'I'm lost. I'm out here on my own. This shocking thing has happened.' Now I saw that the desert was a big hand: I was sitting in the palm of God. I did not need to abort. I could not send my dearest friend away. All I needed to do was to make the next meal. What choice did I have? The most outlandish things had already happened: four months behind on rent, no food in the cupboard, and bill collectors knocking at the door. I felt like the car I was driving might have a blowout any minute.

"During the third month, I began to hemorrhage on an airplane; the pain was horrendous. The gate crew met me with a wheelchair. My children and I rested in a hotel. The hemorrhaging became so intense that I phoned Ellen in the middle of the night. Her husband Jim then picked up the phone and asked, 'Why aren't we calling Bill?' I explained, 'Bill doesn't deserve to know about the pregnancy. This gift has come to me, and it hasn't come to him.' Jim replied, 'Well, it's high time Bill found out.' Bill showed up forty minutes later and set aside our problems and his shock that I had been pregnant without his knowledge. He was wonderful and assisted me. My pregnancy was short-circuited once I went through my transformation. The Soul came when I needed someone. When I did not need her any longer, she felt free to go. Whoever that was, God bless her. She was absolutely what I needed."

A Knock on the Door from Twins

Souls close to perfection may not need a long lifetime.

Judy: "I had no plans for more children. I was a full-time mother in my late thirties with two children under four. At the same time, I received an urgent phone call from Mother Nature. The thought came like a knock on the door following a deep meditation: 'You are destined to have another child and get pregnant right away.' Two Souls put the thought in my head: 'We want in. We want to be born.' Their demand was a total contrast to a conscious desire for a child. I cried because of the awesomeness of the experience. My husband and I succumbed because the request felt sincere. Ken ejaculated. Because he was hardly inside me, we thought, 'We need to try again.' Eight hours later, I woke up feeling nauseated.

"I looked forward to two more children. I thought, 'I have some unfinished business in terms of motherhood.' My heart is normally open to children; yet as time passed, my spirit was far from elevated. My earlier pregnancies had blessed me with another jet engine and heightened awareness. I missed that amplification of energy. Instead, the twins created irritability, insomnia, and nausea. I felt dragged down and barely held things together. The twin's vibrations did not match mine. I felt as if I was carrying another woman's child.

"Six weeks into the pregnancy, I was exhausted and sensed the impending loss. I became irritable because I could not hold them; such a misfit experience. Meanwhile, my husband encountered lots of pressure at work. He began to argue with me. Our quarrel triggered the whole thing to finally let go. Right after that, I started bleeding. The Souls chose to leave. I lay on the bed and witnessed an extraordinary physical sensation gently rippling up from my uterus to my heart. The Souls left one at a time like a gentle burp and then out of my heart.

"I felt powerless to stop it. I felt loss and sadness in their departure. On a deeper level, the miscarriage did not shock me. I had lost the twins on the subtle level before the physical. I knew for a long time the pregnancy was not going to make it. Still, a mother has lost her children. I did not feel any remorse from their side. The twins apparently only needed a faint incarnation to fulfill their desire and to get what they needed. They were grateful to hang in there that long. The loss was part of a plan, rather than an accident. I did my duty by bringing them into the physical world, if only for a short time. Afterward, I was completely free of desire to have more children. I have not heard from them since."

Spiritual Lessons in the Loss of a Baby

A fetus that lived for seven months changed Richard's life.

Christi carried a child in her womb and had trials and discomfort. Then suddenly she found herself "empty," with nothing. Her husband, Richard, shares their experience, starting soon after the honeymoon ended.

The newlyweds settled into a new home where Richard had a "crystal clear" vision: "I saw a newborn when I looked into my wife's eyes. Next, I saw a group of babies playing together like a series of tiny bubbles, layers of babies ready to incarnate. At times, the babies appeared older—four to five years—and then back to babies again. Finally, one child appeared. The child always had the same facial features and hair color. Sometimes it was a boy and other times a girl. Three weeks later, Christi realized she was pregnant. At that moment, a vision of the baby appeared when I looked into her eyes. The after-image lingered, and I felt the child's presence in our home. I shared my visions with Christi. My wife looked forward to motherhood. At thirty-three, she was a long distance runner in excellent health. The strange thing is, I had an inner sense that a problem was looming. I didn't feel totally jubilant.

"Within months, Christi became ill and withdrew into a shell. Christi had zero energy and felt depressed nearly all the time. She seemed like a person who aged rapidly: she had the flu for seven to ten days, would be fine for two days, and then she was sick with a bronchial problem for four days. Christi began to talk about suicide. We sought medical help. Doctors kept saying, 'Everything is fine. Christi's problem is due to psychological pressures of a new marriage and a first pregnancy.' After consulting seven psychologists, the probing only increased Christi's emotional imbalance and worries about her mental state as well as our relationship. Advice from friends suggested, 'Ultimately, there's a larger plan behind all this.' No one knew what the big picture might be. Christi's illness went beyond what I could understand. I felt lost; it was such a deep, dark time."

Chemical Exposure in a New Home

"Christi's pregnancy terminated after seven months due to a medical complication. We had a funeral for baby Jonathan. While we felt some short-term relief, Christi's illness did not end with delivery of our stillborn baby. One year later doctors at an environmental clinic diagnosed her with multiple chemical sensitivity (MCS). She got an insurance settlement for her MCS treatment and felt psychologically relieved about having a legitimate health problem from toxic chemicals.

"Our problems began when we moved into a new home—energy efficient and airtight. The home won awards for energy efficiency. We noted the chemical smell, although we thought it was the natural smell of a new home. Christi's poisoning came from the formaldehyde emitted from the carpet backing. Toxic levels built up in the house when it had been sealed up the month we were on our honeymoon. Triple-paned windows, exterior foam, and doors cut energy bills. Unfortunately it did not create a healthy environment. We had one air exchanger in the living room, and so the bedroom got too little fresh air.

"Moving into a well-insulated home in winter, without fresh air circulating, amplified the formaldehyde levels. Formaldehyde caused my moodiness and depression at the time. The problem is that Christi spent more time at home, thus intensifying her exposure. Finally doctors at an environmental health clinic found traces of formaldehyde and a second synthetic chemical in Christi. Her symptoms resembled classic formaldehyde poisoning. Formaldehyde is a common indoor air pollutant."

Teachings of the Stillborn Baby: Become a Green Architect

Understanding the purpose of a stillborn child is often beyond comprehension. Richard discovered that everything that happens has a purpose: "I was unable to bring my child back. Yet I decided to change the future and clean up our living spaces as an architect. The Soul of our child was conscious of the reason for his incarnation. In my wife's illness, our child screamed at me: 'Wake up. Reject everything you have been taught. Otherwise, many pure Souls may stop incarnating.' I committed myself to serving humanity. I began to construct homes in a life-enhancing way without toxic materials. Architecture was in a degraded state. I found alternatives in the European Baubiologie of nontoxic building using natural materials that create soothing effects essential to a person's well-being. Our child had a message. He knew what was best. His playful innocence had no place for poisons. I feel incredible gratitude for this spiritual lesson."

Message of the Bumblebee

Can the same Soul return to a mother after a miscarriage in the next pregnancy?

Summer, a thirty-five-year-old mother, had more pre-birth communications than any other mother interviewed. Summer is also unique in that she is a very evolved person who recalled pre-birth memories. Summer had a large flock of Souls to bring in. Her pre-birth memories enriched the births of six children. She knew her children were "aware of what they are coming in for."

Summer: "Children are part of our baggage. For me, there was a profound sense of completion with each of my children: a feeling that I had missed these people and they were coming back to be with me. But when I was heading out into the world at eighteen, I expected to have a more worldly life. I didn't foresee motherhood was destined to be my greatest spiritual duty and contribution. So having children wasn't an adventure I consciously set out on. Rather, it unfolded itself to me sweetly and wonderfully. I know now in retrospect that it was well ordained.

"When I was twenty-three, my first child was wonderful, and the mothering feeling was strong. I had been married five years, yet our marriage had become rocky. We hoped to escape a cramped apartment if our marriage survived, and we were saving for a new home. In addition, I was determined to finish a college degree. In spite of this, I felt a strong, gentle presence—a baby's Soul—lingering around our home, a different energy in the air. For several months, someone was constantly over my shoulder. Whenever I'd leave home in the car, the strange feeling came that someone had been left behind. A child was missing. Or we would be sitting at dinner, and I'd feel as if there was someone in the other room who was supposed to be with us.

"I knew I was pregnant right after lovemaking. I perceived a quickening within my body. I was extremely nauseous from day one. I had heightened emotions and sore breasts. The child's presence was strong. This Soul wanted me to be its mother. She was persistent. It was such a painful time with my husband that I could not face another child. Plus Travis and I would be strapped to the limit financially. At the same time, I could not bear losing this Soul forever. I felt close to her already.

"I decided to have a serious talk with her about the obstacles in my life. I sat in the backyard and jotted down goals I wanted to complete before becoming a mother again: (1) my marriage needs to heal; (2) we need a larger home; and (3) I want to finish my degree. I closed my eyes. I felt the girl's Soul listening to my thoughts. Communication took place on that silent level where everything is connected—in the deepest silence of my Soul. With love, I explained it would not be opportune to enter my life at this time. The only solution was to ask her to come back at a better time. I felt like I was talking to someone with intelligence and discrimination. I sensed her response, 'Yes, I have read the demands; I've got it under control. Everything is fine.'

"I opened my eyes to ponder the Soul's response. Immediately, a passing bumblebee flew down to me, landed on my journal, and walked up and down over the three wishes. The bee started buzzing wildly again and flew away. I laughed and thought, 'Well, I hope he knows her.' I didn't tell anyone. I embraced it and kept that one inside. I knew it had been a telepathic communication with someone very dear, a real experience that I didn't want discounted. The next day, my pregnancy ended in a spontaneous miscarriage." For Summer, the bumblebee's symbolism was clear. The little creature represented the Soul, who received her message and flew away.

Sara, Child of Déjà Vu

"One year after the spontaneous miscarriage, I unexpectedly became pregnant. The message of the bumblebee flashed in my mind. I realized that the three conditions I had recorded in my journal had now been satisfied. We had moved into a large, comfortable home, our marriage had stabilized, and I had my graduate degree. Once again, I sensed her Soul and was happy that she had returned. I had the same severe nausea as I had had in the pregnancy the year before. Now that I have had six children, I know each pregnancy is unique. With Sara, unlike my other pregnancies, I was extremely nauseous right after conception."

An additional clue indicated that Sara had made the return trip shortly after the miscarriage. "Sara is extremely advanced—always a year ahead of herself. My daughter could speak at three months. And at one year, my daughter told us things a child that innocent would not normally think about. Perhaps rapid development took place because the wave of her life was supposed to have started the year before. Sara's teachers say that academics will never be a problem for her. Her only difficulty could be boredom."

Summer's ability to form a relationship with her unborn fetus at such an early stage of development is significant. A pregnant woman and her unborn child are of the same flesh and telepathic wavelength. Summer: "When I sense a Soul's presence around me, I explore them in their seed form. Subtle differences in personality and life force become apparent. Then a relationship on the sweetest level starts to develop on a level of intuition that cannot be harmed or changed through many life spans."

Alternative to Abortion

Until recently most doctors would not advise talking to a baby in the womb, considering it to be useless and unrealistic. Experiments with prenatal stimulation and bonding have now validated the possibility for prenatal communications. Prenates are capable of interacting, remembering, learning, and giving meaning to their experiences. The mother can influence whether the fetus stays in the womb or not.

Summer's miscarriage hints that the unborn fetus is aware and telepathic. A serious communication with the Soul can be an alternative to abortion. What happened took place in Summer's consciousness, where the mind influences her own body as well as the body of the sentient fetus. Mothers need to heed the message "Thoughts are things." Thoughts turn into actions at a biochemical level. A mother's thoughts become alive in the baby as it takes form.

The mind-body connection offers explanations for spontaneous miscarriages. First, it suggests a mind-body-Soul connection where physiological and cosmic influences create a pregnancy. Then, as conditions change, they terminate the pregnancy. One theory is that the pregnancy was terminated when the fertilized egg was left unattended by a cosmic influence, a subtle spark of intelligence that energizes it and is the chief architect of embryonic development. As long as the energy attaches to the growing embryo and no outside force intervenes, pregnancy continues. Therefore Summer's desire to end her pregnancy may have prompted a disengagement of cosmic energy from the embryo.

Summer's ability to telepathically talk with the Soul in the womb is not so unusual. Elisabeth Hallett cites parallel cases in several books. Indeed, over thirty years ago, Dr. Gladys McGarey, pioneer of the concept of Soul Communication with the unborn fetus, began to advocate communicating with the unborn, sentient fetus in the womb as an alternative to abortion in cases of an untimely pregnancy.

McGarey's book, *The Physician Within You*, cites the case of a seventeen-year-old girl who explained to the unborn child why the time was not right for her to become a mother, "You will only be away a little while. We will be together again." Susan spontaneously miscarried in the third month of pregnancy. Two years later, a child's voice awoke Susan one night: "Mama, I'm coming back." Susan knew it was her little girl returned. This was the same night her friend birthed a baby girl. A strong love bond unfolded between Susan and her friend's daughter. One day the three-year-old child asked Susan, "Do you remember when I was in your tummy?" "No, honey, you were in your mother's tummy," Susan said. The girl shook her head. "Not that first time." Susan asked, "What did you do in my tummy?" The little girl replied, "I cried. The ones that brought me to you said I couldn't stay; it wasn't the time." The three-year-old touched her navel as she explained: "They pulled me back with a long silver cord."[1]

Returning after a Miscarriage

Reports of a miscarried child remembering a miscarriage are not uncommon. As chapter 3 revealed, a miscarried boy returned as a girl in the same family. In a separate case, John's son, David, recalls being born as their daughter who was stillborn at full term. As a child, David told his parents that he chose them and was ready to become their child, but then his "vehicle" died: "The only difference is, I'm five years younger than I would have been, and I'm a boy instead of a girl. Yet, in the long run, it really doesn't matter."

Carol Bowman's book *Children's Past Lives* cites a case of Desmond who told his mother that he went to Aunty Ruth before he came to her, but he didn't stay there very long. Desmond recalled his time in Aunty Ruth's womb as happy, comfortable, wet, warm, dark, but not scary. It felt bouncy and he turned around and around all the time. One time Desmond fell asleep, and when he woke up, he was no longer with Aunty Ruth. Without knowing it, he was referring to Ruth's birth of a stillborn son ten years before Desmond's birth. The family never spoke about this traumatic event.[2] The trauma of miscarriages makes it a difficult area to research because parents prefer to move on and forget.

Miscarriages in the Light of a Greater Wholeness

Like attracts like. Love attracts love. Parents attract the Soul they need for their growth and the Soul attracts the parents needed for its growth.

Even painful events such as miscarriage can be understood as being part of a greater plan rather than accidental. Each parent and child is drawn to the other in order to learn lessons. Parents sharing stories in chapter 12 felt consoled in the certainty that the loss of a child was not a meaningless fate or an arbitrary occurrence. They realized that they had stepped into this profound life-altering experience for a purpose. A stillbirth or a miscarriage teach lessons. We learn to open up to the preciousness of life. We realize that physical reality is not all that there is. We realize we had done nothing wrong and to not judge ourselves as being irresponsible. We resolve an issue of forgiveness, guilt, or letting go.

Cosmic Cradle looks "outside the veil" to understand a premature death. When we define prenatal loss as "bad," our judgment has its basis in our limited experience in the here and now. A more expansive picture encompasses our world, the pre-birth realm as well as past, present, and future.

CHAPTER 13

Conversations with Unborn Children

⌒

Babies in the womb who have normal hearing and
a normally stimulating environment are prepared
to send and receive messages without benefit of the
words, syllables, and phrases that begin appearing
in a year or two after birth.
— DAVID CHAMBERLAIN, PHD

*Pre-birth communication is a silent invisible spark
preparing the flame of life.*

PRE-BIRTH COMMUNICATION SHOULD BE FILLED with tender loving care as the connection between mother and child intensifies during pregnancy. When a pregnant mother acknowledges that she is carrying a child within her who is aware, her pregnancy becomes more fulfilling. A generation of conscious mothers can generate happier, healthier, and more-realized children on Earth.

Chapter 13 highlights cases where babies in the womb telepathically transferred messages to family members. These babies knew what they needed in order to secure a healthy pregnancy and a safe birth. In the first three cases, a pregnant woman or a sensitive grandmother responded positively to the communications. In the fourth case, Fran suffered regrets for not listening to the soul of the unborn baby who reached out to her.

A Mystical Mother's Journey

Beverly is blessed with pre-birth communications, conception awareness, and a son who recalls his Soul's journey.

"Three months prior to marriage, my doctor said, 'You have cervical cancer. The best option is to have a hysterectomy and blow off having a child.' I replied, 'You don't know the ball game. I'm supposed to have a child, and he's important. My child is pestering me to be his Mommy.' I was going to get one child; I had no doubt. I had a wonderful doctor. She performed a special surgery that gave me a slight possibility of bearing a child. She took off two and a half inches of my cervix and uterus and reformed an artificial cervix. She said, 'The probability of conceiving and giving birth is ten percent, at best.'

"Now, I'm psychic. I have known since I was ten years old that I was going to have one child. I knew his personality, outlook on life, and his sense of humor. He would pop into my awareness unexpectedly, particularly when I was having fun because he is a gas of a child and loves to have a good time. Taylor and I are old friends. He has been my father before. I would hear him and ache for him.

"One morning when my husband and I made love, as we both climaxed, bliss washed through me and I heard Taylor's laugh. I felt the calm I feel when I am alone in the forest with only God. I smiled at my husband. He said, 'What is so funny?' I said, 'It'll be okay. Just chill out.' I knew we were with child. Something had been missing in my life. Now all the pieces of the puzzle meshed at once. Taylor is part of me the same way I am part of him.

"In retrospect, I saw why I had not become pregnant even though my husband and I had sex for six years without contraceptives. My life needed more joy and perception of myself. He came after I went through certain experiences, such as death of loved ones, to help me appreciate the preciousness of life.

"Taylor knew that his body was starting and that he could land any time he saw fit. His Soul fully entered the fetus in the eleventh week. He rocked my body down to my toes. Terry and I were driving to a festival. I said, 'Whoa! Did you feel that?' My husband said, 'Yeah.' I said, 'He is there. I can feel him.' I felt a symbiosis of being from the instant Taylor landed. I had been noticing physical symptoms; but now I felt a being inside me. I was coping with both of us at the festival, deciding what we wanted to do. I was no longer completely in charge. My son and I made agreements on everything.

"There was joy in knowing Taylor was near. I also felt as if I had been living alone in a spacious room with everything arranged the way I wanted and then someone moved in and made the quarters rather tight. We are both dominant with strong opinions. How do you put two like Souls in one body? So, whenever my husband suggested we go somewhere, I said, 'Let me think about it first' and then I asked Taylor, 'Does that sound like a good idea?' If my son kicked and screamed, why bother?

"We treated him like a person from the instant he was there. He was not some foreign little baby yet to be born. I talked to him, sang to him. He talked back, as he calls it now: 'When I was still inside of you, Mommy.' I am acutely sensitive; Taylor is, too. So we were carrying on conversation before he was born via a nonlinear stream of energy—three-dimensional downloaded reality in the now—feelings, sounds, smells, taste, and emotions, all at once. That is how we would talk, much rounder and riper than this little thing called 'verbiage.' He was going to be as clean as a whistle."

A Mother's Validation

"Taylor is the same person today as he was in the womb. Taylor stopped kicking and listened in the womb whenever I sang opera. He also responded to Tchaikovsky, Liszt, Chopin, and funky blues. I felt him bumping in rhythm to the boogie music. As a child he adored jazz and did the same little bonk-bomp he did in the womb.

"I have an acute sense of smell and whenever I shopped for oils, herbs and incense, Taylor registered my tactile sensation of smell. Taylor responded well to exotic aromas. He dragged me over to the cinnamon counter and I stood there sniffing cinnamon for ten minutes. He would tell me, 'Yeah! This is really good.' Today his favorite smells are still cinnamon and cloves. On the other hand, he hated sage, one of my favorites. So during pregnancy, I stayed away from sage. He forever changed my opinion about it. Taylor also disliked licorice and anise. Following his birth, he would make a horrible face and spit out that kind of candy."

Prenatal Sensitivity and Music

"I was at Taylor's beck and call throughout pregnancy. Besides kicking and squirming if he was uncomfortable, Taylor gave his opinion so that I could avoid the source of his irritation. Of course, I wanted to do what pleased me, such as the time I was in the mood to dance. I was six months pregnant. I knew loud noises offended Taylor. I told him, 'I must go to a Christmas party for business reasons; there's going to be loud music. I promise not to stay very long.' Taylor yelled back, 'I don't like this idea. Please don't go.' He was kicking and squirming, squealing, and yelling at me.

"I walked into the party hall and they turned on this stereo. He froze in there and said, 'I am not putting up with this. I am not doing this. This hurts.' Taylor froze and started to kick the stew out of me. I decided, 'Taylor is right. We have to leave. He cannot put up with this.' I didn't even drink three sips of my cola before I told Terry, 'Taylor is making me miserable.' The moment we walked out, my son sighed, 'Aah.' I had not been anywhere for so long. I had dressed up and was in the mood to have fun. Taylor put the kibosh on the whole evening. He knew what was going to happen and tried to tell me not to go. I went anyway, and he made me pay for it."

Grapes and Cottage Cheese

"While I was pregnant I would eat what I wanted for dinner. Ten minutes later, I would be seized with the overwhelming push by Taylor: 'Grapes and cottage cheese. Grapes and cottage cheese!' This was regular, pretty much every meal. I would bring out a bowl of grapes and a bucket of cottage cheese. My husband was disgusted: 'You just ate an enormous dinner.' I said, 'I know, but Taylor is telling me this is what he wants.' This got really loud in the fifth month. The instant I finished, Taylor fell asleep. Taylor's insatiable appetite for grapes and cottage cheese continued for the first eighteen months after his birth.

"I went to the same doctor as my sister during my pregnancy. She is a meticulously conservative doctor. I described my diet. The doctor's eyes became enormous. She said, 'Prenatal vitamins are unnecessary. Your proportions are perfect. Your consumption levels of vitamin C, calcium, and folic acid are the concern.' I said, 'You are kidding me. Everybody takes prenatal vitamins.' Each time she told me, 'If you take vitamins, you'll overdo it. You're eating the perfect diet. I wish I could teach every pregnant woman to eat like you.' My son was getting me off my butt to make sure that he was getting everything he needed.

"Taylor also desired chocolate. By the fourteenth week of pregnancy, I had to eat chocolate all the time—sometimes a box of Godivas in one sitting. My husband said, 'Are you okay?' I told him, 'I'm great. We're having a blast over here.'

"I didn't do pregnancy exceptionally well because I had another person in here with me. It got a little crowded. It wasn't that I was pregnant and carrying another body. Another person was with me, and it left very little room for me, like two minds going at same time. Taylor did not come and go. No way. That would be like telling him to leave his bed without his blanky. He knows where his bread is buttered, and he was perfectly happy there.

"Taylor enjoyed being a constant house guest. When he landed, he landed for real. I often told my husband, 'I am just a walking, talking incubator for this child. I am his host. Boy, will I be glad when he is big enough to hatch.' I was at his beck and call. He overrode and superseded most of my natural inclinations with his will. Occasionally that got frustrating because I am strong-willed. I'm Irish and very direct, and so is he. After Taylor's birth, I thought, 'There is a little breathing room. I like that a lot.'"

Taylor: A Special Spark

"God makes gifts, and this child is a gift. When Taylor was an infant, people commented about his old, wise eyes. Everyone recognized that he was far from baby-like: 'Notice the way your son looks at things. Your son is listening to every word we say. How old is he again, four months?' I thought my son's behavior was normal. They said, 'Your son is so focused. He is not supposed to do that at that age. Babies are typically easily distracted.' By the time Taylor was two, he was stringing mature sentences together with five-syllable words. One day Taylor said, 'What an inexplicable thing.' His words stopped me in my tracks. I wondered, 'Where in the heck did that come from?'

"Taylor started daycare at two. The teacher was stunned at Taylor's language skills. Taylor was talking philosophy. She asked, 'Where did you get this child? Taylor speaks in full sentences like an adult.' When Taylor was eight, he always scored six years ahead in reading, writing, and comprehension and spoke like a forty-year-old.

"My son came into this world knowing that people are wonderful. He is unable to understand violence or greed. As a child, he looked stunned when he saw anger and asked, 'Why are they upset? I see nothing to be upset about.' My son knows what is happening on levels that most people are unaware of. He sees angels and talks to fairies. Despite his maturity, he has never lost his childishness, innocence, or joy. He was a little kid with a child's imagination and enthusiasm. Taylor just came in glued together pretty tight.

"When Taylor was two, I told him, 'Thank you so much for being my son. I am proud that you are my little boy. I appreciate being your Mommy.' Taylor stopped playing with his toys and leaned over and looked up at me. His eyes got these tiny slits and he said, 'But Mommy, didn't you know, I picked you?' He said, 'I picked you because I knew you would be a good Mommy. You would take good care of me. And I love you.' He explained, 'You also picked me to be your son. We can't do this unless we agree.' I said, 'That works fine for me. Does it work for you?' He said, 'Yeah, it's good for me too.' I had never explained karma or reincarnation to him. I walked away thinking, 'This child just had an abstract, advanced Buddhist philosophy conversation, and he is barely old enough to understand the words he is spitting out.'

"Another incident happened when Taylor was three and a half. I told my pregnant girlfriend, 'That due-date business means nothing. Babies come out when they decide to be born. Taylor was due on the first of the month. He stayed in the womb even when the doctor induced labor. She finally yanked him out with a C-section twenty-five days after the due date.' Taylor overheard us and beamed up at me, 'Yeah, it was great in there: your own private swimming pool with all you can eat.'

"When Taylor was twenty-eight months old, he shared his birth memories: 'I remember all the lights and it was cold. I had to go to the bathroom and I peed all over the doctor. I remember her (the doctor's) funny (shocked) face.' So Taylor did a perfect stream of pee and hit the doctor in the chest when she showed him to me. The doctor and nurse cracked up. His birth started with humor. We never told him. He brought that up."

Mother–Child: Relationship of Oneness

Nan's pregnancies involved exchanging at a deep level with unborn children.

Nan is a forty-five-year-old mother of three sons. She is the founder of a non-profit organization dedicated to preserving the wisdom and healing ceremonies of tribal elders. Nan has hosted global gatherings around the world: "I have always been a seer [clairvoyant and clairaudient]. From a young age, I knew I would marry and have three sons. I also knew they would mirror everything that was unlike love within me and what needed to be healed so there were times when I wanted to back out."

First Son: A Blue Shimmering Essence of Energy

"Conception of my first son was fiery and passionate. He pushed to come in: 'I'm ready.' I agreed in my heart: 'Let's go for it.' My intuition had been saying, 'The timing is right.' My sisters were having babies. Twenty-one felt old enough to me. Yet Darien and I had only been married two months. He was still in college and wanted to wait until we were financially comfortable. So conception needed to be an 'accident.' I had my diaphragm in. I felt a slipping energy near the ring of the diaphragm. I perceived my son come in as a pale blue light form. It felt right, good, and exciting. After the doctor confirmed the pregnancy, I apologized to my husband, 'Guess what? I'm pregnant. Well, we were careful. We did everything we were supposed to, and we got pregnant anyway.'

"After conception, I saw my son's body or face in my mind's eye during prayer and meditation. I felt his presence as I was driving down the highway. I also saw his spirit as a blue shimmering essence of energy. Paul's Soul would come and go. He stayed in the fetus as long as necessary and left behind little spurts of energy to keep his body forming, as if to say: 'Life in the womb is boring and confining. I'm not thrilled about being here. I'll do what is necessary to create a healthy body. Then I'll check in with you from time to time.' Today Paul continues to be a venturing-type spirit. He is one of those Souls who is spread throughout the universe. My son has a hard time being in one place. He has lots of energy to go and do.

"Paul is a bright Soul and was clear about what he wanted, what felt right, and what his body needed. He worked with me during pregnancy like a spiritual teacher and gave me mature, advanced messages: 'Mom, your body is out of alignment' or 'Your pelvic floor is weak.' He advised, 'Keep your body strong.' So I walked every day and became healthy and fit. I became especially tired during the last two weeks before his birth; Paul coached me: 'Get up, Mom. Do your pelvic rocks. You'll be glad. It is going to be a long, hard labor.' Paul also told me: 'Mom, go out in the sun and expose your belly. I need light. Take on the solar energy or sit out under the stars.' I remember sunbathing with my big belly in the sixth month out at the lake. Keeping that natural connection and spending time outdoors was important for the creation of his body.

"I did fine with pregnancy cravings. Paul liked Mexican food. I enjoyed it. Sometimes I ate hot spicy food twice a day. Paul also reminded me to be careful about my diet: 'Watch what you eat. Your system is out of balance and weak hormonally. If you eat that, it will throw you over the line.' I paid the price if I failed to pay attention. One time I became ill when I ate chocolate. I could not stop vomiting.

"Paul got me out of a pattern of blindly following advice from men. When my doctor told me, 'Oh, that's normal. No need to worry.' Paul would call him on it: 'Don't listen to the doctor. You know better.' One time, the doctor prescribed white tablets for morning sickness. The message I received from my son was: 'Don't take these pills. They cause birth defects.' I am happy that I listened. Paul's destiny was to have a healthy body. Within a few years, research proved that those pills caused birth defects."

Second Son: Seer Living Parallel Lives

After the birth of Nan and Darien's first son, Darien took several years to settle into fatherhood. He explains: "The responsibility of being a husband was enough. I was overwhelmed and baffled by the prospects of being a father. I needed five years to finish an architecture degree. I freaked out: 'I'm just a kid. I don't feel ready. Having a child to raise is throwing me for a loop.'" With the conception of their next child, Darien felt an overpowering feeling: "We need to have another child right now. I had graduated and felt secure and open to hear a Soul wanting to come through. I assumed having our son was my idea and chalked it up to logic: 'I've finished school. I have a good job.' Looking back, that was not the case."

Nan: "My second son maintained a constant home in the womb for nine months. Gabriel rested a lot and was intrigued with his body's formation. It had been eons since he had been in a physical body. He was involved and excited about the birth process. Lots of communication took place between us. He had such peace, centeredness, calmness, and joy. He coached me: 'You'll do fine. We'll teach each other.' His interactions with me were mature and sober. He was in a state of contemplation. It upped my meditation time and helped me become more focused on doing what I loved to do. He nudged me to do techniques from the East—yogic breath, *prana,* and rebirthing. Teachers in the physical started showing up that knew how to teach it and to help with his birth.

"My second son is very enlightened, and my clairvoyance multiplied when I was pregnant. I thought, 'What are you coming in to teach me? You are opening my psychic gates even further.' I could smell the presence of Gabriel and his Guide, an old oriental Master Soul who smelled like sandalwood. Gabriel came in as a healer and teacher. He activated awareness of unconscious patterns. My husband and I had been heavily programmed to be fine Southern people. When Gabriel came in, we started working on core issues of family-of-origin patterns, addictions, and responding through habit rather than what we are really feeling.

"Gabriel recalls his past lives and is a seer. When he was in kindergarten, he said, 'You need to know that I have another body on Earth.' I freaked out: 'Does it look like you? If both of you came home, would I know which one was you?' He laughed and said, 'No, I live in Asia, and I'm a grown man. I go there all the time; I leave enough of myself in the room to talk and read and take a nap on my little mat. The teacher doesn't know when I come back or when I leave. I go there to see what he's doing.' I asked, 'Why do you need to tell me?' Gabriel said, 'You need to know this happens to more people than me. It is small, limited thinking to believe that we have only one life at a time. Souls can have more than one body if they can handle it. What I am learning there is different from what I am learning here. I deal with international companies and work on world issues.'

"I knew my son was speaking the truth, yet I had no words to respond. I still don't know what to say. Gabriel had never been in contact with that kind of information. He was still a little bitty kid. It has been a real different kind of life. My children have been such teachers. They are far more enlightened than I could ever have dreamed of. So it is like, 'Shut up and listen up.'"

Spiritual Motherhood

"I interacted with the Souls of my children prior to their births and related to them as mature adults rather than innocent babies who know nothing. When the Soul of my child entered my body, I had access to all of his thought forms, understanding, cellular memories, and past life memories. The mother–unborn child relationship is like lovers who exchange sacred sexual energy or like business partners who spend lots of time in each other's energy field. Each helps the other work his case. He becomes your mirror, and you become his. Also, you help take on his addictions or thought forms and help clean them up.

"My relationship with my children is a relationship of Oneness, an unexplainable love and bonding. I am as bonded to my sons as to my husband; however, our marriage took twenty years of getting through walls and making love in sacred ways. Whereas with an unborn child, I am immediately bonded and drinking at the unborn's Soul level, and he is drinking at my Soul level, and our bloods mix."

A Visit from My Unborn Grandson

Affirmations can support the fetus in the womb.

Nan: "My grandson came to me in spirit form when he was in the womb. He told me, 'I'm frightened. I don't know if I can stay. It takes courage for Souls to come in right now. Things have sped up and happening so fast in such a concentrated way. I am having a hard time deciding whether to be born male or female and which lessons I need to learn.' My grandson was in a last-minute panic choice and was clear about his needs. He told me, 'My parents are not saying what I need to hear. I would like them to tell me:

- ❀ Your timing is perfect.
- ❀ Your choice of gender is perfect.
- ❀ You know exactly what your lessons should be.
- ❀ You are loved and wanted.'

"My granddaughter and other family members took turns speaking the prayers and affirmations out loud to my unborn grandson. As a consequence, his natural birth was gentle and short. He is a contented, advanced, happy six-month-old baby.

"Studies have shown that we are heavily influenced and abide in a highly teachable state while in the womb. What our parents and siblings say to us affects our self-worth. Parents can select statements that family members would have loved to have heard from their parents and siblings when they were in the womb. By telling the Soul what it needs to hear, unfulfilled desires for love within the parents and the child are fulfilled."

Prenatal Communication with a Battered Teen

Unborn babies share the world of their mothers'
thoughts, feelings, and actions.

Fran's unborn son began communicating distress signals when she was four months pregnant. The teenage mother believes he had been communicating earlier than that, but she had turned a deaf ear to him. Once the fetus became developed enough to create physical pain, he was better equipped to get her attention.

Fran: "One day I was sitting around with my friends and about to light up a cigarette when I heard the baby in my womb say, 'Oh, my God, please don't smoke.' I thought, 'This kid must be psychic. He can sense my desire for a cigarette.' When I went ahead and lit up, the baby rubbed his elbow or knee back and forth against my womb. It hurt. As soon as I finished the cigarette, he stopped irritating me. Throughout the rest of the pregnancy, as soon as I reached for a lighter, my baby cried out, 'Mom, please don't smoke.' He warned, 'It's killing me. I can't stand this.' I refused to listen even when he was rubbing his elbow or knee into my uterus. I tolerated the pain. I was addicted to smoking thirty cigarettes per day. One time my baby was rubbing his knee against my uterus, and I began moaning, 'Oh, God, it really hurts.' My older sister heard my groans and rushed in to see if I was okay: 'You're really having pain, aren't you?' I said, 'Yeah, I think he really hates it when I smoke.'

"I remember another incident when I was alone and my daughter was sleeping. The baby created so much pain that I put the cigarette out. I lay on the couch and began sobbing. I felt miserable. I was overwhelmed thinking about how terrible my life is: 'I want this baby. Still, I'm hurting my baby, and I'm unable to stop doing that.' My remorse and sense of helplessness continued throughout pregnancy.

"After the nurse brought my newborn son to me, I lit up a cigarette. My sister warned, 'Don't smoke.' I replied, 'I'm smoking, so he'll have to get used to it.' My baby began to sneeze, and he crinkled up his nose. My nicotine habit contributed to my son's poor health. Dan was born with allergies—a stuffy nose, sore throat, earaches. As a child he had migraines, smoker's cough, asthma, and chronic bronchitis. He was also born with an addiction to cigarettes. He smoked for nine years beginning from sixteen.

"Why I ignored my unborn child's cries is imbedded within the cultural milieu of the times. First of all, my mother gave birth to twins when I turned thirteen. I had felt for some time that my mother had emotionally abandoned me. Now the birth of twins made the distance between us complete. At the same time, a nineteen-year-old guy came into my life. Dave's parents owned a tavern, and so he was basically raised on a barstool. He was a crazy drunk when I met him. Dave date-raped me when I was fourteen. I didn't want to be with him, except he enticed me with cigarettes and money. I was born with an addiction because my mother had smoked two packs per day during my womb time. Besides, smoking was cool. Everyone was doing it.

"During the Vietnam War, Dave served in combat as a radio operator in the third Marine division. He was exposed to Agent Orange. He was on pot, smoking dope. During this time, I realized Dave was a jerk, and I dated men who were good to me. Still, my family said, 'That is mean to dump Dave when he's in the war.' When Dave and his friends returned from Southeast Asia, my sister gave them a party. They were intoxicated and miserable. None of them could talk about Vietnam. Dave had warned me beforehand, 'Never ask me what I did over there. I'm never going to tell you.' Yet everyone knows they did atrocities. I am an empath, and their anguish was killing me. I do not drink alcohol, but Dave spiked my grape juice. I fell asleep on the couch because their agony was excruciating. That night Dave and I had sex in my sister's bedroom against my will. I became pregnant with our first child, a daughter. I wanted an abortion, but my mother forced me to get married. I was seventeen.

"A few years later, Dave and I conceived our son. Throughout pregnancy Dave emotionally and physically abused me and cheated on me. The police even arrested him for molesting a fourteen-year-old girl. Dave was a big liar from the get-go but had become worse when he returned from Vietnam. I never understood I was a battered woman and what it was doing to me. I was under too much stress. It wore me down and made me incapable of making good choices. It took years to understand and forgive myself. I feel horrible because I could have made better choices if I had not been demoralized, demeaned. My unborn son wanted me to stop smoking. I was interfering with his growth and destroying his immune system. I was killing him. If only I had listened to his cries from the womb."

Cultural Parallels: A Pregnant Mother's Thoughts and the Unborn

Long before our modern age of ultrasound, people knew that life in the womb is a critical period for the physical, emotional, and mental development of every baby. An unborn baby listens to its mother's thoughts, feelings, heartbeat, and everything she imbibes through her senses.

- ✿ Hippocrates (Greece, 460–370 BCE): what a mother is thinking can transmute the fetus in different ways.
- ✿ Paracelsus (Switzerland, 1493–1541): an infant in the mother's womb is as much in the hands and under the will of the mother as clay in the hands of the potter, who from it makes whatever pleases him. Any strong desire, appetite, or inclination can be impressed upon the fetus.[1]
- ✿ Leonardo da Vinci (Italy, 1452–1519): the things desired by the mother are often found impressed on parts of the unborn child. One and the same Soul governs the two bodies, and the same body nourished both.[2]

Two cases further illustrate how the unborn responds to its mother's actions.

- ❀ Abu Yazid-e Bestami (Sufi master, 804–877 CE): Bestami's sensitivity to toxic food began in the womb. His mother told him: "Every time I put a doubtful morsel in my mouth, you stirred in my womb and would not keep still until I had put it out of my mouth."[3]
- ❀ Abu Sufyan al-Thawri (Sufi master, 715–778 CE): while Sufyan was in the womb, his mother snitched cucumbers from her neighbor's garden. Sufyan was aware of her less than virtuous act. As soon as she put one of the stolen pickles into her mouth, the unborn baby gave such a violent kick that his mother thought she had lost him.[4]

Parents who surround their unborn babies with love and respect are part of a ancient tradition. When an empress in ancient China was pregnant, she avoided looking at unpleasant things, listening to bad music, using abusive language, lest she negatively influence the royal child within. Today, parents who want to communicate with their babies in the womb have many studies to inspire them. In Caracas, Venezuela, prenatal enrichment has been tested via a study led by Dr. Beatriz Manrique on children from the prenatal age of five months gestation with follow up to six years of age. Through attention, affection, caresses, sensory stimulation, and communication in utero, babies experienced an emotional and intellectual head start. The stimulated babies showed superior visual, auditory, language, memory, and motor skills.[5]

PART THREE

༄

Pre-Birth Wisdom
Down through History

ONTEMPORARY ADULTS AND CHILDREN REPORTING pre-
birth experiences in parts One and Two conform with wisdom from spiritual and philosophical traditions. Part Three
presents five chapters representing pre-birth experiences from
around the globe and throughout recorded history:

Chapter 14: Pre-birth communications of the indigenous
peoples of Australia who tuned into a Spirit-Child, the prerequisite for pregnancy and birth of a child.

Chapter 15: Pre-birth memory accounts of indigenous North
American peoples who knew everything about their future
existence prior to conception.

Chapter 16: Concepts from around the world of how pre-
birth planning, rebirth, and the hidden Cosmic Designer who
orchestrates everything from behind the scenes.

Chapter 17: Highlights on the universal notion of the Soul as
an immortal Being imprisoned in a body of flesh and exiled
from its true Home.

Chapter 18: The pervasive wisdom of the Soul's evolutionary
journey as a process of remembering and experiencing ourselves as the divine being we really are.

The universal nature of pre-birth experiences increases our awe
for the journey each of us has taken to this life. Collectively, they

suggest that we are indeed one indivisible wholeness that extended itself as a manifested cosmos to experience itself in a diversity of flavors. The One is the Source; the Many is the creation that emerged from the Source. Source is both the One and the Many: creator and the created.

CHAPTER 14

Spirit-Children Down Under

$\sim$

PSYCHIC PRE-BIRTH DREAMS

They say we have been here for sixty thousand years, yet it is much longer. We have lived and kept the Earth as it was on the First Day.

—ROBERT LAWLOR

The Spirit-Child equates to diverse cultural concepts of the Soul.

IN 1970 A WARLPIRI OF central Australia explained what a newborn would say if he could talk:

We have only one windbreak, one fire, and one blanket each. We huddle together to keep warm in winter. Mum often has to get up to stoke the fire, and it is then that I see her crawl back into my dad's blanket. I hope you don't think I was conceived and born as the result of sexual intercourse that takes place there.... Mum and Dad know that I was created by a Spirit entering her body. Nonsense, you say? Yet I heard you say you were a Christian. If that is so, you must believe in virgin birth, in immaculate conception. Then why laugh at us if we think babies are formed by Spirit-Children who pass into the mother while she sleeps? ... If you want to argue the point ... why not come out here to see us at Yuendumu settlement? We could give you a windbreak and a fire and we'd find a spare blanket for you. Or do you believe babies are found under cabbages?[1]

The pregnancy paradigm of the indigenous peoples of Australia goes beyond modern biology: prior to conception, everyone exists as a Spirit-Child who exhibits freedom in selecting its parents, ethnic group, and social class. A Spirit-Child reveals its name to a prospective father and expresses a desire for birth. The man then chooses an appropriate mother for the Spirit-Child among several wives. A Western researcher who lived with these indigenous peoples describes the Spirit-Child concept: The new life that chooses to enter the woman is "a complete entity who has originated at some time in the long distant past, and is more ancient and completely independent of any living person."[2] The Nibalda explain how a Spirit-Child selects a father. The Spirit-Child throws a tiny club *(weetchu)* before him until he locates a couple belonging to a compatible totem. The Spirit-Child walks behind the couple and throws the weetchu under the woman's thumb or big toenail, and enters her body. The *weetchu* may be a nonphysical sacred wood or stone slab related to a totem. Early anthropologists labeled the Spirit-Child notion as the most elementary belief concerning conception on the planet. The indigenous peoples maintained belief in a Spirit-Child's role even after learning about conception as a union of sperm and egg. They contended that sexual intercourse may prepare the way for the child's entry; however, sex by itself is not the cause of conception—a Spirit-Child is necessary. In the 1940s Ashley Montagu reported: "The world of the Aborigines is essentially a spiritual world, and material acts are invested with a spiritual significance. The spiritual origin of children is the fundamental belief, and among the most important stays of the social fabric. So it is absurd then to think ... intercourse could be the cause of a child."[3]

Chapter 14 presents Spirit-Child dreams—intuitive psychic dreams—as well as accounts of the pre-birth world of the Spirit-Children found in anthropology books and published journal articles from the late 1800s and early 1900s. Chapter 14 concludes with a pre–World War II study highlighting modern culture's impact on Spirit-Child communications.

Messages from the Psychic Dream World

Once the Spirit-Child enters the fetus, it becomes a sperm child.

Indigenous peoples of Australia know how to be lucid in sleep. They act consciously in a dream and bring messages from a Spirit-Child to the waking state. Representative dreams are listed below.

* Tiwi: a departed father brought five Spirit-Children to his son in a dream. The five girls addressed him as "Papa." The son accepted them and said, "Come along." That night the son felt a spear hit his head. He accused his wife of hitting him: "Look here. I got hurt." The wife insisted that she was innocent. The husband realized he had been dreaming of Spirit-Children, and in the coming years, all five children joined their family.[4]

* Tiwi: a young man dreamed that his departed father's spirit placed a tiny Spirit-Child on his knee saying, "This is your daughter." The son directed the Spirit-Child to his wife, who later gave birth to the Spirit-Child.[5]

* Murrinh-Patha: Spirit-Children often appear fleetingly to a prospective father, or call to him "Father" as he hunts or gathers food. A Spirit-Child picks out a suitable father, sits on his shoulder, and rides home with him after the hunt. The Spirit-Child whispers into his father's ear, tweaks his hair, or makes his muscles twitch.[6]

* Forrest River: Spirit-Children ride on the back of the Rainbow Snake, the spirit of fertility along rivers and lakes where men are fishing. When a Spirit-Child sights a man to his liking, he

calls, "Father!" The receptive man brings his child home by securing him in his hair, drawn back, bound with hair string, and smeared with red ocher.

❀ Bloomfield River: a woman saw an empty canoe traveling against the river current. The local people searched for it, but it had disappeared. The woman concluded, "A Spirit-Child seeking a mother paddled a spirit canoe up river. The Spirit-Child saw me and entered my womb. That's why I'm pregnant." An elder, narrating, added, "White people have a different way; these things happen to black people."[7]

❀ Yolngu: a man dreamed of a Spirit-Child passing through his village. The boy thumped on the bark wall of the man's hut calling, "Father! Father! Where are you?" The man replied, "Here I am." The Spirit-Child asked, "Where is Mother?" He directed the Spirit-Child to his wife.[8]

Spirit-Child Concept versus Egg-Sperm Theory

Anthropologists concluded the indigenous peoples were unaware of the role of egg and sperm in biological conception. Interestingly, Lloyd Warner's studies among the Yolngu revealed deeper insights into their understanding. After being told about the Spirit-Child concept, Warner pressed further, "What does the semen do when it enters the uterus of a woman?" The elders looked at him "with much contempt for being so ignorant" and replied: "That was what made babies." Warner concluded that the Spirit-Child conception "looms so large in their thinking that the field worker obtains only these facts."[9] The Yolngu understood physiological conception, and yet discussed perception of a Spirit-Child as the cause of conception. They regarded questions about the intercourse/pregnancy relationship as foolish.

Warner parallels his relationship with the Yolngu to that between a visitor from Mars who came to study the Puritans of Massachusetts in colonial days. Had the Martian asked Cotton Mather, "Where do you believe babies come from?" he would have learned:

"God sent them from heaven and it is the church's special duty to look after them." Or he might be told, "The stork brought them," and discover totemic spiritual conception. The Puritan's answer would be no different than the Yolngu's response that a Spirit-Child causes impregnation.

Spirit-Child Dream and Biological Paternity

Infants are free to form both spiritual and biological paternal relationships. That is why a child may have a biological father whose sperm unites with the mother's egg as well as a spiritual father who meets the child in a dream. A man's psychic dream determines his fatherhood rather than his sperm. So firm was the Spirit-Child mind-set that no man acknowledged paternity unless he had met the Spirit-Child in his dream. In one case, a husband accepted a child born to his wife during their five-year separation, ignoring the lapsed time between sex and birth.

In a case among the Tiwi, Larry's daughter had appeared to him in a dream during the couple's two-year separation and asked, "Where is my mother?" Larry instructed his daughter how to find Dolly at Snake Bay. Upon Larry's return to Dolly, he was ecstatic about their newborn daughter, even knowing he was not the biological father.[10]

Rebirth Down Under

Spirit-Children choose rebirth and intentionally select parents.

❀ Bardi: as Nangor walked home from the tribal son's funeral, he felt the deceased boy's Spirit pull on his belt. His Spirit appeared that night in a dream, asking, "May I be born as your son?" Nangor agreed.

* Mularatara: a dream announced Kanakiji's daughter: a man who looked like her deceased father came toward her and disappeared into her womb.[11]
* Yolngu: after Narnarngo's first son's premature death, Narnarngo's departed father announced in a dream, "I am bringing your son back to you." Nine months later, Narnarngo's wife bore a baby resembling the first son who had died.[12]
* Tiwi: a Japanese Spirit-Child appeared in Muramajua's dream. The boy had died in a plane crash and wanted to join the family. Muramajua purified the Spirit-Child in water and put the Spirit-Child near his wife. (Muramajua fought the Japanese during World War II in the Australian Navy.)[13]

Cultural Parallels: Dreams Announcing Rebirth

Announcing dreams serve as evidence of a cross-cultural pattern.

* Burma: the Soul of deceased friend "petitioned" the potential parents in a dream to be born as their child. The wife refused the request, whereas her husband welcomed the friend to be born as their son. In due course, when Maung Aung was born, he "made statements suggesting this his father's acceptance had prevailed over his mother's attempted veto."[14]
* Tlingit (Indigenous American): a child-to-be appears in a dream of the parents during pregnancy: the child enters the home with a suitcase and sets it in a bedroom or enters the parent's bed and lies between them.[15]

Conception Parallels to the Baoulé in Africa

Indigenous peoples of Australia who refused to accept the medical explanation of conception are identical to cases the Baoulé living along West Africa's Ivory Coast. Father Vincent Guerry, a Benedictine monk, once watched a Western class on sex education geared to illiterate Baoulé. At the end of the session, the Baoulé told Father

Guerry: "We saw a lot of things on that screen, but that is not the way one has children. There is something invisible behind all that, something one cannot see, the mystery of fertility and life. And that is where truth is." Father Guerry comments: "The act of procreation, according to the Baoulé, comes close to divinity. It is communion with the fertility rites that rule the universe." The baby's *wawe,* or Spirit, enters the fetus by the second or third month of pregnancy. The baby's Spirit comes from the land of the ancestors which is not a specific location, like a graveyard. The Baoulé know that the land of the ancestors exists beside, behind, and above the physical plane and therefore typically abandon gravesites. Life comes from and goes to a mysterious reality impervious to death. The Baoulé refer to that world as the village of truth in contrast to the village on Earth, that world of pretense where one never gets to the bottom of things, where men live in lies and deceive each other.[16]

The Great Mother's Maternity Ward

The Great Mother births, nurses, and protects Souls until ready for birth.

Children originate from two ancestral women, the Maudlanami. They live in a world above the blue vault of Heaven, according to the Adnyamathanha. The two sisters nurse the *muri,* "little children from the sky," at their pendulous breasts. When the cluster of Spirit-babies becomes too many, the goddesses advise, "Go to the world below and find a mother."[17] From time to time, a multitude of Spirit-Children descend to Earth on a string as fine as a spider's web or fly down like tiny butterflies. When a kind woman with a pleasant appearance passes by their habitat, a Spirit-Child painlessly creeps under her thumbnail, travels up her arm, and moves down into the womb.

Mulili, an elderly mother, knows "what the white-fellow says"; however, their theory is incorrect. Westerners cannot explain why women who sleep with their husbands are not having babies all the time, or what determines the number of children a woman bears. Mulili says that a woman who bears many children is a favorite of the little children from the sky. When Spirit-Children do not like a woman, they refuse to enter her womb.[18]

Cultural Parallels: The Great Mother

❀ Arnhem Land (Australia): the Great Mother carried the spirits of all people in her uterus "and let them out at intervals." She observed all the Spirit-Children and said, "Ah, I have taken too many out of myself."[19]

❀ Nimbalda (Australia): two Goddesses birth Spirit-Children like infinitely minute drops of golden rain. A Spirit-Child matures and travels until it meets a couple. The Spirit-Child enters her body. She is soon pregnant.[20]

❀ Semang (Malay Peninsula): a Great Mother suckles baby Spirits near the Mapic Tree of Life, located on an island at the center of the world. Baby Spirits cross a bridge when they are ready to come to Earth for birth.

❀ Pitjantjatjara (Australia): the Great Mother camped with her Spirit-babies on a large monolith, Uluru. When one of the Spirit-Children seeks birth, it looks for a friendly, large-breasted woman of the proper ethnic group.[21]

❀ Upanishads (India): the Great Mother is like a female spider who carries the seeds of creation. The spider weaves her thread out of herself and then lives upon it. "As the spider produces the thread and absorbs it into itself again, as herbs grow on the Earth, as hairs come out spontaneously from man, so does creation spring forth from the Imperishable."[22]

Numbakulla's Spirit-Children

*Each Arunta is born into a totem associated with an
animal or plant.*

The Arunta believe that Souls were created at a far distant time, and
humans play no physiological part in their generation. In the beginning, a large number of Souls were inside the body of Numbakulla,
the Creator who arose "out of nothing."[23] He kept them concealed
for a while; eventually Numbakulla inserted the Spirits belonging
to a specific totemic group into stone slabs *(churinga)* belonging to
the appropriate totems: wildcat, emu, and kangaroo.

The Sky Heroes who wandered in bands across the country in a
primordial age carried these decorated stones with them. Each arti-
fact, inscribed with totemic designs, sheltered Spirit-Children who
became the Arunta people. The central design of a stone churinga
represents the doorway passage where the Spirit-Child is "dreamed"
into its mother's womb. The Spirit-Child leaves the churinga behind
when it enters the womb. At a young boy's initiation, he learns about
his metaphysical heritage and is presented with a wooden churinga.
The elders tell him, "You came out of it."[24] The wooden churinga is
then rewrapped in leaves, tied with a hair string, and repositioned in
the totemic center.

Eluding Motherhood

*A woman can attract a Spirit-Child independently of her
husband.*

The primordial ancestors *(tjukurita)* of the Central Australian peoples describe immense superhuman creatures who formed "increase
centers," dwelling places for Spirit-Children, in monoliths, caves,
rocks, artifacts, mountains, sand hills, and trees. Caves in Uluru
(Ayers Rock) house huge phallic-shaped stones whose coarse

surfaces have been rubbed smooth as a result of women massaging their bodies against them, a practice intensifying their earthly magnetism and fertility. On a visit to a fertility cave, an Arunta woman sees a Spirit-Child and says, "Little child, who are you? Come to your friend." The Spirit-Child disappears. She thinks, "The little one has gone away." Later she senses the Spirit-Child entry into her womb, "The child moves. I feel it."[25] Lest a woman attract a Spirit-Child when she does not wish so, she stoops over like an old woman, distorts her face, and walks with a cane when she travels by a fertility stone. She warns the Spirit-Children, "Do not come to me. I am too old to bear children."[26]

When Things Fall Apart: Lost Visions

Dr. Lommel's study revealed why Spirit-Child communications declined.

Indigenous peoples of Australia lived in isolation for fifty millennia before Dutch and Spanish sailors encountered them in 1606. European settlement began in 1788. Europeans named them Aborigines—a Latin term meaning "from the beginning"—and implying that they are the most primitive people on Earth. Ethnologists and anthropologists believed these peoples exemplified what people were like before humanity learned to read and write, domesticate animals, cultivate crops, and use metal tools. They were anxious to learn their worldviews. Clearly anthropologists underrated their wisdom. The absence of clothing and complicated economics did not imply an absence of philosophical power. Indigenous peoples were more advanced than initially suspected. Little did the visitors know that the Euahlayi, "clever men," had gazed into crystals and foresaw the arrival of the Europeans, "filling their minds with dread."

With the invasion of religion, science, and exploitation, the Spirit-Child dream was headed toward extinction, contributing to population decline. In 1938, Dr. Andreas Lommel studied modern culture's impact on assimilated people, those on the fringe of settlements, and the untouched who kept their heritage intact.[27] Lommel discovered that indigenous people who had been raised on Christian missions and government stations knew little about hunting kangaroos or collecting edible roots. These farmers and laborers adopted European dress and preserved only fragments of their original language. The American cowboy, as they saw him in Wild West movies, served as their hero. The assimilated people were unable to have Spirit-Child dreams. Birth rates decreased. Ten percent of the Worrorra population, for example, was under twenty, showing a population in decline. A missionary's advice, "Increase sexual contact with your wives," fell on deaf ears. The Worrorra knew conception depends upon a Spirit-Child even after the men had been educated about male sperm. The Worrorra explained why they were having fewer Spirit-Child dreams: the dreamer must remain alert and sensitive, even as the body rests. Sleep must not be too heavy. The Spirit-Child's name then enters his heart, "goes into his head," and the man becomes conscious of it. If a man lacks strength in his heart or head, he does not catch the Spirit-Child's name in his dream, and is unable to pass that Spirit-Child on to his wife. An alert mind and resting body is the prerequisite for conception. Indigenous peoples accumulated stress once they left the silent life of the bush where there had been time to contemplate and meditate. They lost the zest for living in government missions where "moonlit evenings are silent, or broken only by the muttering of the card-players or a sudden burst of quarreling."

In the case of the Wunambal, a Stone Age hunter-gatherer people who hid in the backcountry, they also complained about their falling birth rate. Their lifestyle remained unchanged and economic conditions were favorable. Instead of Spirit-Child dreams, however, they had nightmares of Europeans who looked like ghosts, devices flying overhead, and strangely lit boats that passed in the night. Although the Wunambal had never seen a European, nightmares and rumors of the approaching invaders upset their peace of mind. They suffered from psychic shock.

Traditionally, if a Spirit-Child did not contact a man aspiring to father a child, the Wunambal shaman encouraged a Spirit-Child to enter the womb of the man's wife. In this case, the shaman's psychic ability had also become disturbed. Due to fear, his power to communicate with Spirit-Children had been lost. The shamans "no longer have the vision." They are "frightened inside like a little child who has lost his mother and with that fear the vision of the spirit world departs." The elders lamented that there were no longer good clever men, and no one knew their secrets.

Knowing from a Distance

Spirit-Child dreams were rooted in the tranquil lifestyle of the Australian bush.

Spirit-Child communications, along with other psychic sensitivities of hundreds of ethnic groups, serve as landmarks on the road to expanded awareness. The ability to tune into Spirit-Children is a faculty of discerning something beyond the five senses. Lommel's study concluded that the Spirit-Child dream may be indispensable for conception and documented how the sensitivity needed for this ability dwindled as the stresses caused by modernization increased.

A vital role in receptivity to Spirit-Child communications is a lifestyle free of time constraints, allowing for opportunities to contemplate, meditate, and daydream. This psychic sensitivity went hand-in-hand with a sophisticated, rich cultural tradition. The Law laid down in the beginning by ancestor Spirits governed every aspect of life. As one example, Charles Mountford's report on the Pitjantjatjara reflects the nature of these desert peoples.[28] The Pitjantjatjara met the hazards of life with five simple tools and limited food-gathering equipment. They quickly and intelligently responded to emergencies. The Pitjantjatjara survived in an arid climate where no European visitor could live unless he took food with him. The Pitjantjatjara were at peace and in harmony with each other and surroundings. Well-balanced laws maintained social equilibrium and eliminated the need for warfare. Their life was rich in philosophy, cultural expressions, and communal living. Among their utopian social conditions were:

✿ People are part of creation rather than masters of creation.

✿ The same mysterious life essence vitalizes all life.

✿ The environment was respected: no hillsides were stripped of trees, no farmlands turned into dust bowls, nor were animals killed for sport.

Muta, a Murrinh-Patha elder, expressed the West's dilemma in appreciating their culture when he said with a cadence almost as though he had been speaking poetic verse: "White man got no dreaming, Him go 'nother way. White man, him go different. Him go road belong himself."[29]

May this chapter create a bridge between the Spirit-Children lined up and ready to return and the living population on Earth. May the elders in the Spirit world establish pre-birth contact and live on Earth with their people once again.

CHAPTER 15

Lodge of the Great Manitou

❦

Indigenous American Preexistence

We regard the Soul as the greatest and most
incomprehensible of all.
— Iglulik Eskimo[1]

Human birth is a passage down from the Great Spirit.

F RAGMENTS OF THE GREATEST JOURNEY, the journey each Soul takes to birth, survived within indigenous North American culture, as documented in multiple cases of pre-birth memories as well as accounts from dozens of ethnic groups describing the world of the Soul. Reports published in ethnological books and journals in the late 1800s and early 1900s document pre-birth regions described by communities from Canada to Mexico.

Children Descend from the Cosmic Abode

Children descend as a gift of the Great Spirit or an emanation of His being.

The Lakota talk in detail about a Great Camp filled with beauty and peace. Inside, Grandfather calls out to a man and woman: "You're going to make a long journey. You will return here and be asked about your journey. Do your best, and never possess more than you need."[2] The Canadian Saulteaux elder Fair Wind likewise remarked, "The ancestors have been on this Earth once, and before that they were sent from above to come on this Earth."[3] Many indigenous groups recognized their origins.

- Chinooks: "The baby's home is in the Sun before being born. All children come from the daylight. That is their home. If their parents don't take good care of them, they think: 'Well, I'd better go back.' Then they get sick and die. Later a child may take pity on its parents and decide to return. 'Maybe my parents will be better to me now.' Then the child is born again to the same mother, but is a different sex."[4]
- Osage: babies are tiny stars who come from the Sky, Spiritland.
- Deg Hit'an (Alaska): there is a warehouse pervaded by Spirits of children, all impatiently waiting to be born.[5]
- Mandan: "Newborn babies are incarnated stars."[6]
- Montagnais: our home is in the Clouds.
- Cocopah: twins have a "supernatural paternity." When they are three or four years old, they name themselves with names they bore in heaven.[7]
- Maricopa: twins have a supernatural origin. Before human birth, they live together in "a mythical village in the northwest."[8]
- Natchez: our chiefs came from the "Luminary," where they will return.[9]
- Miwok: O-lo-win, the vast region of "spiritual genesis and exodus," is "a long, long ways off" from Earth. We all come from there and will return. Even our children know the trail along the fine, fragile bridge, a thousand miles long.[10]
- Pacific Northwestern peoples: unborn children live and play in Babyland before they come to Earth.
- Akwa'ala: newborn twins yearn to return to Twinland, their "own country." Despite a shaman's sales pitch, twins say: "We will visit for a while. Then, we will return to Twinland. We go back and forth and are born to different mothers."[11]

❁ Aztecs: Aztecs "bade a newborn baby welcome from the Ninth Heaven, dwelling place of the supreme gods."[12]

❁ Havasupai: if a child is insulted or mishandled, "its Soul goes back to the land of spirits whence it came."[13]

❁ Kwakiutl: a spiritual Guide and a woman ascended straight up, passing through an interconnecting door in the middle of the upper side of the world. She observed "the hole in the edge of the world." The Guide explained, "Through this hole pass the children when they are born, when they come from the upper side of the world."[14]

❁ Athabaskans: at death their Souls return to the Goddess in the South, whence they proceeded at birth.[15]

❁ Pawnee: "Our people were made by the stars." When creation ends, we become small stars and fly to the South Star, where we belong. The Milky Way is the Soul's pathway beyond death.[16]

❁ Menominee, Iroquois, Ojibwe, Delaware, Otoe, Lenape, Omaha, Cherokee, Winnebago, and Plains Cree: "The soles of the children's moccasins are pierced, so that in the event of their wishing to return to their spiritual abode they may not be able to undertake the long, rough journey, which would require stouter footgear to resist the wear and tear."[17] Thus when unborn children invite a newborn back to the Land of the Spirits, the infants say, "I cannot travel so far, my shoes are bad."[18]

❁ Salish: the after-death realm for adults is the underworld, "but Souls of children are gathered at the rising sun, whence they once came."[19]

❁ Shawnee: unborn children live on the little stars of the Milky Way or they live with the Creator, Our Grandmother. "A soul goes to earth and jumps through the mother's vagina and into the body of the child through the fontanel just before birth."[20]

❁ Menominee: "Some babies are actually manitous in human shape, as in the case of thunder boys, who are nothing less than these powerful god beings come to earth for a while; or girls who personify one of the sacred sisters of the eastern sky. In such circumstances also the name of the person in question is pre-existent, and no other name must be substituted for it during his earthly existence. The reserved character and meditative behavior of a child is a decisive criterion of its supernatural birth."[21] Such a child accurately predicts rainfall, "because coming from above, he has inherited the knowledge of overhead affairs."[22]

❀ Central Algonquin and adjacent Sioux: medicine men were thunder-beings before human birth.[23]

Instead of the Sky World, other peoples located the regions for non-incarnated Souls beneath Earth's surface:

❀ Hidatsa: Makadistati, a cavern extending deep into the Earth is the entryway to the house of infants waiting to be born.

❀ Hopi: the underworld is the house of the sun and Earth goddess. "Here are generated the Souls of the newly born on Earth, and to this home of the sun return the spirits of the dead."[24] The Soul passes through a gateway or *sipapu* located on the wall of the Grand Canyon at birth and death. Thus the place of the Soul's genesis equates with its "postmortem home."[25]

❀ Zuni: villages of the "unborn-made" exist in the underworld. They are ethereal beings and transparent like smoke. Every human passes through successive states of becoming, beginning as a haze being, and passes Raw, Formative, Variable, Fixed [Done], and Finished [Dead] states.[26]

String of Babies: Myth of the San Joaquin Basin

The Mariposa equated the pre-birth realm with the after-death realm.

A man and his wife lived up the canyon. She was a beautiful woman, and he loved her very much. One day they quarreled, and he accidentally killed her. He grieved greatly and found no comfort. He fasted and lay beside her grave. On the fourth night, he was crying for her to come back. As the Great Star stood overhead, the ground trembled and heaved up, and she was pushed to the surface. The clods rolled back, and she arose, loaded with her burial gifts, and stood brushing off every speck of dust until clean. He stared in silence; a man would die instantly if he spoke to a spirit. She started away, and he ran after her, weeping. She warned him to go back to Earth, declaring that she was bound for the home of the ancestors.

He pursued her Spirit for four days until they reached a perilous churning river. She mounted a bridge as fine as a spider's web, on which no human could balance. He fell to the ground, shrieking, and cried with beseeching gestures. She turned and beckoned him. He sprang up onto the bridge. She did not touch him. His living scent was too strong. She guided him safely over the bridge. The other shore was all dark. She said, "Wait a minute. There will be light." Then great blue and red fires flashed up and went out again. They lit up everything, and he saw a great country. The woman said, "Closely observe this wondrous realm, and return to tell our people." He met deceased relatives and friends and saw a rich land with people from all over the world living together peaceably. There was plenty for all. He saw a long string of children moving silently back across the bridge, going to Earth, coming to be born to their women. There was time to see everything before his wife guided him back over the bridge. She bade him to return on the third day. He traveled home and called his kin people together. Three days later, the messenger finished relating all he had seen, and the couple was reunited.[27]

Indigenous American Seers

Shamans knew everything about their future existence before birth.

Medicine men were the philosophers, sages, healers, and psychologists of their society. They functioned from a high awareness, beyond the ordinary states. "Neither men nor gods, death nor life, the wind nor the waves were beyond their control."[28] They were awake "inside" 24/7: "Even while he is asleep, he knows and sees everything; you cannot go near him without being perceived."[29] The shaman's awareness suggests a dual state of being whereby pure awareness is maintained along with waking, sleeping and dreaming. Special abilities were another indication of their advanced consciousness. Medicine men could merely think of a remote place and travel there on the level of consciousness "to find out the secrets of other beings." The Apache Geronimo knew where U.S. soldiers were, making it difficult to track him down.

Titles of medicine men reflect their advanced state of awareness: Dakota: "Dreamers of the Gods"; Algonquin: "Those Knowing Divine Things"; Cherokee: "Those Having the Divine Fire"; Iroquois: "Keepers of the Faith"; and Apache: "Wise Ones."[30]

Dreaming of the Gods

Dakota Sioux considered the medicine man or woman to be the highest expression of the divine essence: "gods in human form, though in diminished proportions."[31] Embryonic medicine men selected their future roles and went through a dress rehearsal before birth. They learned to use the Great Mystery under the tutelage of teacher gods. Reverend Gideon H. Pond's 1889 account of the inspirational process called dreaming of the gods deserves to be quoted:

> The original essence of these men and women, for they appear under both sexes, first wakes into existence floating in ether. As the winged seed of the thistle or of the cottonwood floats on the air, so they are gently wafted by the four winds—Taku-skan-skan—through the regions of space, until, in due time, they find themselves in the abode of one of the families of the superior gods by

whom they are received into intimate fellowship. There the embryonic medicine man remains till he becomes familiar with the characters, abilities, desires, caprices, and employments of the gods. He becomes essentially assimilated to them, imbibing their spirit and becoming acquainted with all the chants, feasts, fasts, dances, and sacrificial rites which it is deemed necessary to impose on men.[32]

Spiritual guides trained the would-be shamans to heal, foretell the future, and find lost objects. Each shaman chose the ethnic group and parents that allowed him to best serve the next generation. Then his Soul rode forth on the "wings of the wind," over the length and breadth of Earth, observing various groups. He selected a womb where he could "fulfill the mysterious purposes for which the gods designed him."

Pre-birth memories commonly cited by medicine men of other ethnic groups:

- ❀ Great Bear Lake (Canada): he learned about medicinal plants before birth as he witnessed elixirs falling like rain from a medicine star to Earth.

- ❀ Huron: a medicine man recalled dwelling as an *oki* (spirit) in a subterrestrial world with a female spirit. They desired to become human beings. They chose to be born as twins, concealed themselves near a path, and took up their abode in a passing woman's womb. The medicine man and his twin fought in the womb. Due to a premature delivery, his sister was stillborn.[33]

- ❀ Winnebago: a medicine man named "G" knew that he was a reincarnated Thunderbird. He came from the home of the Thunderbirds, higher beings with superpowers. "My spirit mother and father were Thunderbirds. The Thunderbirds are beings whose glance can penetrate any object. For that reason I also can do it. For instance, I have seen a man through a tree…. When I was ready to go down among the human beings (i.e., when I became reincarnated), I was given the power to overcome enemies in battle. And this I have already done." When "G" tires of living among human beings, he will return to his original abode.[34]

❀ Dakota: medicine men received their power from messengers of the Supreme Wakan'taka prior to birth, including administering to the needy and tuning into the nature of their illness. During thunderstorms, they scouted "for a choice place for nativity" preferring birth "among Indians, so that they might have Dakota customs and dress." They knew what family they will be born into next and events of their future life.[35] In some cases, they also recalled "what occurred to them in bodies previously inhabited for at least six generations back."[36]

❀ Tlingit: while touring the Milky Way, a shaman peeked through "the cloud door" and observed the Earth below; the tops of the trees looked like countless pins. The vision kindled a desire for rebirth. He pulled a blanket over his head and flung himself down into a forest. He discovered a small home with a door covered with mats. He peeped in and heard a newborn crying. He himself was this child.[37]

❀ Iowa: Wanet'un'je became a great prophet and told of his previous existence. Before birth, his Soul floated about in the air inspecting many ethnic groups before he decided to be born an Iowa. He rejected the Winnebago "because they smelled like fish, and so he circled around until he discovered the Iowa. They suited him because they were clean, kept their camps swept up, and sent their women a long way off to menstruate." He came down and entered a dark lodge with a bearskin door, and after "quite a stay," he came out.[38]

❀ Menominee: Chief Thunder Being sought volunteers for a mission. Rolling Eyes and Moulting Feathers agreed to be born to serve the people. They traveled the world looking for a people with brave honorable men and virtuous women. Rolling Eyes cast his gaze upon the Menominee. He felt satisfied and entered a woman's womb, causing her to become pregnant. Moulting Feathers chose a mother of a nearby people.[39]

❀ Yuma: "If one is to be a great doctor, the spirit appears before the man is born, when he is only one or two months in the womb."[40]

❀ Yuma: Tsuyukwerau, a funeral orator, *keruk* speaker and singer, and a self-appointed repository of true doctrine, a.k.a. Joe Homer, was "unwilling to give a straightforward account of his dreams and power, alleging previous misrepresentations of his statement by others…. It appears, however, that he believes his dreaming to have begun before birth."[41] Joe Homer recalled being present at the beginning of Creation and retained awareness in the womb. "Before I was born, I would sometimes steal out of my mother's womb while she was sleeping. But it was dark, and I didn't go far…. Every good doctor begins to understand before he is born, so that when he is big he knows it all."[42]

❀ Mohave: Mohave believe that dreams are the basis of everything in life. "Not only all shamanistic power but most myths and songs, bravery and fortune in war, success with women or in gaming, every special ability, are dreamed. Knowledge is not a thing to be learned, the Mohave declare, but to be acquired by each man according to his dreams…. Nor is this a dreaming by men so much as by unconscious infants in their mothers or ever earlier, when their *matkwesa,* their shadows [Souls], stood at Avikwame [the sacred mountain] or played at Aha'av'ulypo. 'I was there, I saw him,' a myth teller says of his hero, or of the death of the god Matavilya; and each shaman insists that he himself received his powers from Mastamho at the beginning of the world."[43]

❀ Mohave: "Mohave doctors are born, not trained. Their gifts are supernatural, not acquired. They can talk to the spirits before they have left their mother's womb…. We have women doctors who are born with the gift just as the men; they are regarded as our equals and treated with every consideration."[44] "In the fetal stage, they [ordinary Souls] follow the actions of the mother and dream of 'how to be born.' ... In other intrauterine dreams they [the Souls of medicine men] witness the origin of the world and listen to the instructions handed out to mankind by Paho'tcatc. They already express their shamanistic propensities in the fetal state."[45]

Memories of Embryonic Life and Pre-Birth

Indigenous Americans reported clairvoyant awareness during fetal life.

The fetus is conscious and feels and thinks in the womb. "Sometimes this consciousness is intensified to the point of precognition, prophetic clairvoyance."[46]

* Lenape: "A very sensible Indian, much esteemed by all who knew him, even among the whites" asserted supernatural knowledge that he had obtained before he was born: "He had lived through two generations; he had died twice and was born a third time to live out the then-present race, after which he was to die and never come to this country again. He well remembered what the women had predicted while he was yet in his mother's womb; some had foretold that he would be a boy, and others a girl; he distinctly overheard their discourses, and could repeat correctly everything they had said."[47]
* Lummi: a fetus can hear the conversations of his future family and knows what they think. If they have negative thoughts, he avoids birth into such a family and exits the womb before birth.[48]
* Saulteaux: Kiwitc: "Some people say that a child knows nothing when it is born. Four nights before I was born, I knew that

I would be born. My mind was clear as it is now. I saw my mother and father, and I knew who they were. I recognized the things an Indian uses, their names and what they were good for.... I used to tell this to my father and he replied: 'Long ago, the Indians used to be like that, but the ones that came after them were different.' I have asked my children about this, but there is only one of them that remembers when he was in his mother's womb."[49]

❁ Fox: the child in the womb understands its mother's conversations and abandons her if she becomes quarrelsome.[50]

❁ Yuma: the fetus has "dream-visions" even in the womb.[51]

Pre-Birth Memories of a Winnebago Shaman

Thunder-Cloud shared pre-birth memories with a cultural anthropologist in 1908.

Thunder-Cloud was a virtuous man who loved everyone and adhered to the precepts of the Medicine Rite:[52] "I came from above, and I am holy." Thunder-Cloud recalls past lives and the journey through the interlife realms.

"Many years before my present existence, I lived on this Earth. At that time, everyone seemed to be on the warpath. I was also a warrior and a brave man. Once when I was on the warpath, I was killed." An enemy attacked his people, and innocent lives were lost. "It seemed to me, however, as if I had merely stumbled. I rose and went right ahead until I reached my home. At home I found my wife and children, but they would not look at me. I spoke to my wife, but she seemed to be quite unaware of my presence. 'What can be the matter,' I thought to myself, 'that they pay no attention to me and that they do not even answer when I speak to them?' All at once it occurred to me that I might, in reality, be dead." Thunder-Cloud returned to the battleground where he thought he had been killed. "Sure enough, there I saw my body."

Thunder-Cloud's Spirit was taken to where the sun sets [the west], where people have "the best of times." Whenever he desired to go anywhere, he found himself there at the speed of thought. One day the elder inquired, "My son, did you not speak about wanting to go to Earth again?" Thunder-Cloud had just had the thought. The Chief advised Thunder-Cloud: "You may go and obtain your revenge (upon the people who killed your relatives and you)." Thunder-Cloud was brought down to Earth: "I did not enter a woman's womb, but I was taken into a room. There I remained conscious at all times. One day I heard the noise of little children outside and some other sounds. I thought I would go outside. Then it seemed to me that I went through a door, but I was really being born from a woman's womb. As I walked out, I was struck with the sudden rush of cold air and I began to cry."

In Thunder-Cloud's second past life, he prepared for warfare by fasting. He took full revenge for the lives of innocent people lost in the earlier life. His life ended painlessly due to natural causes: his bones became disjointed and his ribs caved in. Loved ones wrapped his body in a blanket and set it on sticks over a grave. His spirit lingered near the burial site until a voice said, "Come; let us go away." A Guide escorted him in the direction of the sun to a village where they met the ancestors. His Guide instructed, "Stay here for four nights." In reality, he enjoyed himself and stayed four years. From that place, he ascended to Earthmaker's realm and talked to Him face-to-face. He saw the Spirits too. "Indeed, I was like one of them."

Between his second past life and his current life, Thunder-Cloud incarnated in animal bodies. He became transformed into a fish. They are happy beings and have many dances. Their life is much worse than humans for they are frequently in lack of food. At another time, he became transformed into a bird. Bird life was pleasant so long as the weather was good. He underwent hardships when it became cold and had to steal meat from the racks at the camp of some humans. A boy stood guard at the racks. Thunder-Cloud feared him and flew away in fright when he shot with a bow and arrow, making a dreadful noise. He slept in a hollow tree at night. If he entered the tree first, he would be nearly crushed to death by the rest of the flock who entered afterward. If he waited until the last, there was no room and he slept outdoors. "At another time I became a buffalo. The cold weather and food did not worry me much then; but as buffalos, we would always have to be on the alert for hunters.

"From my buffalo existence, I was permitted to go to my higher Spirit home, from which I originally came. The one in charge of that home is my grandfather. I asked him for permission to return to this Earth again. At first he refused, but after I had asked him for the fourth time, he consented. Before I left, he told me, 'Grandson, you had better fast before you go, and if any of the Spirits take pity on you [i.e., bless you], you may go and live in peace on Earth.' So I fasted for four years, and all the Spirits above, even to the fourth heaven, approved of my coming." Earthmaker granted him a boon—to select his earthly mission. He chose to join the Medicine Rite again.

Before incarnating, a council of Spirit Teachers, including Spirit grizzly bears, taught him to be a healer. First, the Bears danced and performed, and then they wounded themselves and were "badly choking with blood." They demonstrated how to become "holy again." The Bears blessed him with songs and holy claws, and promised to assist him in times of trouble. An additional set of Spirit Teachers tested Thunder-Cloud to be sure he could serve people properly:

* A sick person, represented by a dead rotting log covered with weeds, lay in the middle of the lodge. Thunder-Cloud "breathed four times on the log and sprinkled water on it. The dead log arose and walked away as a young man. 'Human, very holy he is,' they said to me."

❀ The Spirit Teachers taught Thunder-Cloud chants and a healing breath by placing "an invulnerable spirit-grizzly bear" in the lodge. "Then I walked around the lodge, holding a live coal in my palm, and danced around the fireplace saying *'wahi!'* and striking the hand containing the coal with the other hand. The invulnerable bear fell forward, prone upon the ground." Thunder-Cloud circled the bear and breathed on it four times; then the Spirit Teachers breathed with him. The spirit-bear walked away in the shape of a human. The teachers said, "This is good. You will always do the same on Earth."

❀ Thunder-Cloud breathed on a black stone four times and blew a hole through it. The Spirits said, "Good. You can blow pain away when someone seeks healing."

❀ Thunder-Cloud blew on the mighty ocean waves at a shamans' village in the middle of the ocean; they became as quiet as water in a tiny saucer. The Teachers piled the waves one upon the other in the ocean. He blew on the choppy ocean, and it became silent.

The Spirit Teachers offered a final blessing: "Whatever illnesses all [the people] may have, you will be able to cure them." Thunder-Cloud then descended to Earth for the third time as a human. "Even in my prenatal existence, I never lost consciousness."

CHAPTER 16

The Cosmic Designer

⟶⟶

PLANNING OUR EARTHLY LIVES

"My parents are old and have been waiting for me
so long," says the child anxious for birth. Father
Time explains, "No, you will start at the proper
hour, your proper time."
—MAURICE MAETERLINCK, *THE BLUE BIRD*

*Shakespearean Theme Portrays the World as a Colossal
Drama.*

THE PRELUDE TO LIFE IN the womb is filled with mystery. Religion, philosophy, and mythical legends describe how birth country, parents, life purpose, even the time and circumstances of death are chosen prior to conception.

Each actor arrives on the stage of life with the most appropriate script. Some philosophers propose that this is a free-will universe and each Soul actor previews the coming life and chooses the family that best reflects its need. A second perspective related to reincarnation emphasizes that the Soul's ability to influence pre-birth choices varies with spiritual maturity. Every actor selects a script in the light of balancing out accumulated past actions from previous lives. Still a third theory proposes that a Cosmic Designer working behind the scenes writes the script for the grand play of life and sets the stage. The Cosmic Designer orchestrates the grand entrance of roughly 130 million children born on Earth each year and, in addition, the

252

exit of millions of others. Chapter 16 presents teachings from religious and philosophical sources, indigenous legends, and visionaries representing these three diverse perspectives.

You Get the Body of Your Choice

References to the Soul's ability to design its own lesson plan appear worldwide.

Seldom do people stop to think they are actors who chose a script for the colossal stage of life. Yet, within the seed of our destiny, we have a grain of free will. Human life is the beginning of an intentional, purposeful experience as an ancient legend from India illustrates: "I choose to be free," the Soul announced. "So be it," answered the Supreme Voice, "but you will encounter suffering. Pride will seduce you. And you will know death." "I must contend with death to conquer life," the Soul explained. God loosened the shining cord, and the Soul ventured forth to make mistakes and grow in strength and wisdom.

Philosophers, poets, and mystics have long felt inspired to write about the lesson plan for each child coming into this world. Ten examples are cited among the hundreds in the literature in the East and West.

❋ Plato (Greece, circa 424–347 BCE): each Soul contemplates pure and perfect knowledge when it is a companion with God in the upper regions "before the influx of matter intoxicated our Souls." Life scripts correspond to how much Souls retain of the Eternal Truths: Justice, Temperance, Knowledge, and Beauty. Nine levels are noted. At the first level is the Soul who has seen the most and is born as a saint, a philosopher. He or she seeks wisdom and yearns for higher realities. The second level is the Soul born as a righteous monarch or warrior. The Soul who retains the least of the Eternal Truths is born as a tyrant.[1]

"Each Soul, according to its nature, clothes itself in certain circumstances ... which it has itself chosen, circumstances which are to be regarded not as forcing it, or dominating it mechanically from without, but as being the environment in which it exhibits its freedom or natural character as a living creature."[2]

* Plotinus (Egypt, circa 205–270 CE): when its moment comes, the Soul descends and enters of its own accord. Each Soul has its own time, and like a herald summoning it, the Soul comes down and goes into the appropriate body.[3]

* Macrobius (Rome, fifth century CE): the Soul gravitates toward the appropriate earthen garment [body].[4]

* Tibetan Buddhism: the Second Dalai Lama (1475–1542) pondered where he should be reborn in order to enlighten humanity. Tsongkhapa tossed a white flower toward Earth, saying to reincarnate where the flower falls. After birth, the young boy told his family that the flower landed in Yolkar Dorjeden. Therefore, he chose that place and them as his parents.[5]

* Emily Dickinson (United States, 1830–1886): "The Soul selects her own Society / Then shuts the Door; / On her divine Majority / Obtrude no more."[6]

* C. W. Leadbeater (theosophy, 1854–1934): "Each man is his own absolute lawgiver, the dispenser of glory or gloom to himself, the decreer of his life, his reward, his punishment."[7]

* Rudolf Steiner (anthroposophy, Austria, 1861–1925): the ego of the unborn and the spiritual hierarchies of the cosmos worked hundreds of years to prepare the spiritual blueprint for the developing body.[8]

* Kahlil Gibran (Lebanon, 1883–1931): "We choose our joys and sorrows, long before we experience them."[9]

* Swami Prabhupada (India, 1896–1977): "The living entity creates his own body by his personal desires, and the external energy of the Lord supplies him with the exact form by which he can enjoy his desires to the fullest extent."[10]

✿ Swami Satchidananda (India, 1914–2002): We decide on our number of births and the duration of each birth. Each of our actions has a consequence that we must face. If we do not have enough time to face all these reactions, we are given another body."[11]

The idea that our Souls have hand-chosen our pains and sorrows can be found worldwide. Spiritual insights help us see deeper into pre-birth choices.

✿ Stewart C. Easton (1907–1989): "Whenever we bemoan our destiny … we are railing against our own choice." No one with knowledge of karma permits himself to be envious of anyone's life situation, talents, fortune, or friends. We each experience what we have chosen and earned.[12]

✿ Swami Chinmayananda (1916–1993): "If God is sitting and writing our individual histories—all these sorrows and tragedies—he must be a mental pervert. Right? This idea of God is a poetic point of view; it has no philosophical support. The creator endows the mental and physical equipment and situations in the creation according to your own instructions, so that you can fulfill your desires."[13]

Cultural Parallels: South America, Africa, Asia, North America

When anthropologists first studied small-scale societies, they learned about pre-birth planning. Let us begin with examples from South America and Africa.

✿ Brazil: a Tapirapé shaman guides unborn children to their mothers. The Spirit Baby curls up in different wombs looking for the perfect fit and says, "No, this one is not right," or "Yes, I will stay here. This woman will be my mother." The Spirit Baby selects the womb as if each mother and her baby were meant for each other.[14]

✿ Bangwa (Cameroon): a Bangwa elder's memories include being in an immense dark cave where Spirit Babies floated in search of parents. He and his buddy chose a twin birth and penetrated their father's belly; they were transferred to their mother's womb via his semen. Prior to birth, the elder's twin returned to the spirit world and tormented the peaceful twin for not joining him. The renegade ultimately located another mother who birthed him as a girl in a nearby village, one day after the elder's birth.[15]

✿ Dagara, West Africa: a baby's Soul chooses parents and a purpose on Earth. For the incoming Soul, the choice is always conscious; for the parents, this contract may be conscious.

✿ Yoruba (West Africa): before birth, everyone chooses a guardian. Some enjoy successful material lives. Others encounter misfortune and wonder where they erred in planning their journey to Earth.[16]

✿ Ijaw (Nigeria): each Soul chooses a life as male or female as well as the manner of life they will lead and the circumstances of death.

✿ Zulu: after death, the Soul is cleansed during a deep slumber in the spirit world, Esilweni. The Soul sleeps until it dreams of something to learn on Earth. The Soul proceeds back to Earth, retracing its previous steps.

Indigenous peoples of Asia believe that Souls preselect their lives:

✿ Karen (Thailand and Burma): the Soul determines life span and how, when, and where death will occur. Even if death is premature or violent, no one laments, since it was the person who chose it.

✿ Native Indonesians: a physically disabled man prays to God to change his sad fate. The Creator tells him to choose again. On reflection, the man makes the same choice again.[17]

❁ Batak (Sumatra): each Soul picks his or her lot-determining leaf; each leaf is inscribed with lessons to be learned, life span, and circumstances of death. Thus destiny is what our Souls have asked for.

❁ Iban (Borneo): the Soul chooses the tool it desires to use on Earth. If it selects a sword, the heavenly counselors declare it to be male. If it selects cotton and a spinning wheel, it is a female.[18]

❁ Tontemboan (Sulawesi): Souls select a match connected to a particular destiny from a myriad of long-burning matches.

Indigenous American references to Souls previewing human life are interesting:

❁ Great Plains Lakota: Souls wandered around in the nearby hills, peeking into tepees until they found appropriate parents.

❁ Dakota (Sioux): a medicine man selects a birthplace where he can serve others. When he dies, he returns to a divine abode, where he receives a new inspiration, to serve a new generation of people somewhere else in the world.

Cultural Parallels: Pre-Birth Scripts and Longevity

Whether we literally understand the beliefs of indigenous peoples or not, the message is clear: babies enter the world with a purpose, even if they don't stay long. Five examples reveal:

❁ Nias (Sumatra): if someone desires longevity, he or she chooses a Soul with the heaviest weight, one-third of an ounce. If miscarriage or a premature death is desired, he or she chooses a slightly lighter Soul. When life ends, the Nias say, "What he asked for is gone."

❁ Finno-Ugric peoples: a Great Mountain Mother holds a wooden staff from where countless threads hang. Each thread represents a newborn's life. At the time of someone's birth, she ties a knot in his or her thread. The distance between the knot and her staff determines longevity.

✣ Khanty (Siberia): a Goddess protects the Spirits of future children in her mountain home in the sky world. She inscribes each child's lifespan in a golden book, or a golden seven-branched tree.[19]

✣ Koryak (Siberia): Souls hang suspended from the rafters by cords in the home of "The-One-on-High" before He sends them into the wombs of their mothers. Longevity is related to the length of the mystical strap connecting them to the ceiling. A short cord means an early death of the child to be born; a long strap means longevity.

✣ Finno-Ugric peoples: the goddess Vagneg-imi rocks the cradles of unborn children hanging from her rooftop on a seven-storied mountain. If a cradle accidentally overturns, that child's destiny is a short life on Earth.[20]

Soul Groups

"Birds of a feather flock together" applies to the Soul's pre-birth state.

According to the Pistis Sophia, an important Gnostic text discovered in 1773, and possibly written as early as the second century, Christ coordinated his birth time with helpmates to accompany him to Earth. He selected twelve Disciples before He came into the world. He cast these twelve powers "as light sparks, into the wombs of their mothers" and continued to oversee their pregnancies and births.

Christ played the same role in Saint John the Baptist's birth. He looked down on the world, observed Elizabeth, and infused her with a power from the Good, ensuring that prophet Elias's Soul entered John the Baptist's body.

Cultural Parallels: Soul Groups

Souls elect to work together with earthly companions who think alike.

* Baal Shem Tov, a.k.a. Rabbi Yisroel ben Eliezer (Hasidism, 1698–1760): sixty disciples agreed to be born as a support to this rabbi who had refused to be born because the rabbi feared evil people might destroy his courage.[21]
* Joseph Smith Jr. (Mormonism, United States, 1805–1844): humanity lived as eternal intelligences in Heaven. The assembly volunteered to bring goodness to Earth. Each Spirit coordinated covenants, with companions to be his parents, spouse, and children.
* Ramakrishna Paramahansa (India, 1836–1886): before taking human birth, Ramakrishna prayed to be blessed with companions who would be devotees of God. "How can I go to Earth if I do not have pure-minded companions uncontaminated by lust and gold to talk with?" A flock of spiritual companions, including Sarada Devi (Ramakrishna's wife) and Swami Vivekananda, were born in answer to Ramakrishna's prayer.[22]

Island of Perpetual Youth

Trobriand Islanders in Papua New Guinea select an appropriate clan prior to rebirth.

Anthropologist Bronislaw Malinowski lived among the Trobriand Islanders in the early 1900s and recorded accounts of reincarnation, although he did not call it that.[23] He studied their beliefs about the Soul's after-death state in Tuma, a subterranean paradise, characterized by perpetual youth preserved by constant rejuvenation. Whenever the Soul shows signs of aging, the Soul simply sloughs off its old covering and takes on a fresh, young appearance with black hair, smooth skin, and no bodily hair. Trobriand Islanders believe that in primeval times humanity knew how to live eternally young before this ability was lost.

Despite the Soul's pleasant life in Tuma, after a long spell "underneath," the Soul becomes bored with paradise and desires to come back to Earth. To do so, the Soul bathes in a salty ocean where it transforms itself into a beautiful tiny Spirit-Child. The Spirit-Child floats in the sea emitting drawn-out wailing sounds as it approaches the seashore. Each "rejuvenated spirit" surveys the women bathing on the shore and selects a mother who belongs to the Spirit-Child's clan and subclan. Pregnancy can also occur when an ancestor places the Spirit-Child on a woman's head; it flows slowly down into her body, and she is with child.

Er's Tour of the Land of Cosmic Contracts

Mature Souls preselect their life plan more wisely.

Souls make choices before being born on Earth based on their levels of spiritual progress. New Souls are less able to make wise decisions in choosing life plans, while older Souls are able to plan a life path of greater wisdom. Much like advanced graduate students who have more freedom to select a curriculum than grade school students who follow a prescribed set of courses, the ability to make pre-birth choices varies with spiritual maturity. The more evolved the Soul, the greater is its freedom to choose.

The early Greeks subscribed to this philosophy. In *The Republic* of Plato (circa 424–347 BCE), Socrates relates the fate of a bold warrior, Er, the son of Armenius, who had an NDE and observed the pre-life planning of a flock of Souls getting ready to be born on Earth.[24] Er was left for dead on the battlefield. Ten days later, when the warrior's body was collected, Er's remains were not decomposed. Two days later, Er revived and narrated his NDE. Er's account contains seven out of sixteen elements accepted as characteristic of an NDE: out-of-body experience; passage toward a bright light; an otherworldly, beautiful landscape; encounter with departed Souls; life review; encounter with a boundary; and forced return to the body.

Once Er regained mortal consciousness, he related the account of the Soul's journey between one life and the next. His mystical world tour began where Souls who had just completed their earthly lives were undergoing a life review. Four openings appeared—two into and out of the sky and two into and out of the Earth. Judges sat between these openings and ordered mature Souls to take the path in the sky to Heaven. Souls who lived at cross-purposes with universal law were directed to a nasty underground called Tartarus. Like the rest, Er stood before the judges, who advised him, "You are not here for judgment. You have come as Earth's messenger and must convey to other mortals otherwise inaccessible wisdom about the posthumous fate of Souls."

Er's unique task continued in a meadow mingling with a gathering of Souls like a festival crowd. Luminous shining Souls floated down from the opening in the sky; they recounted beautiful visions of Heaven. Haggard and tired Soul dwellers from the underworld, covered with dust and grime, wept in despair as they recounted their sufferings. After seven days, Er ascended through a heavenly gate and traveled to the outer rim of the sky. He encountered an impersonal Being of Light: a towering band of light resembling a bright, pure rainbow. The luminous column stretched through Heaven and Earth, a passageway for the Souls' journey back and forth to Earth. Within this scene, Souls prepare for rebirth. Souls previewed tablets inscribed with life patterns of every creature and condition. Everyone had an opportunity to choose a good life. Number one had the first choice, and so on, according to the numbers they held, until all had chosen. The overseer advised, "Even the last Soul to pick will find a tolerable life, if he chooses with intelligence." Er witnessed how each Soul chose a script. Advanced Souls selected wisely. Pleasurable lives tempted less mature Souls. Young Souls grabbed scripts without examining the fine print, such as great wealth followed by bankruptcy, or years of sensual pleasure followed by years of pain. The true character of the first Soul who chose his life plan was revealed when he grabbed the script of an absolute dictator. He realized too late that he was destined to take the life of his children, among other atrocities. He beat his breast, blaming God, the planets—everyone except himself. Wise Souls, such as Odysseus, king of Ithaca, contemplated previous lives before making a decision. This time he looked for less heartache and tragedy: a quiet man's life, the one rejected by all the other Souls. Although Odysseus happened to be the last to make a choice, he said, "I would have done the same even if I had drawn the first lot."

After each Soul was assigned a guardian to aid them through life, Er witnessed one final step prior to the takeoff spot for the journey to Earth. The Souls marched through a burning heat and cold frost across the Plain of Amnesia, where the River of Forgetfulness flowed. Souls satisfied their thirst. Foolish Souls drank more than the rest. The more they drank, the deeper they slept—and the more they forgot. Unlike the rest, Er chose to forgo the waters in order to remember all that he had seen and heard. Thus Er remained wide awake at midnight and witnessed a lightning and quaking of the universe to awaken the Souls, propelling them to the waiting wombs of earthly mothers—leaping upward like shooting stars. Before he knew it, Er opened his eyes and found himself lying on a funeral pyre, able to recall his journey through the afterlife.

Cross-Cultural Parallels: Soul Maturity and Pre-Birth Choices

The belief that mature Souls make better pre-birth choices and less mature Souls need more guidance is a common thread within the framework of reincarnation. Four literature sources serve as examples.

* ✤ Tibetan Buddhism: because spiritually advanced individuals remain conscious through the transition from death to rebirth, they can control the circumstances they are born into. These

high "incarnates" have no karma and choose to be born to alleviate suffering in the world.[25]

❉ Edgar Cayce (United States, 1877–1945): mature Souls can preselect their life plan; young Souls have made poor choices in the past and are "dangerously subject to earthly appetites." Less mature Souls are therefore born under circumstances best suited for their growth.[26]

❉ Amma Mata Amritanandamayi (India, born 1953): individuals who achieve enlightenment decide whether to be born again or advance to another dimension: "You can decide what you should be, where you should be, and how you should be in your next life. Or if you do not want to come at all to this world, that too is possible."

❉ Zulu (South Africa): Souls advance through stages of human birth: pupil, disciple, brother, elder, master, *isangoma* (those who know), and *abakula-bantu,* perfect human beings. When someone attains the highest grade, "instead of being but himself, apart, he is truly all the tribe and the tribe is he." After death, his Soul no longer "dreams" of returning to earthly life. The perfected Soul becomes one with the Source. Even so, he can choose rebirth and retain the human form.[27]

Cultural Parallels: NDEs and Souls Choosing Life Scripts

Like Er's description of the Souls previewing an array of life scripts, pre-birth plans are noted in other NDEs.

❉ Plutarch's account of Thespesius (Greece, 46–120 CE): a desire for human life is engendered in a flock of Souls dwelling in a heavenly world. A soft gentle breeze carrying a delectable odor attracts the Souls to a gaping chasm. The sweet scent produces an intoxicating mood. The laughter, party atmosphere, festivity, and merrymaking dissolve reason and engender the Soul's desire for human birth by reviving nostalgic memories of life in a physical body.[28]

❉ Shri Dhyanyogi Madhusudandas (India, 1877–1994): two flocks of Souls were waiting to be born. Standing on the right, people were weeping and crying; a happy and peaceful crowd lined up on the left. Those who cried realized that they had received a precious human body and had wasted time in harmful pursuits instead of doing good. Now they feared a rebirth with little chance of self-realization. The virtuous Souls were singing in anticipation of a rebirth, where they would have the chance to realize God.[29]

Insights into the Cosmic Designer

The Cosmic Dreamer needs actors to play both good and evil characters in the earthly drama.

At our core, each of us is an eternal Light Being who temporarily masquerades as one of the actors on the earthly stage. The Bhagavata Purana offers glimpses into how earthly life is merely a playacting, like a movie. The roles of good and evil characters in the human drama are the means whereby the Soul learns, eventually finding Truth beyond opposites. This ancient scripture from India relates countless stories. Of interest here is the story of the travels of the Kumara brothers[30] (Sanaka, Sananda, Sanatana, and Sanat-Kumara) through the three worlds. They desired to pay respects to the Lord. Despite being the four sons of Brahma, they appeared to the gatekeepers as small, naked children. The gatekeepers Jaya and Vijaya forbade them to enter. The brothers said, "We are great devotees of God. Please let us in." The doorkeepers ignored their pleas.

The brothers became angry and said: "Foolish doormen, since you are agitated by passion and ignorance, you cannot remain in this heavenly place. Descend to Earth and take birth in a wicked family." Vishnu then appeared. He could not rescind the curse; however, he blessed the doorkeepers before they fell to Earth: "You will remember Me even when you become demonic, but not as a devotee normally does, but as an enemy in hatred. Your demonic existence will be limited to three births. After that, you shall return to Heaven duly purified by your death at my hands."

In this way, Jaya and Vijaya took three births as Hitler-like beings, as haters of God in the world: (1) Hiranyaksha and Hiranyakasipu, (2) Ravana and Kumbhakarna, and (3) Sisupala and Dandavaktra. Their human incarnations as evil kings are recorded in ancient Sanskrit texts. Despite maintaining feelings of enmity for the Lord, Jaya and Vijaya regained the shelter of the Lord after three earthly incarnations.

Tweedledee Teaches Alice

We project an illusion on the screen of our consciousness when we dream; like that, the divine projects the movie of Creation on the screen of its Being.

How are the life scripts created and planned out? Lewis Carroll (1832–1898) uses fairy-tale fantasy to give an answer to that question in *Through the Looking-Glass,* a sequel to *Alice's Adventures in Wonderland.* The central character is Alice, a child who ponders whether she is real or not. She hears a sound like the puffing of a large steam engine as she is walking through the forest. The noise is the Red King snoring. One of her fairy-tale companions, Tweedledee, explains: "The King is in the middle of a dream. What do you think he is dreaming about?" Alice answers, "I don't know." Tweedledee exclaims: "He's dreaming about you! And if he stopped dreaming about you, where would you be? You would be nowhere. Why, you are merely an illusion in his dream! And if the King wakes up from his dream, you would dematerialize—bang!—out like a candle!" Alice becomes upset. Then again, Alice is already in her own dream; only she does not realize it.

Symbolism in *Through the Looking-Glass*

Cloaked within this child-like fairy tale is a teaching about the Soul and the nature of cosmic reality as a dream.

- Alice: each of us is Alice. She represents the Soul encased in a body who is trying to figure out its true nature and to wake up to what reality is.
- Sleeping Red King: a cosmic designer who ultimately writes life plans like the roles in a grand movie script. Without a director behind the scenes, the "drama of life" is impossible.
- Tweedledee and Tweedledum: ironically, these supporting characters have been twisted and viewed in a negative light. Perhaps Carroll used these names to protect himself from religious persecution of the day. In actuality, they are teachers who open us up to cosmic insights.

Cultural Parallels: All the World's a Stage

Carroll's notion that the whole cosmos is the by-product of divine dreaming appears as a common theme throughout religion and philosophy.

- Plato (Greece, circa 424–347 BCE): whether we have been constructed to serve as playthings of the divine or for some serious purpose is beyond human understanding.[31]
- Plotinus (Rome, circa 205–270 CE): analogous to an actor on stage getting a mask and costume, a stately robe or rags, a Soul is allotted its fortunes before birth, and always with a Reason.[32]
- Muhammad (Islam, 570–632 CE): "Men who are living here are in a dream and when they die then shall they be awake; for all this world is a mere thought—the thought of Him who is the True, whose thought is Truth."[33]
- Ibn 'Arabi (Sufism, 1165–1240): the world is God's shadow.

❦ Reverend John Gregorie (England, 1598–1652): "Creation is but a Transcript." God created the world out of that copy which He had "in His divine understanding from all Eternity."[34]

❦ Bishop Berkeley (Ireland, 1685–1753): we are all aspects of the dream of a divine power. Man and the universe exist as part of the imagination of the divine. The world is God's dream.

❦ Thayumanavar (India, 1706–1744): we are like wound-up tops. The "Player" winds the string around us, pulls it, and we spin. How tightly He winds the top and how fast He plays determines how long we rotate before we fall down.[35]

❦ Reverend Phillip Brooks (United States, 1835–1893): unborn things exist as divine ideas in God's Mind.[36]

❦ Albert Einstein (Switzerland, 1879–1955): "Everything is determined, the beginning as well as the end, by forces over which we have no control. It is determined for the insect as well as the star. Human beings, vegetables, or cosmic dust, we all dance to a mysterious tune, intoned in the distance by an invisible piper."[37]

❦ Paramahansa Yogananda (India, 1893–1952): the Cosmic Director writes scripts for His super-colossal entertainment and summons "tremendous casts for the pageant of the centuries." God makes His motion picture very complex, full of contrasts of good and evil.[38]

❦ Swami Satchidananda (India, 1914–2002): "The Lord is a great economist. He will not waste even an ounce of extra breath on you. Yes, it is all measured; He sent you packaged with a certain amount of breath."[39]

❦ Advaita Vedanta (India): just as tragedies and comedies, romances and satires, mysteries and farces are designed to keep the attention of a theatre audience spell bound, something similar is occurring in the universe. The analogy of drama-cinema to world-universe is astonishingly accurate.[40]

✤ Maharaj Charan Singh (Sikhism, 1916–1990): Souls are like dancing puppets. "Realized" Souls and "unrealized" Souls are dancing in the same way. The realized Souls know that God is pulling the strings according to our karmas, whereas the unrealized Souls think that they are dancing by their own effort.

Golden Book of Destiny

Our life scripts are a projection from the divine Dreamer according to small-scale societies as well as the great religions of the world.

✤ Judeo-Christian: You formed my inward parts. You wove me in my mother's womb. My Soul knows it very well. My frame was not hidden from You when I was made in secret. Your eyes saw my unformed substance and all the days that were ordained for me were already written in Your book.[41]

✤ Judaism: in the prenatal state, our sex, constitution, size, shape, appearance, social position, livelihood, spouse, and all that may befall us, are pre-ordained.[42]

✤ Finno-Ugric peoples (Europe): the Great Mountain Mother holds a wooden staff. Each of the countless threads hanging from her staff represents someone's life. At the time of birth, she ties a knot in his thread. The distance between the knot and her staff determines longevity.

✤ Kabbalah: all Souls were initially woven into a mystical fabric, the "curtain of souls," that hangs before the Throne of Heaven. Each Soul's past and future is woven into the spiritual ether making up this curtain. Adam viewed this curtain and witnessed future generations.[43]

✤ Islam: Allah sends an angel to a woman's womb to "breathe" the Soul into the fetus when the embryo is forty-two days old. The angel asks God: "Will this be a boy or girl? What will be life span, location, and circumstances of death? Children? Occupation? Happy or sad?" The angel inscribes God's decree onto a scroll.[44]

❀ Sufism: Allah created a green beryl Tablet and an emerald Pen filled with an ink of white light. He said, "Write, O Pen!" The Pen of Fate asked: "Lord, what shall I write?" Allah answered: "Write the destinies of all things until the Final Hour."[45]

❀ Hazrat Inayat Khan (Sufism, 1882–1927): angels set unborn Souls to certain rhythms that determine the path they will tread in the future. This event is known as *Azal*, the Day of Tuning, when the life plan of a Soul is designed.[46]

"Creation Is a Vast Motion Picture"

One day during World War I the great spiritual master from India Paramahansa Yogananda was shocked by a newsreel showing the carnage on the battlefields of France. Yogananda prayed: "Lord, why do you permit such suffering?" An answer came in the form of an inner vision of the actual battlefields filled with dead and dying soldiers. The scene far surpassed the horrors of the news-reel. A Voice spoke: "Look intently. These battlefield scenes are an illusory play of light and dark. They are the cosmic motion picture, as real and as unreal as the theater newsreel—a play within a play. Creation is light and shadow; otherwise no picture is possible. Good and evil must alternate. Without suffering, man scarcely cares to recall that he has forsaken his eternal home. Pain is a prod to remembrance. The way of escape is through Wisdom. Those who shudder at death are like an ignorant actor who dies of fright when nothing more than a blank cartridge has been fired at him on the stage."[48]

Yogananda's mystical encounter convinced him that creation is a vast motion picture, and that reality lies beyond it. In the same way that a movie audience sees one imageless beam of light coming from the projection booth as the source of the images on the screen, the super-colossal entertainment in our planetary theater issues from the white light of a Cosmic Source. We are actors as well as audience in this universal drama.

When we can see behind the scenes of the world, Yogananda says that we will realize that "life on earth is a puppet show.... The concept of life as a changing, passing show is not pessimistic; it should teach us not to take life seriously at all. Maya, cosmic delusion, makes us feel that the body is so real, such a necessary part of our being. Yet in a moment, the body may be taken away from the soul by death, and the separation is not painful at all. When that 'operation' is over, you have no need of time, dress, food, or shelter, for you no longer have to carry this bodily bundle of flesh. You are free of it. And you are still you."[49]

CHAPTER 17

Travelers from the Light

❦

"I Am Not of This World"

My Soul remembers its lost Paradise.
— Francis Thompson

Our earthbound journey emerges from a world of transparent light and timelessness. The voyage down to Earth is part of a sojourn through heavenly dwellings of the Creator. When seen as a whole picture, birth is a cosmic event, a fantastic voyage charted to a blue pearl called Earth.

THE NOTION OF OUR PREEXISTENCE as beings of intelligence and glory has captivated the hearts and minds of poets, philosophers, and visionaries of all cultures. They remind us that we are immortal beings whose bodies are simply external wrappings—light trapped within matter. Chapter 17 explores this immortal life hidden within physical life.

Plato, Father of Western Philosophy

Plato's discourses tell the account of the Soul's descent from a higher reality.

Plato (circa 424–347 BCE) regarded our Soul as truly divine and far more real than the physical body. According to Plato, the Soul's divine transcendent world is foreign and remote from the earthly world perceived with human senses. The Soul preexisted in the world where only eternal forms and Souls exist.

Before our Souls fell from the universe of being into the mundane realm, we saw the universe and understood the laws of destiny. Every Soul "beheld true Being; this was the condition of her passing into the form of man." We witnessed beauty shining in all its brilliance—the beatific spectacle and (divine) vision. Our Souls were initiated into the holiest of mysteries and enjoyed mystic ecstasy. We were still pure, "in the state of wholeness and unconscious of the evils that awaited us in the future." We were not yet "imprisoned in the body," bound to it "like an oyster in his shell."[1]

Once shown the nature of reality, Souls begin the rounds of earthly existence. In *Timaeus,* Plato says: the Soul is sown into the "instrument of time."[2] The physical realm is a world of trial and opportunity for our Soul. We chose our life with open eyes, when we were in a position to see things as they are.[3] Because we drank the waters of Lethe before our descent to Earth, we have become bewildered and oblivious of our true nature. Souls therefore do not easily recall the things of the other world.

Plato's *Republic* describes how most people function like captives chained within a cave. A "Light" is behind them. They look ahead and assume the "shadow-show," the flow of appearances upon the wall, is the true reality. The prisoners do not turn around to see the Light behind them. They never realize that the Light is the true reality. They become slaves to the senses.[4] Their earthly sojourn is a dreamy exile from "Home."

Treasury of Souls, the Chamber of Creation

Jewish traditions describe the Souls of unborn generations awaiting human birth.

According to rabbinic and kabbalistic texts, Souls await birth in the Guf, a pristine Treasury of Souls or Chamber of Creation. *Guf* means "body"; thus the storehouse of Souls is literally "a body of Souls." These Souls exist in their primal Soul bank, untouched by existence in the physical world.

⚘ Talmud: the repository is located in Aravot, the Seventh Heaven, where angels guard the Treasury of Peace, Blessing, etcetera.

⚘ Shimon ben Lakish (Syria Palaestina, third century CE): the Messiah will arrive once the guf is empty and every Soul has been born on Earth.

⚘ Rashi (France, 1040–1105): Souls awaiting birth are kept in a chamber, a Heavenly partition (Pargod) separating the Shechinah (Divine Presence) from the habitat of angels.

⚘ Essenes: Souls emanate from the subtlest ether and are enfolded in bodies as prisons due to a natural enticement for human life. Following the sojourn in physicality, Souls rejoice and are carried upward once again.

⚘ Philo of Alexandria (1st century CE): most Souls were attracted by material desires and fell from Heaven into the body's prison.

⚘ Slavonic Book of Enoch (circa fourth–third century BCE): "For every Soul was created eternally before the foundation of the world."

⚘ Kabbalah: all Souls originated in the world of Emanation. They know everything they will learn on Earth. Since the Soul is part of the divine, it feels lost and out of place in human form and longs to return Home.

Christianity and the Soul

Biblical sources refer to existence before conception.

Biblical figures in the Old Testament refer to their "prenatal antiquity":

⚘ King Solomon: "The Lord possessed me in the beginning of his way, before his works of old. I was set up from everlasting,

from the beginning, or ever the earth was.... When He prepared the heavens, I was there. When He established the clouds
above, when He appointed the foundations of the earth.... I
was daily His delight, rejoicing always before Him."[5]

✿ Job says he was there when God "laid the earth's foundations."[6]

✿ Jeremiah: "Before I formed you in the womb I knew you for
my own; before you were born I consecrated you, I appointed
you a prophet to the nations."[7]

Verses in the Old and New Testaments refer to the Soul and its
embodiment:

✿ The Soul wears its "coats of skins"—a human body constructed from earth, air, fire, and water.[8]

✿ "I have said, 'ye are gods; and all of you are children of the most
High.' Is it not written in your laws, 'I said, ye are gods'?"[9]

✿ "The Kingdom of God is within you."[10]

When Was the Soul Created?

Early Christianity faced a growing enigma dealing with the definition of the Soul and its origin, with church leaders raising questions.
Christian theologians knew they needed to probe into basic aspects
of the Soul. One leader was Saint Gregory of Nyssa (335–395 CE),
who pointed out four unanswered questions: (1) Who understands
his own Soul? (2) Is the Soul's essence material or immaterial? (3)
How do Souls come into being? (4) How does the Soul unite with
the human form?

Certain church leaders proposed a simple theory: "If the Soul
exists eternally after the body's dissolution, must not the Soul
exist eternally prior to the body's formation, as well?" This group
explained: if the Soul is endless, the Soul must be without a beginning. The parents' role is merely to prepare a material body for an
"immaterial preexistent inhabitant."

❋ Saint Clement of Alexandria (Greece, 150–215 CE): before the world's foundation, we exist in the "eye of God."[11]
❋ Saint Jerome (Roman province of Dalmatia, 347–420 CE): Souls enjoyed a former blessedness, a divine habitation before descent to Earth.
❋ Synesius, Bishop of Cyrene (Greece, 370–430 CE): the Soul exists in the heavenly region before coming into a human body.

The Precosmic Spiritual Universe—Father Origen

Father Origen (Egypt, 185–254 CE), theologian, biblical scholar, and the primary advocate of preexistence, synthesized Christianity with Greek philosophy. He theorized that every Soul has existed from the beginning with God in a precosmic spiritual universe. "Every Soul has therefore passed through some worlds already, and will pass others before it reaches its final consummation. The Soul comes into this world strengthened by the victories or weakened by the defects of its previous life." His theory outlines the steps between the Soul's exile from Heaven to conception.

❋ Spiritual Fall: some Souls in Heaven turned aside from the path of duty and passed into the human race.
❋ Pre-birth plan: the degree of the Soul's offenses in the spiritual world determine earthly circumstances.
❋ Conception: the embryo receives its Soul at conception from an angel.
❋ Return of the Soul: Souls become purified and recover the angelic condition by righteous and noble living, and return to a purely spiritual state—apocatastasis.

Father Origen found two errors in the Bible's translations of the Souls' fall from Heaven.[12] To begin with, the Greek word *katabole,* meaning "to cast downward," was mistranslated into the Latin word *constitutio,* meaning "beginning." The standard translation of Matthew 24:21 contrasts with that of Origen:

❈ Standard translation by the Church: "And there will be tribulation in those days, such as was not since the beginning of the world."
❈ Father Origen: "And there will be tribulation in those days, such as was not since the Souls were cast downward."

In a separate passage (Ephesians 1:4), *katabole*—"to cast downward"—is mistranslated into the Latin word meaning "foundation":

❈ Standard translation by the Church: "Who hath chosen us before the foundation of the world."
❈ Father Origen: "Who hath chosen us before the Souls were cast downward."

Origen's theory survived intact for three hundred years until the church decided he had gone too far. He was never formally branded a heretic because his opinions always bore on points not settled by the church. Even so, the Second Council of Constantinople in 553 CE censored his doctrine of the preexistence of the Soul due to its obvious link with reincarnation. Preexistence does not require the doctrine of reincarnation; nonetheless, Origen was misunderstood as supporting reincarnation since he believed the Soul does not begin with the life of the body. Since that turning point, Christian doctrine has frowned upon preexistence and instead upheld the theory that creation and infusion of the Soul coincides with the moment of conception.

Homesick Traveler

In the *Enneads,* Plotinus (circa 205–270 CE), the Egyptian-born philosopher, religious genius, and great mystic, writes about the Soul's preexistence: "Before we had our becoming here we existed There."[13] We walked the lofty ranges with the complete Soul and were made perfect. We were immune from care and trouble. Souls rush down to Earth due to having seen their images [in matter].

Each Soul descends at its own special moment. "Like a herald summoning it," the Soul penetrates to Earth in a "voluntary plunge" and goes into the appropriate body.

The physical world is the remotest realm from the "One." It is still the best place to advance and become prepared for a higher exaltation—knowledge of, and unification with, the "One," portrayed as an ecstatic state. Plotinus talked about his mystical awakenings: "Many times it happened: lifted out of the body into myself; becoming external to all other things and becoming self-encentered; beholding a marvelous beauty; then, more than ever assured of community with the loftiest order." Plotinus lamented that his consciousness could not sustain that "sojourn in the divine" indefinitely. So he wondered "how did the Soul ever enter my body, the Soul which, even within the body, is the high thing it has shown itself to be."

Plotinus was so ashamed his Soul had become imprisoned in a body that he refused to have his portrait painted. He never spoke about his birthday, parents, or country of origin. He wrote: "Life here, with the things of Earth, is a sinking, a defeat." Once our Souls drift from home, we are like infants taken from our parents and brought up at a distance. "The Soul is a deserter from the All."

Gnosticism: We Have Come from the Light

*According to Gnosticism, human Souls are
"allogenous"—of another race.*

The root of every human being is not of this world. Thus the human body holds a divine seed as a prisoner. This Spark is a portion of the eternal light realm that accidentally fell into the material world. Gnostic texts refer to preexistence:

✿ Pistis Sophia (second century CE): Christ: "I have indeed said to you from the beginning that you are not from the world; I also am not from it."

- Book of Thomas: Jesus said, "If they say to you, 'Where did you come from?,' say to them, 'We came from the light, the place where the light came into being on its own accord and established [itself] and became manifest through their image.' If they say to you, 'Is it you?,' say, 'We are its children, and we are the elect of the living father.'"[14]
- Manichaeus, a.k.a. Manes (Persia, 216–276 CE): the Soul's true home, tents of joy, Father, Mother, and brethren dwell "on high." Manichaeism is a late Gnostic religion dating to the second to the eighth centuries.

"We Lived with the Lord"

The belief in preexistence makes Mormons unique in modern Christianity.

Like most Christians, Mormons believe in immortality beyond death. At the same time, they believe in life before birth. According to Joseph Smith (1805–1844), founder of Mormonism, everyone existed as spirit children of God and lived in the Heavenly Father's house and dwelt with Him in their true Home. Our Spirits lived as free rational intelligences in the heavens, pure and holy as angels: "Man was also in the beginning with God."[15] The pre-mortal world offers limited opportunities for learning how to triumph over evil and suffering. Earthly life, in contrast, allows people to gain wisdom and to become glorious resurrected beings, with incorruptible bodies of flesh and bone. Joseph Smith also taught that the prophets and "noble and great" leaders who have served mankind were foreordained to these missions. As God revealed to Abraham: "You were chosen before you were born."[16]

Pre-Birth Existence: Cross-Cultural References

The Soul is a wandering heir to a lost inheritance.

Whether we study Eastern or Western religion, we find the motif of the Soul's descent from a higher dimension into human bodies: Judeo-Christian story of the fall; the Buddhist idea of *dukkha,* or suffering; and the Hindu *avidyā,* or ignorance. All Souls pine for that Paradise from where we have been exiled. Descriptions of a subtle dimension where we preexist as spiritual beings and negotiate the circumstances of our lives can be found scattered throughout religious, philosophic, and poetic teachings.

Ancient Greek Philosophy

* Orphism (6th century BCE): our body is a living tomb in which our Soul is enshrined.
* Pythagoras (570–495 BCE): "I am not of this world, for it is not sufficient to explain me." The Soul descends to Earth from the World of ethereal constellations, translucent Souls, and oceans of light.[17]
* Anaxagoras (500–428 BCE) and Heraclitus (535–475 BCE): Souls make their pilgrimage to Earth from other planets.
* Empedocles (490–430 BCE): the philosopher wept at being born on Earth, the region of "furious discord." He was an exiled divinity who fell to Earth from his high estate due to his mistakes. The "decree of necessity" required that he endure human lifetimes for thirty thousand seasons.[18]

Western Philosophy and Mysticism

* Plotinus (Egypt, 205–270 CE): "Souls of men see their images as if in the mirror of Dionysus, and come down to that level with a leap from above. Still their tops remain firmly set above in Heaven."[19]

❉ Macrobius (Rome, early fifth century CE): a longing for a body overtakes the Soul. The weight of this earthly thought causes the descent through seven celestial spheres whereby the Soul acquires faculties such as reasoning power from Saturn, practicality and morality from Jupiter, and sensuality from Venus.[20]

❉ Leibniz (Germany, 1646–1716): Souls preexist in a sort of organized body.

❉ Immanuel Kant (Germany, 1724–1804): our Soul "neither began in birth, nor will end in death."[21]

❉ Johann Wolfgang von Goethe (Germany, 1749–1832): our higher Soul seeks to rise with mighty throes to those ancestral meadows whence it came. "As long as you are not aware of the continual law of Die and Be Again, you are merely a vague guest on a dark Earth."[22]

❉ Thomas Taylor (England, 1758–1835): the Soul, while an inhabitant of Earth, is in a fallen condition, an exile from the orb of light.[23]

❉ Amos Bronson Alcott (United States, 1799–1888): to conceive a child's acquirements as dating from birth seems an atheism that only a shallow metaphysical theology could entertain.[24]

❉ Ralph Waldo Emerson (United States, 1803–1882): the human Soul is a ray from the source of light and comes into a temporary abode, the human body.[25]

Western Poetry

Poets wistfully lament the Soul's exile from its "true home" of higher consciousness:

❉ John Webster (England, 1580–1634): the Soul in the body is like a bird in a cage: "This world is like her little turf of grass, and the heaven o'er our heads like her looking-glass, only gives us a miserable knowledge of the small compass of our prison."[26]

❋ Thomas Vaughan (Wales, 1621–1666): a Soul in the body is "like a candle shut up in a dark lantern" or "a fire almost stifled for want of air."[27]

❋ Edward Bulwer-Lytton (England, 1803–1873): why does our Soul descend from its "eternal, starlike" sphere to shrink into a "dark sarcophagus [the body]?"[28]

❋ Epes Sargent (United States, 1813–1880): "The human Soul is like a bird that is born in a cage. Nothing can deprive it of its natural longings, or obliterate the mysterious remembrance of its heritage."[29]

❋ Laurence Binyon (1869–1943): where is that world I fell from? "Surely I was rather native there, where all desires were lovely."[30]

Religions of the East

Hinduism, Zoroastrianism, and Sufism embrace the idea of the Soul's original status:

❋ Hinduism (India): we came from Source. We are divine Souls on a wondrous journey. We are the Truth we seek. Deep inside we are perfect this very moment.

❋ Zoroastrianism (ancient Persia): "Happy are you, starry brethren, who from heaven do not roam / In the eternal Father's mansion from the first have dwelt at home…. Me, he has cast out to exile in a distant land to learn."[31]

❋ Adi Shankara (India, 788–820 CE): Souls enjoy the ecstatic life and intuitively know everything in their Primordial Home, Turiya.

❋ Paramahansa Yogananda (India, 1893–1952): we are the King of the Universe's children and we ran away from home. We forgot our divine heritage due to being locked up in human bodies for so long.[32]

❋ Sufi poets: Sufi metaphors express the relationship between body and Soul: a fish on dry land, a caged parrot, a moaning dove that has lost her mate, and a reed torn from its bed and fashioned into a flute whose melancholy music fills the eye with tears.

Return to the Source: The Goal of Life

The Soul returns to the pre-birth dimension after death.

Many religious leaders, philosophers, and mystical poets give the same answer to the questions "Where am I from?" and "Where will I go after death?" Alongside the flow of Souls from the eternal realm to Earth, a current carries us back. Heaven is our original home. Souls consciously or unconsciously pine to return to that paradise from where we have been temporarily exiled. Sooner or later, each wanderer returns Home because all Souls are part of that Source.

Ancient Greek Philosophers

❁ Orphism (6th century BCE): Orphics believed if they purified themselves, they could return to a semicorporeal, semi-spiritual state where everything is full of splendor, charm, and the harmony of the spheres. The Soul simply lives, drinking in sounds, forms, and light, floating like a dream.

❁ Pythagoras (570–495 BCE): the Soul can return to its divine state by contemplating the form, order, proportion, limit, and harmony in the universe.[33]

❁ Heraclitus (535–475 BCE): "The way up and the way down are one and the same."[34]

❁ Empedocles (490–430 BCE): he was an exiled divinity who fell to Earth from his high estate and lived a series of human lifetimes. He expected to rejoin the immortals after this life ended.

❁ Plato (circa 424–347 BCE): the Soul is guaranteed immortality as a "pure intelligence" in the birthplace of Souls after being purified through a series of human births.

Judaism, Christianity, Gnosticism

❊ Judaism: what does God do after creating all the Souls that are to enter human bodies? God continues making ladders for Souls to ascend and other Souls to descend, until all the Souls in the heavenly repository experience human life.

❊ Kabbalah: since the Soul is part of the Creator, it feels lost and out of place in the body, and yearns to return to the palace of the divine king, the place where our Souls were created. Everything in this world, spirits as well as bodies, will return to the principal root from where they originated.

❊ Judeo-Christian: because man goes to his eternal home, and the mourners go about the streets; before the silver cord is snapped, or the golden bowl is broken, or the pitcher is broken at the fountain, or the wheel broken at the cistern, and the dust returns to the earth as it was, and the spirit returns to God, who gave it.[35]

❊ Christianity: Jesus alludes to our Soul's outgoing and return via the Prodigal Son parable.[36] Our Souls leave our true home of the spirit and eventually return to our lost estate.

❊ Father Origen (Egypt, 185–254 CE): "Origen imagined salvation not in terms of the saved rejoicing in heaven and the damned suffering in hell, but as a reunion of all souls with God."[37]

❊ Pope Dionysius of Alexandria (Egypt, late second century CE): "All things flow out from God, and all will ultimately return to Him."[38]

❊ Gnosticism: words of the risen Christ to his disciples: "You are to say to him: 'I am a son, and I am from the Father.' He will say to you, 'What sort of son are you, and to what father do you belong?' You are to say to him, 'I am from the Preexistent Father, and a son in the Preexistent One.... When he also says to you, 'Where will you go?,' you are to say to him, 'To the place from which I have come, there shall I return.'"[39]

❁ Gnosticism: the disciples said to Jesus, "Tell us how our end will be." Jesus said, "Have you discovered, then, the beginning that you look for the end? For where the beginning is, there will the end be. Blessed is he who will take his place in the beginning; he will know the end and will not experience death."[40]

Islam and Sufism

❁ Muhammad (Saudi Arabia, 570–632): "From Allah do we come, for Him we are, and to Him verily is our return."[41]

❁ Abdul Qadir Gilani (Persia, 1077–1166): the pilgrim returns to the home of his origin. This is all that can be explained, as much as the tongue can say and the mind grasp. Beyond this is the inconceivable and indescribable.

❁ Rumi (Persia, 1207–1273): I am like a bird from another continent, sitting in this aviary. I did not come here of my own accord. Whoever brought me here will have to take me back.

❁ Aziz al-Nasafi (Persia, died 1300 CE): the final goal is returning to one's origin. Everything that reaches its origin has reached its goal. A farmer sows grain in the ground and tends it. Then it begins to grow, seeds, and again becomes grain. The grain has returned to its original form. Completing the circle is freedom.

❁ Abdul Khaliq Gajadwani (Naqshbandi order, died 1179): our journey is toward our Homeland. We are traveling from the world of appearances [Earth] to the world of reality.

Western Philosophers and Poets

❁ Aristotle (Greece, 384–322 BCE): every natural thing longs for the divine and desires to share in the divine life.

❁ Plotinus (Egypt, 205–270 BCE): "To real Being we go back, all that we have and are; to That we return as from That we came."[42] On his deathbed, Plotinus said, "Now I seek to lead back the self within me to the All-self."[43]

❀ Dante (Italy, 1265–1321): the Soul's supreme desire "is to return to its first Source," the First Cause of our Souls.[44]

❀ Leonardo da Vinci (Italy, 1452–1519): "Behold now the hope and desire to go back to our own country, and to return to our former state. How like it is to the moth with the light."[45]

❀ Henry Vaughan (Wales, 1621–1695): "How I long to travel back, and tread again that ancient track. But my Soul with too much stay is drunk, and staggers in the way. And when this dust falls to the urn, in that state I will return."[46]

❀ Leo Tolstoy (Russia, 1828–1910): birth is a rebirth from the "more real life" to which later, in old age, we prepare ourselves to return.[47]

Teachings from the East

The Soul's longing to regain its forgotten, lost Self is an integral part of Hinduism, Buddhism, Taoism, and Zoroastrianism:

❀ Bhagavad Gita (India): Krishna: "After a Soul has passed through untold births, it knows, and comes back to Me, in the end."[48]

❀ Dr. Bhagavan Das (India, 1869–1958): the Upanishads of ancient India teach: "This Whirling Wheel of Brahma vast, immense; this 'Planetarium, Asterarium,' in which all Souls are circling without rest, and being born and dying over and over, so long as they believe they are the 'whirled,' fixed on the spokes and tires, all separate from the Fixed Whirler at the Central Nave—whoever glimpses his Identity with it, at once gains Immortality, seeing that Twirled and Twirler are the Same, that the One Self, Dances around Its-Self, and finds Him-Self at Rest in Heart of Peace."[49]

❀ Lao-tzu (Taoism, sixth century BCE): "Life is a going forth, death is a returning Home."[50]

❀ Jianzhi Sengcan (Third Chinese Zen patriarch, died 606 CE): "When the ten thousand things are viewed in their oneness, we return to the Origin and remain where we have always been."[51]

❀ Saint Honen (Japan, 1133–1212): "I came from the Land of Bliss and I am sure I am going back there."[52]

❀ Zoroastrianism (mid-seventeenth century): "Search thou the path of the soul, whence she came, or what way, after serving the body, by joining work with sacred speed, thou shalt raise her again to the same state whence she fell." The eternal and infinite Souls come from above. If distinguished for knowledge and sanctity while on Earth, they return above, are united with the sun, and become empyreal sovereigns.[53]

Indigenous Peoples

❀ Lakota (North America): Grandfather summons a man and woman before they descend to Earth: "You are going to make a long journey; do the best you can. You will return and be asked about how your journey fared."

❀ Caribs (Venezuela): Louquo, the first human, descended from the sky home and returned after reproducing numerous offspring. His descendants ascend to the heavens and become stars after death.

❀ Baoulé (West Africa): departed Souls return to the "Village of Truth," where everyone knows ultimate truth and deception is unthinkable.[54]

CHAPTER 18

Journey from Forgetting to Remembering

⌒

Our birth is but a sleep and a forgetting: / the
Soul that rises with us, our Life's Star, / Hath had
elsewhere its setting, / And cometh from afar: /
Not in entire forgetfulness, / And not in utter
nakedness, / But trailing clouds of glory do we
come / From God, who is our home.

—WILLIAM WORDSWORTH[1]

*A toddler laments: "Mom, I am starting to forget
Heaven and how angels sound."*

LIFE IS A CONDITION OF spiritual amnesia for the vast majority
of Souls. Most of us forget our passage to birth and our cosmic status as sparks of consciousness. Physical embodiment
and social conditioning dull awareness, causing us to believe that
sensory perception is the only reality. Human birth is analogous
to watching a movie and becoming identified with one of the characters. We become immersed in our own Hollywood drama, the
earthly illusion. Pre-birth amnesia is acknowledged by ancient and
modern peoples. Chapter 18 focuses on theories from Buddhism,
Pythagoras, ancient Indian medical treatises, Judaism, Gnosticism,
and Sufism.

Four Ways of Descent into the Womb

The Soul's passage through a veil erases and blocks pre-birth memories.

Why are we suffering from amnesia of our spiritual origins? Buddhism suggests four ways of descent into the fetus ranging from no pre-birth memory to full pre-birth memory.[2] Most people are born in the forgetful levels. The four levels are:

1. No pre-birth memory: one enters the fetus unaware and unknowing and is born with amnesia.
2. Pre-birth memory is forgotten in the womb: one deliberately enters the fetus. Pre-birth memory is intact, but is lost while in the womb and continues after birth.
3. Pre-birth memory is lost at birth: one deliberately enters the fetus. Pre-birth memory remains intact until birth trauma induces forgetfulness.
4. Full pre-birth memory: one deliberately enters the fetus. Pre-birth memory is intact, and one is born fully conscious of the Soul's journey.

An individual who is born retaining full pre-birth memory, the most advanced level, is considered a person of great wisdom, in an enlightened state. The Buddhist commentary considers someone to be a bodhisattva in its last rebirth if he or she "enters the mother's womb knowing, stays there knowing, and leaves it knowing." Other Buddhist scriptures describe a bodhisattva's entry into the womb as "mindful and fully aware."[3]

The Greatest Mystery: Descent and Incarnation

Pythagoras described the fading of pre-birth memory.

Pythagoras (570–495 BCE) laid out the step-by-step process of the Soul's descent when its time is up in the spiritual realm. First, the Soul is overcome with heaviness, giddiness, and melancholy. An invincible force attracts it to earthly life. This desire is mingled with dread and grief at leaving divine life. Nonetheless, the time for human birth has come. Next, heaviness increases; a sensation of dimness is felt. The Soul no longer sees its companions of Light except through a dense veil. It hears the sad farewells and tears of its loved ones. "Then, with solemn oaths, it promises to remember: to remember the light when in the world of darkness, to remember truth when in the world of falsehood, and love when in the world of hatred."[4]

The Soul descends and finds itself in the dense atmosphere of Earth. A guide points out its mother-to-be. The baby in her womb will live only if the Soul animates the fetus. The Soul plunges into that warm womb cavern. Memory of divine life flickers out: "For between it and the light above are interposed waves of blood and tissues of flesh, crushing it and filling it with darkness." The fusion of the Soul with the fetus "operates slowly with perfect wisdom: organ by organ, fiber by fiber." Finally at birth, the newborn cries over its veiled "memory of the celestial regions."[5]

This analogy that a frequency shift to a lower vibration blocks out memories is expressed by early Greek philosophers and is found in other cultures as well.

- ❁ Hesiod (Greece, circa 750 BCE): the gods cover human life with a thick veil.[6]
- ❁ Plato (Greece, circa 424–347 BCE): "Socrates argues that the soul is immortal and continually moves between our world and the underworld. When the soul entered our world we call it birth and when it leaves we call it death, but in reality the soul never perishes. Since it has over time seen all things, both in this world and the underworld, the soul knows everything— there is nothing it has not learned. Thus what we generally call learning is nothing but the soul recollecting what it already knows."[7]

❁ Sufism: each Soul descends through seventy thousand veils in our journey to be born. Passage through the veils brings amnesia. The inner half are thirty-five thousand veils of light. The outer half are thirty-five thousand veils of darkness. For every veil of light passed through, the Soul loses a divine attribute; the Soul accumulates an earthly quality for every dark veil. The child weeps at birth for the Soul realizes its separation from God.[8]

❁ Adi Shankara (India, 788–820 CE): amnesia increases as Souls traverse the four spheres separating primordial Oneness from the human realm.[9]

❁ Parley P. Pratt (Mormonism, 1807–1857): "a veil" is thrown over "the scenes" of our "primeval childhood in the heavenly mansions."[10]

❁ Yoruba (West Africa): "We knelt down [in heaven] and chose our destinies, but when we arrived on Earth we became impatient."[11]

Sleeping Soul in a Body

For the most part, pre-birth memories become embedded within the subconscious mind once the Soul becomes captive in a bodily costume. Additional examples describe how the body and senses "intoxicate" the Soul and overshadow awareness of pre-birth memory. We become identified with the body.

❁ Zoroastrianism (Persia, 6th century BCE): "I lie here, a star of heaven, fallen upon this gloomy place. Scarce remembering what bright courses I was once allowed to trace. Still in dreams it comes upon me that I once on wings did soar."[12]

❁ Gautama Buddha (India, circa 563–411 BCE): the world is a dark dungeon, and people are unable to see that they are prisoners. However, their will can be awakened and set in motion.[13]

❁ Plato (Greece, circa 424–347 BCE): every Soul has beheld true Being; this was the condition of its passing into human form.

Souls forget the other world once they become fastened and glued to earthly bodies.[14] When the Soul uses the body to see, hear, and so on, the Soul is "dragged into the region of the changeable" and becomes confused: "the world spins round her." Each pleasure and pain acts like a nail that rivets the Soul to the body, and makes her believe whatever the body affirms to be true.[15]

❀ Hermes Trismegistus (ancient Egypt): a child's Soul is connected to its Source, while its body is small and unspoiled by bodily passions. When the body increases in size and has drawn the Soul down into its material mass, it generates oblivion. The Soul separates from "the Beautiful and Good."[16]

❀ Ovid (Rome, circa 43 BCE–18 CE): Souls remain at peace "above" until, like Narcissus, they became enamored with physical form and mistake the image for reality. The Soul becomes a captive in a bodily costume and no longer remembers its immortal nature.[17]

❀ Gnosticism (Egypt, second century CE): the Soul turned toward matter and fell in love with it, and burning with desire to enjoy bodily pleasures, wished no more to be separated from it. The Soul forgot its true center.

❀ Macrobius (Rome, early fifth century CE): the Soul enters the fetus staggering as if it is intoxicated. Hence oblivion, the companion of intoxication, begins to creep into the recesses of the Soul.[18]

❀ Solomon ibn Gabirol (Judaism, 1021–1058): once the Soul enters the fetus, this union and mixture with the flesh confuses it like applying mud onto a transparent mirror. The Soul forgets "true knowledge" which remains concealed within.[19]

❀ Rumi (Persia, 1207–1273): the Soul "is wrapped in the slumber of this world, like a star covered by clouds."

❀ Parley P. Pratt (Mormonism, 1807–1857): we will never be fully awake to the intelligence of our premortal state.[20]

❀ Paramahansa Yogananda (India, 1893–1952): a bird confined in a cage hesitates to fly away once the door is opened because it has forgotten the joy of flying in the sky. So too our Souls become locked up in the human cavity, attached to our physical veils, and forgetful of our divine heritage.[21]

❊ Chögyam Trungpa Rinpoche (Tibetan Buddhism, 1939–1987): every child should remember the pre-birth state. The memories are deep impressions, yet they fade away due to indoctrination by family, school, and society.[22]

Prenatal Life According to India's Scriptures

Ancient texts outline the Soul's condition in the fetus until birth.

Medical treatises and spiritual texts from India (Garbha Upanishad, Markandeya Purana, Srimad Bhagavatam) explain that the Soul enters the fetus in the seventh month. The Soul remains like a bird in a cage without freedom of movement and observes the movie of hundreds of past lives. The Soul prefers the freedom of being without form and finds the idea of rebirth distasteful. "He thinks: I have seen thousands of wombs, eaten several kinds of food and sucked many breasts. Born and dead again and again, I am immersed in grief but see no remedy. Thinking of my good and bad deeds, I am suffering alone, although the bodies that enjoyed the fruits are gone. When I get out of this womb, I will take refuge in Sānkhya-Yoga, which destroys misery and yields liberation; when I get out of this womb, I will take refuge in Maheśvara, who destroys misery and grants liberation. When I get out of this womb, I will take refuge in Nārāyana, who destroys misery and grants liberation. When I get out of this womb, I will meditate on the eternal Brahmin."[23]

The fetus pleads for help: "Lord, let me out of this prison! I cannot see. I cannot hear. I am bound." God teaches the fetus how to become aware of a higher truth: to meditate on the mantra *soham,* meaning "I am Pure Being." The fetus meditates and realizes its true identity and settles down. Alas, once the baby is squeezed and delivered from the womb, he is touched by Vishnu's all-pervading illusory force (Maya) and emerges veiled of memory of his past. He forgets soham, "I am Pure Being." Instead the newborn is expelled from the womb, wailing, "kwanh, kwanh" (koham, koham), meaning, "Who am I?" The memory loss is the result of the brain being forcibly squeezed from the womb.

In the womb, the Soul fears rebirth. Once out of the womb, he or she is in full life and good health and no longer takes the miseries of birth seriously. The Soul forgets that he or she is a spiritual being having a human life and identifies with the body *(deham):* I am a male or female; I am a child, a youth, or an old person; I am a physician, teacher, artist, and so on. The Soul is covered with the cosmic delusion that existence depends on body and breath.

Cultural Parallels: Mystical Potions of Amnesia

Parallels reminiscent of Vishnu's magical power that rubs out the newborn's memory involve a potion of forgetfulness:

⚘ Plato (Greece, circa 424–347 BCE): incarnating Souls preview future life. As they are about to pass into the flesh, someone gives them a cup of amnesia. They forget the Holy things they once saw. Few Souls arrive with memory intact once they enter the flesh.[24]

⚘ Virgil (Rome 70–19 BCE): Aeneas journeys to the Valley of Amnesia where Souls that are to receive bodies in due time wander along the banks of Lethe. Meanwhile they drink amnesia of former lives.[25]

⚘ NDE of Thespesius (Plutarch, 46–120 AD, Greece): Thespesius reached a giant chasm where a mellow breeze carrying fragrant scents had attracted an assembly of Souls. This was the Place of Lethe (amnesia) where sweet odors arouse an intoxicating mood. Nostalgic memories of earthly revelry, festivity, and merrymaking trigger an overpowering desire, dragging the Soul down into a human body.[26]

❖ Chinese mythology: before Souls reincarnate, Granny Meng serves a broth spiked with a drug ensuring that Souls start birth with a clean slate. On feeling the amnesic effects, a torrent of red foaming waters precipitates Souls into the human realm.[27]

❖ Gnosticism (second century CE): the immature Soul drinks a cup of amnesia and forgets "all the regions to which it hath gone." That human being will be "continually troubled" in his heart. By contrast, the "purified Soul" drinks a potion full of intuition, wisdom, and prudence and is cast into a body that will be unable to forget. The mature Soul seeks "the Mysteries of Light."[28]

❖ Macrobius (Rome, early fifth century CE): the muddy drink from Lethe causes Souls to stagger, forget their previous state, and undergo rebirth.[29]

❖ Ralph Waldo Emerson (United States, 1803–1882): "Where do we find ourselves? In a series, of which we do not know the extremes. We wake and find ourselves on a stair; there are other stairs below us. There are stairs above us. But the Genius which stands at the door by which we enter, and gives us the Lethe to drink mixed the cup too strongly, and we cannot shake off our lethargy."[30]

Modern Theories: Oxytocin-Induced Amnesia

Modern medical understanding of the baby's forgetfulness dovetails with the foregoing ancient accounts from Greece, Rome, India, and China. Today, the mystical potion of amnesia is the hormone, oxytocin. In high levels, oxytocin produces a biochemical amnesia in well-trained lab animals. Oxytocin leaves them unable to recall previously mastered tasks under the hormone's influence.

During human birth, the baby and the womb are bathed in oxytocin once contractions begin. Oxytocin remains high in the brain for an hour or more after birth. Oxytocin is the mother's hormone for triggering uterine contractions and the flow of breast milk.

According to Thomas Verny, MD, oxytocin accounts in part for the amnesia related to birth. Oxytocin causes the mother and baby to forget birth trauma and induces feelings of trust, calm, and well-being. Dr. Verny notes that this amnesic effect continues when a baby is breastfed if sufficient oxytocin is in the mother's milk.[31]

Another cause of pre-birth amnesia may be excessive fluoride. According to some sources, fluoride added to public drinking water may block the pineal gland. By the age of five, a child's pineal may be impaired by a calcification process that fluoride promotes. This may be one factor explaining why children stop talking about pre-birth memories around this age.

Lailah, Midwife of Souls

An angel ensures each child's amnesia begins at birth.

Jewish texts describe the Tree of Life in Paradise, which has Souls as its blossoms.[32] As the Souls ripen, they fall into the Treasury of Souls where they await human birth. At the time a woman conceives a child, God advises the angel named Lailah, "Bring me the Soul whose name is so-and-so, and whose form is so-and-so." God commands the Soul, "Go to a certain place and enter that sperm." The Soul pleads, "Why must I, who am holy and a part of your glory, enter an impure sperm? I do not wish to be enslaved and corrupted." God attempts to convince the Soul that earthly life will be better than Paradise and explains, "I have created you for this purpose. I have blessed you with gifts in order to carry out a role in the Divine Plan." Lailah encourages the Soul to obey and places the drop of semen before God, asking, "Sovereign of the universe, what is the fate of this drop?" One thing is left undecided and up to each Soul: moral character. After that, Lailah places the Soul in the womb of the mother. The Soul reluctantly enters, with its life mapped out before it.

Further details about prenatal life can be found in Babylonian

Talmud[33] and *Legends of the Jews,*[34] where it relates how angels place a lighted candle at the head of the unborn infant so it can see from one end of the world to the other until it is born. During womb time, the angel teaches the unborn infant the Torah and all that it will ever need to know in life, both the good and the bad.

As birth approaches, the angel says, "The time has come to enter the world." The Soul hesitates to exit the shelter of security and rest. Alas, the angel extinguishes the light at the head and brings the Soul forth against his or her will. When the newborn takes its first breath, the angel lightly fillips the baby above the lips. At that instant, the infant forgets all that the Soul has seen and learned. That is the origin of the vertical groove everyone bears on the upper lip — the philtrum or infranasal depression.

Hymn of the Pearl

A Gnostic poem portrays human life as suffering from amnesia or being asleep.

The Hymn of the Pearl is a masterpiece of spiritual poetry composed by Bardaisan in the second or third century CE and preserved in the *Acts of Thomas.* This hymn is magnificent poetry as well as an allegory of the Soul's journey, narrated by a young prince, who says: "When I was a little child, I dwelled in my Father's Kingdom and delighted in wealth and glories." The young prince's parents required him to leave his heavenly home and provided him with provisions for a long journey. Before departing, his parents removed their son's Robe of Glory and Purple Mantle: "Bring back the pearl, encircled by the terrible loud-breathing serpent, lying in the middle of the sea. When you complete your mission, you will return and wear your Mantle and Robe of Glory again." The young prince agreed and surrendered his garment of Light.

No one suspected his foreign heritage when the prince arrived in

Egypt: "Yea, they provided me their food to eat. I forgot that I was a King's son and became a slave to their king. And from the weight of their food, I sank into a deep sleep." His parents, anxiously waiting, dispatched a message to his sleeping Soul. The letter arrived in the form of a great eagle telling him to remember who and what he is: "You have fallen into bondage. Wake up. See whom you serve. Remember the pearl, your glorious robe, and your splendid mantle. You will wear them again, and we will inscribe your name in the book of heroes."

The prince reawakened from his amnesia and recalled that he was a king's son. He snatched the pearl by charming the serpent into a deep slumber. He recovered his spiritual Robe of Light "with sparkling splendor of colors," "the Glory looked like my own self." He ascended and bowed "to the Glory of Him who had sent it," his mission now accomplished.[35]

Symbolism of the Hymn of the Pearl

The Hymn of the Pearl tells the story of how our Souls fell into human bodies from the realm of Light, the transcendent reality, and how we eventually awake from our slumber of amnesia of who we are and where we come from:

* ❀ Prince: the Soul cast out from the realm of Pure Being.
* ❀ Egypt: physical embodiment, the materialistic world of limited awareness.
* ❀ Sleep: ignorance; the Soul lowers its frequency by taking on a physical body, enters an amnesic state, and forgets its purpose.
* ❀ Pearl: awakening to higher awareness after learning certain lessons.
* ❀ Serpent: guardian of the pearl, who represents distractions, attachments, and pre-birth amnesia.
* ❀ Robe of Light: the Soul's return to Source. The limited "I" merges back into True Being, recognizing its real nature.

Snow White and the Seven Dwarfs

References to pre-birth amnesia pop up in great literature, even in fairy tales.

"Snow White and the Seven Dwarfs" is the story of a beautiful princess who is forced to flee her father's castle. Snow White found sanctuary with the seven dwarfs. Later she enters into a narcotic sleep after eating a poisoned apple given her by the wicked queen. The dwarfs place her body in a glass coffin. The handsome prince arrives, and after the dwarfs give him the coffin, the poisoned apple pops out from her throat as the servants are transporting the coffin. Snow White awakens, marries the prince, and returns to a happy life.

This fairy tale originated in the Middle Ages, an age of spiritual censorship and oppression, when Giordano Bruno was burned at the stake by the Roman Catholic Church in 1600. He was condemned for his heretical view that the sun is the center of the solar system and is a model of stars with life-giving planets. Snow White's story reveals the steps of our Soul's journey:

- ⸙ Snow White: Soul with a divine heritage originating in a luminous world.
- ⸙ Forest: the earthly dimension.
- ⸙ Seven dwarfs: although they do not look human, the dwarfs are mortals who are also lost in matter, in physical bodies. Adding fantasy aspects like seven dwarfs dwelling in a forest makes the real message of the fairy tale less obvious. The religious authorities of the day would not persecute someone teaching fairy tales.
- ⸙ Throat: a metaphysical location for poison. In a tale from India, a compassionate being, Shiva, drank poison in order to save the Angels and humanity from death. That is why Shiva's throat is blue, signifying the poison in his throat. In a similar account in Genesis, Adam stopped swallowing the forbidden

apple after Eve's warning. That is how, according to folk legends, the Adam's apple got its name.

❀ Poison apple dislodged by accident: Snow White's reawaken-
ing from the amnesia of her true nature comes about due to an
accident: divine intervention, a free blessing of the gods.[36]

❀ Marriage to Prince: a happy ending: return to Source.[37]

Sleeping Memory of Immortality

Wiser Souls slip through the cracks of forgetfulness.

Why is it that some people remember? Heraclitus, the Greek philosopher, noted differences between "wet" Souls who remember and
"dry" Souls who suffer pre-birth amnesia when he said "a dry beam
of light is wisest and best."[38] Wet and dry Souls are easily understood
in the context of Plato's myth of Er, where incarnating Souls journey
through a dry, torrid region before reaching the plain of Lethe. Only
the wise Soul resists the drink of amnesia (dry Soul). These 'better'
Souls retain pre-birth memories once they are born on Earth, whereas
a veiled or "wet" Soul has become so gorged with the Lethean bever-
age that it has no pre-birth recollection.

Dr. Ian Stevenson's past life research uncovered a curious example
of a "dry" or a wiser Soul: a Vietnamese man who refused to drink
the spiritual soup of amnesia in the pre-birth world, surreptitiously
slipped it to his dog instead. Consequently, the man recalled his
interlife journey as well as a past life.[39]

Plato correlates pre-birth memory to the Soul's awareness of its
true status: purified Souls retain memory of the universal arche-
types, patterns, or potentials they saw in the super-celestial sphere
before coming to Earth.[40] Such a concept bears close resemblance to
the thinking of sages in India who connect pre-birth memory reten-
tion to higher consciousness. The greater one's super-conscious
mind, the greater is one's pre-birth memory:

❊ Sage Patanjali (Father of yoga, India): when a yogi has mastered the quality of nonpossessiveness in relation to this gross level of reality, his energy of appreciation shifts to the subtle reality. Thus he perceives the reason for the births he recently took. Knowledge of past and future existences arises. The prerequisite for remembering the reason for birth is a virtue called *aparigraha:* a life without greed, covetousness, nonpossessiveness, and nonexcess. In being consistent in nonpossessiveness, there is manifested the reason and the correct perception regarding one's birth.[41]

❊ Paramahansa Yogananda (India, (1893–1952): mature Souls retain self-consciousness without interruption during the transition between lives.[42]

❊ Sadguru Sant Keshavadas (India, 1934–1997): perfected Souls pierce the veil of ignorance that hides the innumerable pasts in the subconscious.[43]

Dr. Ian Stevenson's research of children's past life recall aligns with this position. These children remembered being unusually pious and generous in their past lives. "The subjects of these cases themselves often showed precocious piety and generosity when they were young children, thereby suggesting that they had behavioral as well as imaged memories of the previous personality's spirituality.[44]

Theories posited by philosophers and religious leaders explain why pre-birth amnesia is necessary:

❊ Giordano Bruno (Italy, 1548–1600): amnesia lessens the burden of incarnating Souls. Youths forget their infancy; infants do not desire to be in the womb again; and nobody longs for pre-birth life. Everyone is eager to remain in his current state.[45]

❊ Rabbi Barukh of Mezbizh (Hasidism, 19th century): "If there were no forgetting, a man would incessantly think of his death. He would build no house, he would launch no enterprise."[46]

❀ Maharaj Charan Singh (Sikhism, 1916–1990): Kal, the Lord of justice, has received certain boons essential for the continuation of this universe. One boon is that all creatures forget their past.

Future Pre-Birth Choices

If you could choose your next life, what choice would you make?

A theory held by great wisdom teachers is that choices we make today ripple into the future, including our interlife and future lifetimes. If future lifetimes are an option, we need to be open minded about future choices. Every culture and religion has its description of the life-between-life state or beyond-death state. According to reincarnation theory, this is where the decision is made for rebirth. While they appear on the surface contradictory, each description is actually valid. Inelia Benz, described in chapter 2, explains why our interlife experience is exactly what we believe it will be: "A teacher in the astral world took me under his wing. I asked, 'What happens to people after death?' He answered me by giving me a tour of the Soul realms. He pointed to Jesus and said, 'That is where people go who believe in Jesus.' And right next to Jesus, he said, 'This is where Muslims go.' And then my teacher showed me, 'This is where the Jewish people go.' As we went on, he said, 'And this is the locality where people who believe in hell hang out.' Besides all of the realms related to the different religions, my Guide showed me how people who come to do a specific task on Earth, whether it is a drama or a mission, do it, and after death they all go together to the same interlife realm:

❀ Souls who had come to Earth to play war games and have lives in combat.
❀ Souls who had chosen a life of humanitarian service and Souls who had chosen a life of helplessness.

❀ Souls who believe the purpose of life on Earth is to learn lessons.

❀ Souls who say: 'We are eternal beings; we do not have to learn a thing; life is an experience."

Inelia elaborates on the fourth group of Souls listed above: "These Souls understand that they are simply having experiences for the sake of having experiences, and not to learn, or pay karma. An eternal being does not need to learn. An eternal being knows its true nature and knows all of existence. Most Souls forget that they are eternal beings and that they do not need to learn a thing. They dive into the human experience, at which point they need to validate that experience. So they put meaning and purpose to it, such as karmic debt and learning. In actuality, there is no meaning or purpose to life. It is just life. Souls who realize that life has no purpose or meaning often know that life is about the construction of physicality and having an existential experience in physical reality."

Inelia explains: "The collectively-agreed constructed realities in the different interlife realms support whatever the incarnated Soul's physical life experience and beliefs were in their earthly lives. Much like we have on Earth, these areas are put together from agreed templates, experiences wanted to be experienced, and interpretations of what those individuals believe happens in between physical life moments. They are outside time and space. All of these places were right next to each other and were just constructs that Souls went into. Eventually they came out and were reborn.

"*Cosmic Cradle* will bring empowering energy into the rebirthing process. Readers will remember these ideas after they die. They will say, 'Hold on a minute. I have choices. I don't just have to go back to whatever. I might have done it quite unconsciously before.' People who remember choosing their life plan already have that level of awareness. It is important that this knowledge goes into the collective mind; it is very empowering for the in-between life state."

Remember When You Were a Babe in the Arms of God

Cosmic Cradle increases our insights into the timeless journey our Souls have all taken — to remember when we were a babe in the arms of God. All major spiritual traditions offer ways to restore memory of our true cosmic nature through Self-study, Self-remembering, and awakening. Wisdom teachings inspire us with the same eternal message:

⚜ Christianity: seek the Kingdom of Heaven within.
⚜ Judeo-Christian: you are gods, and all of you are children of the Most High.
⚜ Ancient Greece: know Thyself and you will know the universe and the gods.
⚜ Buddhism: know Self: no problems.
⚜ Zen Buddhism: return to your original state, go back Home.
⚜ Vedic Tradition, Rishi Brighu: transcend, transcend, transcend.
⚜ Bhagavad Gita: go beyond illusion and find ultimate Freedom.

Awakening is an antidote for stress, worry, and fear. When we remember and experience ourselves as Light Beings, we feel centered, self-aware, blissful, supremely loved, and safe.[47] As more people realize their innermost core is rooted in Love and Light, the world will be a better place.

Notes

❧

Prologue

1. Jewish novelist Sholem Asch (1880–1957), quoted in Joseph Head and Sylvia L. Cranston, *Reincarnation: The Phoenix Fire Mystery* (New York: Julian Press, 1977), 124.

Introduction: Amnesia of Our Spiritual Origins

1. John Alexander Stewart, *The Myths of Plato* (Carbondale, IL: Southern Illinois University Press, 1960), quoting *Phaedo* 114d.
2. Kenneth Chandler, *Origins of Vedic Civilization* (2012), http://Sanskrit.safire.com/pdf/ORIGINS.PDF, 28.
3. Elisabeth Hallett, *Stories of the Unborn Soul* (San Jose, CA: Writers Club Press, 2002), 5.
4. Elisabeth Hallett, *Soul Trek: Meeting Our Children on the Way to Birth* (Hamilton, MT: Light Hearts Publishing, 1995); Hallett, *Stories of the Unborn Soul.*
5. Sarah Hinze, *Coming from the Light: Spiritual Accounts of Life Before Life* (New York: Pocket Books, 1997).
6. Arvin S. Gibson, *Echoes from Eternity* (Bountiful, UT: Horizon Publishers, 1993); Arvin S. Gibson, *Glimpses of Eternity* (Bountiful, UT: Horizon Publishers, 1992).
7. P. M. H. Atwater, *Children of the New Millennium: Children's Near-Death Experiences and the Evolution of Humankind* (New York: Three Rivers Press, 1999).
8. See http://www.prebirthexperience.com and http://www.BeyondReligion.com.
9. Thomas Verny and John Kelly, *The Secret Life of the Unborn Child: How You Can Prepare Your Baby for a Happy, Healthy Life* (New York: Dell, 1981).
10. Gladys Taylor McGarey, *Born to Live: A Holistic Approach to Childbirth* (Phoenix: Gabriel Press, 1980).
11. Verny and Kelly, *Secret Life*, 12, 19–20.

12. David Chamberlain, "Communication before Language" (1995), http://www.birthpsychology.com.
13. William James, *Psychology*, American Science Series, Briefer Course (New York: Henry Holt, 1892), 176.
14. Jonathan Shear, *The Inner Dimension, Philosophy and the Experience of Consciousness* (New York: Peter Lang Publishing, 1990), 4–5.
15. Henry David Thoreau, *Walden, or Life in the Woods* (Princeton, NJ: Princeton University Press, 2004).
16. Martin Buber, *Chinese Tales* (Atlantic Highlands, NJ: Humanities Press International, 1991), 4.
17. Burton Watson, *Chuang Tzu* (New York: Columbia University Press, 1964), 97.

Part One: Pre-Birth Memory

1. Hallett, *Stories of the Unborn Soul*, 4.

1. Children as Messengers

1. David Chamberlain, *Babies Remember Birth* (Los Angeles: Jeremy P. Tarcher, 1988), xiii, xxv.
2. Ibid., xiii.
3. Carol Bowman, *Children's Past Lives* (New York: Bantam Books, 1998), 199.
4. Bhagavan Das, *The Essential Unity of All Religions* (Bombay: Bharatiya Vidya Bhavan, 1990), 227.
5. Maurice Maeterlinck, *The Blue Bird: A Fairy Play in Five Acts* (1906; repr. New York: Dodd, Mead and Co., 1961).

2. Memories of the Cosmic Cradle

1. Hallett, *Stories of the Unborn Soul*, 14.
2. James Hastings, *Encyclopedia of Religion and Ethics*, vol. VII (Edinburgh: T. & T. Clark, 1914), 186.
3. Walter Yeeling Evans-Wentz, *The Tibetan Book of the Dead* (New York: Causeway Books, 1973), xxxvi; G. C. C. Chang, *Six Yogas of Naropa and Teachings on Mahamudra* (New York: Snow Lion, 1963), 105–6; Alexandra David-Neel, *Magic and Mystery in Tibet*

(Delhi: New Age Publishers, 1985), 39; Philip Kapleau, *The Wheel of Life and Death* (New York: Doubleday, 1989), 257.

4. Raymond Moody, *Life after Life: The Investigation of a Phenomenon—Survival of Bodily Death* (Harrisburg, PA: Stackpole Books, 1976).

3. "I Was in Your Tummy Twice"

1. McGarey, *Born to Live*, 11.
2. David B. Chamberlain, "The Fetal Senses: Twelve, Not Five: A New Proposal," n.d., http://www.birthpsychology.com.
3. Verny and Kelly, *Secret Life*, 89.
4. McGarey, *Born to Live*.
5. Wendy Anne McCarty, *Consciousness: Supporting Babies Wholeness from the Beginning of Life—an Integrated Model of Early Development* (Santa Barbara, CA: Wondrous Beginnings Publishing, 2009).

4. Scanning Soul Plans

1. Mahatanhasankhaya Sutta, Majjhima Nikaya 38, trans. Thanissaro Bhikkhu, "The Greater Craving-Destruction Discourse," 2011, http://www.accesstoinsight.org/tipitaka/mn/mn.038.than.html.

5. Welcome to Planet Earth

1. Lorenzo Caravella, *Mouth of God: Your Cosmic Contract* (Fairfield, IA: Sunstar Publishing, 1999).

6. Shirley Temple and the Blue Bird

1. Howard Storm, *My Descent into Death: A Second Chance at Life* (New York: Doubleday, 2005).
2. Lee W. Bailey and Jenny Yates, eds., *The Near-Death Experience: A Reader* (New York: Routledge, 1996).
3. P. M. H. Atwater, *Coming Back to Life: The After-Effects of the Near-Death Experience the Light* (New York: Dodd, Mead & Company, 1988).

7. Our Soul as a Tiny Spaceship

1. Ian Stevenson, *Cases of the Reincarnation Type,* vol. IV (Charlottesville, VA: University Press of Virginia, 1983); Jim Tucker, *Life before Life: Children's Memories of Previous Lives* (New York: St. Martin's Press, 2005).
2. Ian Stevenson, *Children Who Remember Previous Lives: A Question of Reincarnation* (Charlottesville: University Press of Virginia, 1987), 214.
3. Tucker, *Life before Life,* 176–77.
4. Stevenson, *Cases of the Reincarnation Type,* 249.
5. Bruce Leininger and Andrea Leininger, *Soul Survivor: The Reincarnation of a World War II Fighter Pilot* (New York: Grand Central Publishing, 2010), 153–54.
6. Ibid
7. Genesis 1:26, as quoted in The Holy Bible, English Standard Version (Wheaton, IL: Crossway Bibles, 2001).
8. Rigveda, Aitareya Araiujaka 2.3, quoted in Bhagavan Das, *The Science of Social Organization or Laws of Manu in the Light of Atma-Vidya* (Adyar, India: Theosophical Publishing House, 1932).
9. Chiggala Sutta, Samyutta Nikaya 56.48, trans. Thanissaro Bhikkhu, *Access to Insight* (July 1, 2010), http://www.accesstoinsight.org/tipitaka/sn/sn56/sn56.048.than.html.
10. Das, *Essential Unity,* 298–99.
11. Atwater, *Coming Back to Life.*
12. Storm, *My Descent into Death.*

8. I Saw All My Costumes

1. Krishnalal Chatterji, *The Guiding Light, A Treatise on Thakur Sree Sree Anukul Chandra* (Calcutta: Indian Progressive Publishing, 1978); Rabindra Nath Sarkar, *Latest Revelation in the East* (Calcutta: Sanskrit Pustak Bhandar, 1987).
2. John 1:1.
3. Chāndogya Upanishad 6, quoted in Mary Pat Fisher, *Living Religions* (London: Pearson, 2010), 79.

4. Mundaka Upanishad 1.3.1, quoted in Swami Yatiswarananda, *The Divine Life, Its Practice and Realisation* (Madras: Sri Ramakrishna Math Mylapore, 1939).

5. Hans Jonas, *The Gnostic Religion* (Boston: Beacon Press, 1963), 44, 55.

6. A Hadith Qudsi, quoted in Das, *Essential Unity*, 348.

7. Z'ev ben Shimon Halevi, *A Kabbalistic Universe* (Boston: Red Wheel, 1977).

8. Cherry Shai, *Torah through Time: Understanding Bible Commentary from the Rabbinic Period from the Rabbinic Period to Modern Times* (Philadelphia: Jewish Publication Society, 2007), 29.

9. Kahlil Gibran, *A Third Treasury of Kahlil Gibran* (New York: Carol Publishing, 1975).

10. "Cosmic Creation," quoted in Paramahansa Yogananda, *Whispers of Eternity* (Los Angeles: Self Realization Fellowship, 1929).

11. Proverbs 8:22–31.

12. Job 38:4–21.

13. Moses ben Nachman, "From the Beginning, Before the World Ever Was (from Before the World Ever Was)," trans. Peter Cole, http://www.poetry-chaikhana.com/N/NachmanidesN/Frombeginnin.htm.

14. E. H. Whinfield, *Masnavi of Rumi* (London: Kegan Paul, 1898).

15. Martin Buber, *For the Sake of Heaven* (Philadelphia: Jewish Publication Society, 1945), 5.

16. Ibid., 65.

17. Elizabeth M. Carman and Neil J. Carman, *Cosmic Cradle: Souls Waiting in the Wings for Birth* (Fairfield, Iowa: Sunstar Publishing, 1999).

18. Creation Hymn from the Rigveda, Mandala 10, *sūkta* 129.

9. Souls Waiting in the Wings for Birth

1. Geoffrey Hodson, *The Miracle of Birth, A Clairvoyant Study of a Human Embryo* (Wheaton, Illinois: Theosophical Publishing House, 1981), 85

10. Soul as a Sphere of Light

1. Paramahansa Yogananda, *Man's Eternal Quest* (Los Angeles: Self Realization Fellowship, 1992) 63–64.
2. Inder L. Malik, *Dalai Lamas of Tibet: Succession of Births* (New Delhi: [no publisher], 1984).
3. Hallett, *Soul Trek,* 159.
4. Plutarch, *On the Delays of the Divine Vengeance;* George Robert Stow Mead, *Doctrine of the Subtle Body in Western Tradition* (Wheaton, IL: Theosophical Publishing, 1967), 41; Stewart, *Myths of Plato,* 331–32; Lawrence E. Sullivan, ed., *Death, Afterlife, and the Soul* (New York: Macmillan, 1989), 110; P. H. De Lacy and B. Einarson, *Plutarch's Moralia,* vol. VII (London: Wm. Heinemann, 1959), 285, 291.
5. Atwater, *Coming Back to Life.*
6. Storm, *My Descent into Death,* 26.
7. Glenn H. Mullin, *Mystical Verses of a Mad Dalai Lama* (Wheaton, IL: Theosophical Publishing House, 1994), 47–54.
8. Murshida Vera Justin Corda, *Cradle of Heaven: Psychological and Spiritual Dimensions of Conception, Pregnancy and Birth* (Lebanon Springs, NY: Omega Press, 1987), 17.
9. R. S. Ramabadran, "Sri Ramakrishna as Siva," *Koshur Samachar* (March 1994), http://www.koausa.org/KoshSam/Ramakrishna.html.
10. Proverbs 20:27.
11. Thomas Carlyle, *Sartor Resartus* (London: Chapman and Hall, 1894; first published 1836), 73.
12. E. W. Emerson, ed., *The Complete Works of Ralph Waldo Emerson: Essays,* vol. II (Boston: Houghton Mifflin, 1909), 66, 358.
13. Julian P. M. Johnson, *The Path of the Masters: The Science of Surat Shabd Yoga* (Punjab, India: Radha Soami Satsang Beas, 1939), 320.
14. Åke Hultkrantz, *Conceptions of the Soul among North American Indians* (Stockholm: Caslon Press, 1953), 260–62.
15. Ibid.
16. Sanderson Beck, *History of Peace,* vol. I: *Guides to Peace and Justice from Ancient Sages to the Suffragettes* (Santa Barbara, CA: World Peace Communications, 2005).
17. Atwater, *Coming Back to Life.*

11. Cosmic Conception

1. Harold W. Percival, *Thinking and Destiny* (Dallas: Word Foundation, 1974), 164.
2. Zohar 3.104a, as quoted in Isaiah Tishby, *The Wisdom of the Zohar*, vol. II (New York: Oxford University Press, 1989).
3. Corda, *Cradle of Heaven*, 24.
4. Hallett, *Soul Trek*, 36.
5. Hallett, *Stories of the Unborn Soul*, 31.
6. Hallett, *Soul Trek*, 36.
7. Torkom Saraydarian, *Woman, Torch of the Future* (Cave Creek, AZ: T. S. G. Publishing, 1999), 84.
8. Hallett, *Soul Trek*, 32.
9. See pages 207, 158.
10. See page 142.
11. See page 43.
12. See page 29.
13. H. N. Banerjee and William Oursler, *Lives Unlimited* (Garden City, NY: Doubleday, 1974), 87.

12. Miscarriages and Stillbirths in the Light of Pre-Birth Plans

1. Gladys Taylor McGarey and Jess Stearn, *The Physician within You: Discovering the Power of Inner Healing* (Deerfield Beach, FL: Health Communications, 1997), 70.
2. Bowman, *Children's Past Lives*, 70.

13. Conversations with Unborn Children

1. Franz Hartmann, *The Life of Philippus Theophrastus Bombast of Hohenheim, Known by the Name of Paracelsus, and the Substance of His Teachings* (London: Kegan Paul, Trench, Trubner, & Co., 1896).
2. Leonardo da Vinci, *Leonardo on the Human Body*, trans. Charles D. O'Malley and J. B. de C. M. Saunders (New York: Dover Publications, 1983), 460; Aidan MacFarlane, *The Psychology of Childbirth* (Cambridge, MA: Harvard University Press, 1977), 6.

3. Farid al-Din 'Attar, *Muslim Saints and Mystics: Episodes from the Tadhkirat al-Auliya'*, trans. A. J. Arberry (Ames, IA: Omphaloskepsis, 2000), 155.
4. Ibid, 201.
5. Beatriz Manrique, M. Contasti, M. A. Alvarado, Monica Zypman, N. Palma, M. T. Ierrobino, I. Ramirez, and D. Carini, "A Controlled Experiment in Prenatal Enrichment with 684 Families in Caracas, Venezuela: Results to Age Six," *Journal of Prenatal and Perinatal Psychology and Health* 12:3–4 (1998), 209–34.

14. Spirit-Children Down Under

1. Douglas Lockwood, *I, the Aboriginal* (New York: Meridian Books, 1970), 66–67.
2. James G. Cowan, *The Elements of the Aborigine Tradition* (Rockport, MA: Element, 1992), 25.
3. Ashley Montagu, *Coming into Being among the Australian Aborigines: A Study of the Procreative Beliefs of the Native Tribes of Australia* (London: Routledge & Kegan Paul, 1974), 63.
4. Jane C. Goodale, *Tiwi Wives: A Study of the Women of Melville Island, North Australia* (Seattle: University of Washington Press; 1971), 141.
5. Charles P. Mountford, *The Tiwi: Their Art, Myth and Ceremony* (London: Phoenix House, 1958), 147.
6. Robert Lawlor, *Voices of the First Day* (Rochester, VT: Inner Traditions, 1991), 160.
7. U. McConnel, "A Moon Legend from Bloomfield River," *Oceania* 2 (1931), 16.
8. Lloyd Warner, *A Black Civilization: A Social Study of an Australian Tribe* (New York: Harper & Brothers, 1937), 21.
9. Ibid.
10. Montagu, 117.
11. G. Roheim, "Women and their Life in Central Australia," *Journal of the Royal Anthropological Institute*, 63, (1933), 241.
12. Warner, *A Black Civilization*, 22.
13. Mountford, *The Tiwi*, 147.
14. Stevenson, *Children Who Remember*, 99.

15. Ibid.
16. Vincent Guerry, *Life with the Baoulé* (Washington, DC: Three Continents Press, 1975), 40, 120.
17. Montagu, *Coming into Being*, 211–12.
18. Ibid., 212; Charles P. Mountford, *Brown Men and Red Sand: Wanderings in Wild Australia* (Melbourne: Robertson and Mullens, 1948), 159.
19. Donald A. M. Gebbie, *Reproductive Anthropology* (New York: John Wiley & Sons, 1981), 341.
20. G. Taplin, *Folklore of South Australian Aborigines* (Adelaide: Johnson Reprint Corp., 1879), 88.
21. Charles P. Mountford, *Ayers Rock: Its People* (Honolulu: East-West Center Press, 1965), 152.
22. Mundaka Upanishad 1.7, as quoted in Swamin Yatiswarananda, *Divine Life.*
23. S. B. Spencer and F. J. Gillen, *Arunta* (Oosterhout, Netherlands: Anthropological Publications, 1966), 358.
24. Montagu, *Coming into Being*, 101; ibid., 116.
25. Spencer and Gillen, *Arunta*, 272.
26. Edwin Sidney Hartland, *Primitive Paternity*, vol. I (London: David Nutt, 1909), 240.
27. Andreas Lommel, "Modern Culture Influences on the Aborigines," *Oceania* 21 (1950); Andreas Lommel, "Notes on Sexual Behavior and Initiation," *Oceania* 20 (1949).
28. Mountford, *Brown Men.*
29. William Edward Hanley Stanner, *White Man Got No Dreaming: Essays, 1938–1973* (Canberra: Australian National University Press, 1979).

15. Lodge of the Great Manitou

1. Hultkrantz, *Conceptions of the Soul.*
2. Marla N. Powers, *Oglala Women: Myth, Ritual, and Reality* (Chicago: University of Chicago Press, 1986), 53.
3. A. Irving Hallowell, "Spirits of the Dead in Saulteaux Life and Thought," *Journal of the Royal Anthropological Institute of Great Britain and Ireland* 70 (1940), 29–51.

4. Verne F. Ray, *Lower Chinook Ethnographic Notes,* Publications in Anthropology vol. 7 (Seattle: University of Washington Press, 1938), 67.
5. John W. Chapman, "Tinneh Animism," *American Anthropologist* 23:3 (1921), 302.
6. Hultkrantz, *Conceptions of the Soul,* 418.
7. Ibid., 420.
8. Ibid.
9. John R. Swanton, *Indian Tribes of the Lower Mississippi Valley and Adjacent Coast of the Gulf of Mexico* (1911; repr. Mineola, NY: Dover Publications, 1998), 181.
10. J. W. Hudson, "Indian Myth of San Joaquin Basin," *Journal of American Folklore* 15 (1902), 106.
11. Edward W. Gifford and Robert H. Lowie, "Notes on the Akwa'ala Indians of Lower California," *University of California Publications in American Archeology and Ethnology* 23:7 (1928), 338–52.
12. Hultkrantz, *Conceptions of the Soul,* 423.
13. Ibid., 428.
14. Franz Boas, *Contributions to the Ethnology of the Kwakiutl* (New York: Columbia University Press, 1925), 47–49.
15. Hultkrantz, *Conceptions of the Soul,* 417.
16. Hartley Burr Alexander, *Mythology of All Races—North American* (New York: Cooper Square Publishers, 1964), 117.
17. Hultkrantz, *Conceptions of the Soul,* 428–29.
18. Alanson Skinner, "Social Life and Ceremonial Bundles," *Anthropological Papers of the American Museum of Natural History* 13:1 (1913), 40; Alanson Skinner, "Songs of the Menomini Medicine Ceremony," *American Anthropologist* 27 (1925), 290–314.
19. Hultkrantz, *Conceptions of the Soul,* 417.
20. Ibid., 417, 422.
21. Ibid., 419.
22. Ibid., 427.
23. Ibid., 419.
24. Jesse Walter Fewkes, "An Interpretation of Katcina Worship," *Journal of American Folklore* 14 (1901).
25. Jesse Walter Fewkes, *The Prehistoric Culture of Tusayan* (Washington, DC: Judd & Detweiler, 1896).

26. Frank Hamilton Cushing, "A Zuni Folk-tale of the Underworld," *Journal of American Folklore* 5 (1892), 50–51.
27. Hudson, "Indian Myth."
28. Daniel Garrison Brinton, *Myths of the New World* (Philadelphia: David McKay, 1896).
29. Powers, *Oglala Women.*
30. Brinton, *Myths of the New World.*
31. Gideon H. Pond, *Dakota Superstitions* (St. Paul, MN: Minnesota Historical Society, 1889).
32. Hultkrantz, *Conceptions of the Soul,* 419.
33. Henry Rowe Schoolcraft, *Historical and Statistical Information Respecting the History, Condition, and Prospects of the Indian Tribes of the United States* (Philadelphia: Lippincott, Grambo, 1851).
34. Paul Radin, "Winnebago Tribe," *Annual Reports of Bureau of American Ethnology* 37 (1923).
35. Wilson D. Wallis, "Canadian Dakota," *Anthropological Papers of the American Museum of Natural History* 41:1 (1947).
36. Hartland, *Primitive Paternity,* 222.
37. Franz Boas, "Indians of British Columbia," *Fifty-Ninth Meeting of British Association for the Advancement of Science* (London, 1889).
38. Alanson Skinner, "Traditions of the Iowa Indians," *Journal of American Folklore* 38:150 (1925), 479.
39. Skinner, "Social Life."
40. C. Daryll Forde, "Ethnography of the Yuma Indians," *University of California Publications in American Archaeology and Ethnology* 28 (1931), 182.
41. Forde, "Ethnography of the Yuma Indians," 203.
42. John Peabody Harrington, "A Yuma Account of Origins," *Journal of American Folklore,* 21, (1908) 326; Jackson Steward Lincoln, *The Dream in Primitive Cultures* (Baltimore: William Wilkins, 1935).
43. A. Kroeber, "Mohave," *Handbook of Indians of California,* Bulletin of American Ethnology no. 78 (1925), 754.

44. John G. Bourke, "Notes on the Cosmogony and Theogony of the Mojave Indians of the Rio Colorado, Arizona," *Journal of American Folklore* 2:6 (1889).

45. George Devereux, "Mohave Soul Concepts," *American Anthropologist* 39:1 (January–March 1937), 417–18.

46. Hultkrantz, *Conceptions of the Soul*, 424.

47. John Heckewelder, *History, Manners, and Customs of the Indian Nations Who Once Inhabited Pennsylvania and the Neighboring States*, Memoirs of the Historical Society of Pennsylvania, vol. XII. Historical Society of Pennsylvania, 1881.

48. Bernhard J. Stern, *The Lummi Indians of Northwest Washington: The Cycle of Life, Tribal Culture, Legend and Lore* (New York: Columbia University Press, 1934), 14.

49. Hallowell, "Spirits of the Dead," 49.

50. Truman Michelson, "Notes on Fox Mortuary Customs and Beliefs," *Annual Reports of the Bureau American Ethnology* 40 (1925), 343.

51. Forde, "Ethnography of the Yuma Indians," 202.

52. Radin, "Winnebago Tribe"; Paul Radin, "Personal Reminiscences of a Winnebago Indian," *Journal of American Folklore* 26 (1913); Paul Radin, "Religion of the North American Indians," *Journal of American Folklore* 27 (1914); Paul Radin, *The Road of Life and Death* (New York: Pantheon Books, 1945).

16. The Cosmic Designer

1. Stewart, *Myths of Plato*, quoting *Phaedrus* 246a–254e.

2. Ibid., 176.

3. A. H. Armstrong, *Plotinus* (London: George Allen & Unwin, 1953), 132, quoting *The Enneads* IV.3.12–13.

4. Jonas, *Gnostic Religion*, 158, quoting Macrobius, *Commentary on the Dream of Scipio* II.11.

5. Mullin, *Mystical Verses*, 47–52.

6. Emily Dickinson, *Complete Poems* (Boston: Little, Brown, 1924), 13.

7. Charles Webster Leadbeater, *A Textbook of Theosophy* (1912; repr. New York: Cosimo Classics, 2007), 89.

8. Paul E. Chu, *Life before Birth, Life on Earth, Life after Death* (Fort Lee, NJ: World View Press, 1972), 80–81.
9. Kahlil Gibran, *Sand and Foam* (New York: Alfred A. Knopf, 2008).
10. A. C. Bhaktivedanta Swami Prabhupada, *Coming Back* (Los Angeles: Bhaktivedanta Book Trust, 1986).
11. Sita Bordow, *Sri Swami Satchidananda* (Yogaville, VA: Integral Yoga Publications, 1986), 3; Sri Swami Satchidananda, *Golden Present* (Yogaville, VA: Integral Yoga Publications, 1987).
12. Stewart C. Easton, *Man and World in the Light of Anthroposophy* (Spring Valley, NY: Anthroposophic Press, 1975).
13. Nancy Patchen, *The Journey of a Master: Swami Chinmayananda—the Man, the Path, the Teaching* (Berkeley, CA: Asian Humanities Press, 1989), 308.
14. Carroll Dunham, *Mamomato* (New York: Penguin Books, 1993).
15. Robert Brains, *Friends and Lovers* (New York: Basic Books, 1976), 239.
16. Ulli Beier, *Yoruba Myths* (Cambridge, UK: Cambridge University Press, 1980), 4; 'Wande Abimbola, *Ifa* (Ibadan, Nigeria: Oxford University Press, 1976), 125.
17. Carman and Carman, *Cosmic Cradle.*
18. Edwin H. Gomes, *Seventeen Years among the Sea Dyaks of Borneo* (London: Seeley & Co., 1911).
19. Uno Holmberg, *The Mythology of All Races,* vol. IV, Finno-Ugric, Siberian (Boston: Marshall Jones Co., Archaeological Institute of America, 1927), 260, 415.
20. Ibid., 260.
21. Carman and Carman, *Cosmic Cradle,* 383.
22. Eastern and Western Disciples, *Life of Swami Vivekananda,* vol. I (Calcutta: Advaita Ashrama, 1979); Lex Hixon, *Great Swan, Meetings with Ramakrishna* (Boston: Shambhala Publications, 1992).
23. Bronislaw Malinowski, "Baloma," *Journal of the Royal Anthropological Institute of Great Britain and Ireland* 46 (1916).
24. *Republic* 10.614–621, as quoted in Raymond Larson, *Plato, The Republic* (Arlington Heights, IL: AHM Publishing, 1979), 277, and Stewart, *Myths of Plato,* 176.

25. Roger Hicks and Ngakpa Chögyam, *Great Ocean, An Authorized Biography of the Buddhist Monk Tenzin Gyatso, His Holiness the Fourteenth Dalai Lama* (London, England: Penguin Books, 1984), 3.
26. Thomas Sugrue, *There Is a River: The Story of Edgar Cayce* (New York: Henry Holt, 1945), 376.
27. Patrick G. Bowen, "The Ancient Wisdom in Africa," *Theosophy* 82:8 (June 1994), 237–40. Originally published 1927.
28. Plutarch, *On the Delays of the Divine Vengeance*, as quoted in Mead, *Doctrine of the Subtle Body*, 41; Stewart, *Myths of Plato*, 331–32; Sullivan, *Death, Afterlife*, 110; and De Lacy and Einarson, *Plutarch's Moralia*, 285, 291.
29. Shri Dhyanyogi Madhusudandasji, *Death, Dying and Beyond* (Antioch, CA: Dhyanyoga Centers, 1979).
30. Bhagavata Purana 3.12.4, as quoted in *Narayaneeyam—for the Young*, episode 8, http://www.geocities/tvnswamy/narayaneeyam.html.
31. Ananda K. Coomaraswamy, "Lila," *Journal of the American Oriental Society* 61 (1941), 98, quoting Plato's *Laws* 644–45, 803–4.
32. Edward Dwight Walker, *Reincarnation: A Study of Forgotten Truth* (New York: John W. Lovell Co., 1888), 323, quoting Plotinus's *Enneads* III.2.17.
33. Das, *Essential Unity*, 335.
34. Isaac Myer, *Qabbalah, The Philosophical Writings of Solomon Ben Yehudah Ibn Gebirol or Avicebron* (Philadelphia: MacCalla & Co., 1888), 115.
35. Satchidananda, *Golden Present*, February 11.
36. George Arthur Gaskell, *Dictionary of Sacred Language of all Scriptures and Myths* (New York: Lucis, 1930), 265.
37. George Sylvester Viereck, "What Life Means to Einstein: An Interview," *The Saturday Evening Post* (October 26, 1929), 17.
38. Paramahansa Yogananda, *Autobiography of a Yogi* (Los Angeles: Self Realization Fellowship, 1972), 241.
39. Satchidananda, *Golden Present*, September 18.
40. John A. Ward, "The Universe as Theatre" (nisaragatta-advaita-vedanta.blogspot.com).

41. Psalm 139:13–14.
42. *Niddah* 16b; Isodore Singer, ed., *The Jewish Encyclopedia*, vols. X–XI (New York: Funk & Wagnalls, 1905), 182, quoting Hanina, Hullin 7b; Hastings, *Encyclopedia of Religion*, 793.
43. Zohar I.90b–91b, as quoted in Tishby, *Wisdom of the Zohar.*
44. Mohammed Marmaduke Pickthall, *The Glorious Koran* (New York: New American Library, 1959), 73, quoting Koran III.143.
45. Elias J. W. Gibb, *A History of Ottoman Poetry*, vol. I (London: Luzac and Co.,1958), 35.
46. Hazrat Inayat Khan, *The Sufi Message of Hazrat Inayat*, vol. I (London: Barrie and Rockliff, 1968), 181.
47. Yogananda, *Autobiography of a Yogi.*
48. Yogananda, *Man's Eternal Quest*, 218.

17. Travelers from the Light

1. Benjamin Jowett, *The Dialogues of Plato* (New York: Random House, 1937), 254, quoting *Phaedrus* 250c.
2. Larson, *Plato;* Stewart, *Myths of Plato;* and ibid, quoting *Timaeus.*
3. Jowett, *Dialogues of Plato*, and Benjamin Jowett, *Republic of Plato* (Oxford, UK: Clarendon Press, 1888), quoting *The Republic.*
4. Ibid., quoting *The Republic* 514a–520a.
5. Proverbs 8:22–31.
6. Job 38:4.
7. Jeremiah 1:4–5.
8. Genesis 3:21.
9. Psalm 82:6.
10. John 10:34; Luke 17.
11. Saint Clement of Alexandria, *Exhortation to the Heathen* (www.gutenberg.us: World Public Library and Project Gutenberg Consortia Center).
12. Walker, *Reincarnation*, 212, quoting Origen's *De Principiis.*
13. Grace H. Turnbull, *The Essence of Plotinus* (New York: Oxford University Press, 1948), quoting Plotinus's *Enneads* VI.4.14.
14. Book of Thomas, Nag Hammadi, Logion 5, quoted in James M. Robinson, ed., *The Nag Hammadi Library in English* (New York: Harper & Row, 1988), 132.

15. Joseph Smith, *Doctrine and Covenants of the Church of the Latter Day Saints: Carefully Selected from the Revelations of God* (Kirtland, OH: F. G. Williams, 1835), 93:29.

16. Gibson, *Glimpses of Eternity*, 285, quoting *Pearl of Great Price*, 65.

17. Edouard Schuré, *Pythagoras and the Delphic Mysteries* (London: Wm. Rider & Son, 1906), 108–128.

18. William Ralph Inge, *The Philosophy of Plotinus*, vol. I (London: Longmans, Green and Co., 1918), 4–5; M. R. Wright, *Empedocles: The Extant Fragments* (New Haven, CT: Yale University Press, 1981), vol. 270, fragment 115.

19. Armstrong, *Plotinus*, quoting *Enneads* IV. 3.12–13.

20. Jonas, *Gnostic Religion*, 158, quoting Macrobius, *Commentary on the Dream of Scipio* II.11.

21. Timothy Dwight and Julian Hawthorne, eds., *The World's Great Classics: Critique of Pure Reason by Immanuel Kant* (New York: Colonial Press, 1899), 438.

22. Head and Cranston, *Reincarnation, The Phoenix Fire Mystery*, 280.

23. Thomas Taylor, *Eleusinian and Bacchic Mysteries* (New York: J. W. Bouton, 1891), 135.

24. Amos Bronson Alcott, *Concord Days* (Boston: Roberts Brothers, 1872), 83.

25. Ralph Waldo Emerson, *The Journals and Miscellaneous Notebooks of Ralph Waldo Emerson*, vol. 1 (Cambridge, MA: Belknap Press, 1960), 341 quoting Pythagoras.

26. John Webster, *The Duchess of Malfi* (New York: P. F. Collier, 1909), 4.2.

27. Arthur Edward Waite, *The Works of Thomas Vaughan* (Whitefish, MT: Kessinger Publishing, 1992), xxix.

28. Edward Bulwer-Lytton, *Zanoni* (Boston: Little, Brown, 1932), I.2.4.

29. Tryon Edwards, *Useful Quotations* (New York: Grosset & Dunlap, 1933).

30. Laurence Binyon, *The Secret: Sixty Poems by Laurence Binyon* (London: E. Mathews, 1920), 61.

31. Quoted in Walker, *Reincarnation*, 257–58.

32. Yogananda, *Man's Eternal Quest*, 216.

33. Schuré, *Pythagoras*,

34. Philip Ellis Wheelwright, *Heraclitus* (Princeton, NJ: Princeton University Press, 1959), Fragments of Heraclitus 61.

35. Ecclesiastes 12:5–7.

36. Luke 15:11–32.

37. Edward Moore, "Origen of Alexandria," http://www.iep.utm.edu /origen-of-alexandria, 2005.

38. Quoted in William Ralph Inge, *Christian Mysticism: Considered in Eight Lectures Delivered Before the University of Oxford* (London: Methuen, 1899), 107.

39. Apocryphon of James 34.17–18, quoted in Robinson, *Nag Hammadi Library*, 265–66.

40. The Gospel of Thomas, trans. Thomas O. Lambdin, http://gnosis.org/naghamm/gthlamb.html, 18.

41. Koran, quoted in Das, *Essential Unity*, 305.

42. Turnbull, *Essence of Plotinus*, quoting *Enneads* VI.5.7.

43. Quoted in Thomas Taylor and G. R. S. Mead, *Plotinus and the Theosophy of the Greeks* (Whitefish, MT: Kessinger Publishing, 2005), 20.

44. Dante Alighieri, *Il convito: The Banquet of Dante Alighieri*, trans. Elizabeth Price Sayer (London: George Routledge, 1887), 210.

45. Edward McCurdy, *Leonardo da Vinci's Note-books: Arranged and Rendered into English with Introductions* (London: Duckworth & Co., 1907), 50.

46. Henry Vaughan, "The Retreat," in Henry Charles Beeching, ed., *Lyra Sacra: A Book of Religious Verse* (London: Methuen, 1903).

47. Leo Wiener, *The Complete Works of Count Tolstoy*, vol. 19 (New York: Colonial Press, 1904), 193.

48. Bhagavad Gita 8.16, quoted in Das, *Essential Unity*, 305.

49. Das, *Essential Unity*, 460.

50. Lao-tzu, Tao Te Ching 50, quoted in Henri Borel, *Lao-tzu's Tao and Wu Wei: An Interpretation*, trans. M. E. Reynolds (New York: Bretano's, 1919), 30.

51. Larry Chang, *Wisdom for the Soul: Five Millennia of Prescriptions for Spiritual Healing* (Washington, DC: Gnosophia Publishers, 2006), 522.

52. Harper Havelock Coates, *Honen, the Buddhist Saint: His Life and Teaching* (Kyoto: Chionin, 1925).
53. Quoted in Walker, *Reincarnation,* 172.
54. Guerry, *Life with the Baoulé.*

18. Journey from Forgetting to Remembering

1. William Wordsworth, "Ode on the Intimations of Immortality," in *Poems in Two Volumes* (London: Longman, Hurst & Co., 1807).
2. Sampasadaniya Sutta (DN 28); Sangiti Sutta (DN 33), quoted in Head and Cranston, *Reincarnation,* 50.
3. Mahapadana Sutta (DN 14); Acchariya-abbhuta Sutta (MN 123); Pathama-tathagata-acchariya Sutta (AN 4.27); Bhumi-cala Sutta (AN 8.70), http://groups.yahoo.com/group/Pali/message/7751?viscount=100.
4. Schuré, *Pythagoras,* 128.
5. Ibid., 128–29.
6. Hesiod, *Works and Days* 42, as quoted in Thomas Moore Johnson, *The Platonist: An Exponent of the Philosophic Truth* 4 (1888): 1–6 (Cambridge, MA: Harvard University Press), 213.
7. Plato, *Meno* 81a8–e3, as quoted in David Diener, "An Inquiry into Teaching in the *Meno,*" Ohio Valley Philosophy of Education Society, 2007, http://www.ovpes.org/2007/Diener.pdf, 141.
8. W. H. T. Gairdner, *"The Way" of a Mohammedan Mystic: A Contribution to the Study of Esoteric Sufism, its Theory and Praxis* (Leipzig: O. Harrassowitz, 1912), 9.
9. George Robert Stow Mead, *Plotinus, Select Works,* trans. Thomas Taylor (London: G. Bell & Sons, 1914), xxv–xxvii, quoting Adi Shankara's treatise *Tattvabodha.*
10. Parley P. Pratt, *Spirituality: The Key to the Science of Theology* (Project Gutenberg Ebook, #35470, Mormon Texts Project, http://bencrowder.net/books/mtp.March 3, 2011), 85.
11. Abimbola, *Ifa,* 113.
12. Quoted in Walker, *Reincarnation,* 258.
13. Gautama Buddha, First Sermon, quoted in B. R. Ambedkar, *The Buddha and His Dhamma* (Bombay: Government of Maharashtra, 1995), http://www.columbia.edu/itc/mealac/pritchett/00ambedkar/ambedkar_buddha/02_2.html.

14. Plato, *Phaedrus* III.23.28, quoted in Stewart, *Myths of Plato.*
15. Ibid., quoting *Phaedo* 82d–84a.
16. John David Chambers, *The Theological and Philosophical Works of Hermes Trismegistus, Christian Neoplatonist* (Edinburgh: T. & T. Clark, 1882), 61–62.
17. Radcliffe Edmonds, *Myths of the Underworld Journey: Plato, Aristophanes, and the 'Orphic' Gold Tablets* (New York: Cambridge University Press, 2004), quoting Ovid, *Metamorphoses* III.
18. Joseph Head and Sylvia L. Cranston, *Reincarnation in World Thought* (New York: Julian Press, 1967), 222.
19. Myer, 196.
20. Pratt, *Spirituality,* 86.
21. Kamala, *Priceless Precepts* (Oakland, CA: Kamala, 1979), 151.
22. F. Freemantle and Chogyam Trungpa, *The Tibetan Book of the Dead* (Boulder, CO: Shambhala, 1975).
23. Garbha Upanishad, trans. Subhash Kak, www.omtemple.com/kak.html.
24. Stewart, *Myths of Plato,* 287.
25. Virgil, *Aeneid* VI. 703–23, as quoted in Thomas Etherbert Page, *The Aenid of Virgil,* vol. I (Cambridge, MA: Loeb Classical Library, 1938).
26. Plutarch, *On the Delays of the Divine Vengeance,* quoted in Mead, *Doctrine of the Subtle Body,* 41; Stewart, *Myths of Plato,* 331–32; Sullivan, *Death, Afterlife,* 110; and De Lacy and Einarson, *Plutarch's Moralia,* 285, 291.
27. Vera Schwarcz, *Bridge Across Broken Time, Chinese and Jewish Cultural Memory* (New Haven, CT: Yale University Press, 1998), 40.
28. Pistis Sophia, as quoted in Head and Cranston, *Reincarnation in World Thought,* 111.
29. Head and Cranston, *Reincarnation in World Thought,* 222.
30. Ralph Waldo Emerson, "Essay II: Experience," in *Essays and Lectures* (Lawrence, KS: Digireads, 2009), 242.
31. Verny and Kelly, *Secret Life.*
32. Midrash Tanhuma, Pekudei 3, as quoted in Howard Schwartz, *Tree of Souls: The Mythology of Judaism* (Oxford, UK: Oxford University Press, 2004).

33. *Niddah* 30b, Singer, *The Jewish Encyclopedia;* Hastings, 793.
34. Louis Ginzberg, *Legends of the Jews,* vol. II (Philadelphia: Jewish Publication Society, 1913).
35. G. R. S. Mead, *Echoes from the Gnosis, Vol. X: The Hymn of the Robe of Glory* (Wheaton, IL: Theosophical Publishing House, 1908).
36. Norman J. Giradot, "Initiation and Meaning in the Tale of Snow White and the Seven Dwarfs," *Journal of American Folklore,* 90: 357. (July–Sept. 1977), 296.
37. Neill Edgar, "Mystery Teachings Through the Ages," in *Theosophical Guide for Parents* by Schultz, Karen (Ojai, CA: Parents Theosophical Research Group, 1984), 153.
38. Wheelwright, *Heraclitus,* 144.
39. Carman and Carman, *Cosmic Cradle,* 479.
40. Jowett, *Dialogues of Plato,* 254, quoting *Phaedrus* 250.
41. Michael Beloved (Yogi Madhvācārya), *Yoga Sutras of Patañjali* (Michael Beloved, 2007), verse 39.
42. Yogananda, *Man's Eternal Quest,* 215.
43. Sadguru Sant Keshavadas, *Liberation from Karma and Rebirth,* 79
44. Stevenson, *Children Who Remember,* 214.
45. Arthur D. Imerti, *Expulsion of the Triumphant Beast, Giordano Bruno* (New Brunswick, NJ: Rutgers University Press, 1964).
46. Martin Buber, Tales of the Hasidim, the Early Masters (New York: Schocken Books, 1945).
47. Deepak Chopra, Life After Death: The Burden of Proof (New York: Three Rivers Press, 2006), 78.

Bibliography

Abimbola, 'Wande. *Ifa.* Ibadan, Nigeria: Oxford University Press, 1976.

Alcott, Amos Bronson. *Concord Days.* Boston: Roberts Brothers, 1872.

———. *Tablets.* Boston: Roberts Brothers, 1868.

Alexander, Hartley Burr. *Mythology of All Races—North American.* New York: Cooper Square Publishers, 1964.

Ambedkar, B. R. *The Buddha and His Dhamma.* Bombay: Government of Maharashtra, 1995.

Armstrong, A. H. *Plotinus.* London: George Allen & Unwin, 1953.

'Attar, Farid al-Din. *Muslim Saints and Mystics: Episodes from the Tadhkirat al-Auliya'.* Trans. A. J. Arberry. Ames, IA: Omphaloskepsis, 2000.

Atwater, P. M. H. *Beyond the Light.* New York: Carol Publishing Group, 1994.

———. *Children of the New Millennium: Children's Near-Death Experiences and the Evolution of Humankind.* New York: Three Rivers Press, 1999.

———. *Coming Back to Life: The After-Effects of the Near-Death Experience.* New York: Citadel, 2001.

Bailey, Lee W., and Jenny Yates, eds. *The Near-Death Experience: A Reader.* New York: Routledge, 1996.

Banerjee, H. N. and Oursler, William. *Lives Unlimited.* Garden City, NY; Doubleday, 1974.

Bates, Daisy. *Passing of the Aborigines.* London: John Murray, 1940.

Beck, Sanderson. *History of Peace,* vol. I: *Guides to Peace and Justice from Ancient Sages to the Suffragettes.* Santa Barbara, CA: World Peace Communications, 2005.

Beier, Ulli. *Yoruba Myths.* Cambridge, UK: Cambridge University Press, 1980.

Beloved, Michael (Yogi Madhvācārya). *Yoga Sutras of Patañjali.* Michael Beloved, 2007.

Berndt, R. M., and C. Berndt. *First Australians.* Sydney: Ure Smith, 1952.

Bhikkhu, Thanissaro, trans. "The Greater Craving-Destruction Discourse." Translated from the Pali. 2011.www.accesstoinsight.org /tipitaka/mn/mn.038.than.html.

———. Chiggala Sutta. Translated from the Pali. *Access to Insight* (July 1, 2010). www.accesstoinsight.org/tipitaka/sn/sn56/sn56.048.than. html.

Binyon, Laurence. *The Secret: Sixty Poems by Laurence Binyon.* London: E. Mathews, 1920.

Boas, Franz. "Chinook Texts." Smithsonian Institution Bureau of Ethnology nos. 14–20, 1894.

———. *Contributions to the Ethnology of the Kwakiutl.* New York: Columbia University Press, 1925.

———. "Indians of British Columbia." *Fifty-Ninth Meeting of British Association for the Advancement of Science.* London, 1889.

Bordow, Sita. *Sri Swami Satchidananda.* Yogaville, VA: Integral Yoga Publications, 1986.

Borel, Henri. *Lao-tzu's Tao and Wu Wei: An Interpretation.* Trans. M. E. Reynolds. New York: Bretano's, 1919.

Bourke, John G. "Notes on the Cosmogony and Theogony of the Mojave Indians of the Rio Colorado, Arizona." *Journal of American Folklore* 2:6 (1889).

Bowen, Patrick G. "The Ancient Wisdom in Africa." *Theosophy* 82:8 (June 1994), 237–40. Originally published 1927.

Bowman, Carol. *Children's Past Lives.* New York: Bantam Books, 1998.

Brains, Robert. *Friends and Lovers.* New York: Basic Books, 1976.

Brinton, Daniel Garrison. *Myths of the New World.* Philadelphia, PA: David McKay, 1896.

Buber, Martin. *Chinese Tales.* Atlantic Highlands, NJ: Humanities Press International, 1991.

———. *For the Sake of Heaven.* Philadelphia: Jewish Publication Society, 1945.

———. *Tales of the Hasidim.* Trans. Olga Marx. New York: Schocken Books, 1948.

Bulwer-Lytton, Edward. *Zanoni.* Boston: Little, Brown, 1932.

Caravella, Lorenzo. *Mouth of God: Your Cosmic Contract.* Fairfield, IA: Sunstar Publishing, 1999.

Carlyle, Thomas. *Sartor Resartus.* London: Chapman and Hall, 1894. First published 1836.

Carman, Elizabeth M., and Neil J. Carman. *Cosmic Cradle: Souls Waiting in the Wings for Birth.* Fairfield, IA: Sunstar Publishing, 1999.

Carroll, Lewis. *Alice's Adventures in Wonderland.* London: Macmillan, 1865.

———. *Through the Looking-Glass, and What Alice Found There.* London: Macmillan, 1871.

Chamberlain, David. *Babies Remember Birth.* Los Angeles: Jeremy P. Tarcher, 1988.

———. "The Expanding Boundaries of Memory." *Pre- and Perinatal Psychology Journal* 4:3 (Spring 1990), 171–89.

———. "The Fetal Senses: Twelve, Not Five: A New Proposal." n.d. http://www.birthpsychology.com.

Chambers, John David. *The Theological and Philosophical Works of Hermes Trismegistus, Christian Neoplatonist.* Edinburgh: T. & T. Clark, 1882.

Chandler, Kenneth. *Origins of Vedic Civilization.* 2012. http://Sanskrit .safire.com/pdf/ORIGINS.PDF,.

Chang, G. C. C. *Six Yogas of Naropa and Teachings on Mahamudra.* New York: Snow Lion, 1963.

Chang, Larry. *Wisdom for the Soul: Five Millennia of Prescriptions for Spiritual Healing.* Washington, DC: Gnosophia Publishers, 2006.

Chapman, John W. "Tinneh Animism." *American Anthropologist* 23:3 (1921).

Chatterji, Krishnalal. *The Guiding Light, a Treatise on Thakur Sree Sree Anukul Chandra.* Calcutta: Indian Progressive Publishing, 1978.

Chu, Paul E. *Life before Birth, Life on Earth, Life after Death.* Fort Lee, NJ: World View Press, 1972.

Clement of Alexandria. *Exhortation to the Heathen.* www.gutenberg .us: World Public Library and Project Gutenberg Consortia Center.

Coates, Harper Havelock. *Honen, the Buddhist Saint: His Life and Teaching.* Kyoto: Chion-in, 1925.

Coomaraswamy, Ananda K. "Lila." *Journal of the American Oriental Society* 61 (1941).

Corda, Murshida Vera Justin. *Cradle of Heaven: Psychological and Spiritual Dimensions of Conception, Pregnancy and Birth.* Lebanon Springs, NY: Omega Press, 1987.

Cowan, James G. *The Elements of the Aborigine Tradition.* Rockport, MA: Element, 1992.

Cushing, Frank Hamilton. "A Zuni Folk-tale of the Underworld." *Journal of American Folklore* 5 (1892), 50–51.

Dante Alighieri. *Il convito: The Banquet of Dante Alighieri.* Trans. Elizabeth Price Sayer. London: George Routledge, 1887.

Das, Bhagavan. *The Essential Unity of All Religions.* Bombay, India: Bharatiya Vidya Bhavan, 1990.

———. *The Science of Social Organization or Laws of Manu in the Light of Atma-Vidya.* Adyar, Madras, India: Theosophical Publishing House, 1932.

David-Neel, Alexandra. *Magic and Mystery in Tibet.* Delhi: New Age Publishers, 1985.

Da Vinci, Leonardo. *Leonardo on the Human Body.* Trans. Charles D. O'Malley and J. B. de C. M. Saunders. New York: Dover Publications, 1983.

De Lacy, P. H., and B. Einarson. *Plutarch's Moralia,* vol. VII. London: Wm. Heinemann, 1959.

Devereux, George. "Mohave Soul Concepts." *American Anthropologist* 39:1 (January–March 1937).

Dickinson, Emily. *Complete Poems.* Boston: Little, Brown, 1924.

Diener, David. "An Inquiry into Teaching in the Meno." Ohio Valley Philosophy of Education Society, 2007. http://www.ovpes.org/2007/Diener.pdf.

Doresse, Jean. *The Secret Books of the Egyptian Gnostics.* Rochester, VT: Inner Traditions International, 1986.

Dunham, Carroll. *Mamomato.* New York: Penguin Books, 1993.

Dwight, Timothy, and Julian Hawthorne, eds. *The World's Great Classics: Critique of Pure Reason by Immanuel Kant.* New York: Colonial Press, 1899.

Eadie, Betty. *Embraced by the Light.* Placerville, CA: Gold Leaf Press, 1992.

Eastern and Western Disciples. *Life of Swami Vivekananda,* vol. I. Calcutta: Advaita Ashrama, 1979.

Easton, Stewart C. *Man and World in the Light of Anthroposophy.* Spring Valley, NY: Anthroposophic Press, 1975.

Edgar, Neill. "Mystery Teachings Through the Ages," in *Theosophical Guide for Parents* by Schultz, Karen. Ojai, CA: Parents Theosophical Research Group, 1984.

Edmonds, Radcliffe. *Myths of the Underworld Journey: Plato, Aristophanes, and the 'Orphic' Gold Tablets,* New York: Cambridge University Press, 2004.

Edwards, Tryon. *Useful Quotations,* New York: Grosset & Dunlap, 1933.

Elkin, A. P. "Totemism in North-Western Australia." *Oceania* III (1933).

Ellis, Alfred Burton. *Ewe-Speaking Peoples.* London: Chapman and Hall, 1890.

Emerson, E. W., ed. *The Complete Works of Ralph Waldo Emerson,* vols. I and II. Boston: Houghton Mifflin, 1909.

Emerson, Ralph Waldo. *Essays and Lectures.* Lawrence, KS: Digireads, 2009.

——. *The Journals and Miscellaneous Notebooks of Ralph Waldo Emerson,* vol. 1. Cambridge, MA: Belknap Press, 1960.

Erny, Pierre. *Child and His Environment in Black Africa.* Nairobi: Oxford University Press, 1981.

——. *Childhood and Cosmos.* Washington, DC: New Perspectives, 1973.

Evans-Wentz, Walter Yeeling. *The Tibetan Book of the Dead.* New York: Causeway Books, 1973.

Fewkes, Jesse Walter. "An Interpretation of Katcina Worship." *Journal of American Folklore* 14 (1901).

——. *The Prehistoric Culture of Tusayan.* Washington, DC: Judd & Detweiler, 1896.

Fisher, Mary Pat. *Living Religions.* London: Pearson, 2010.

Forde, C. Daryll. "Ethnography of the Yuma Indians." *University of California Publications in American Archaeology and Ethnology* 28 (1931), 83–277.

Freemantle, F., and Chögyam Trungpa. *Tibetan Book of the Dead.* Boulder, CO: Shambhala, 1975.

Gairdner, W. H. T. *"The Way" of a Mohammedan Mystic: A Contribution to the Study of Esoteric Sufism, its Theory and Praxis.* Leipzig: O. Harrassowitz, 1912.

Garvan, John M. *Negritos of the Philippines.* Schwanenstadt, Austria: Ferdinand Berger, 1964.

Gaskell, George Arthur. *Dictionary of Sacred Language of all Scriptures and Myths,* New York: Lucis, 1930.

Gebbie, Donald A. M. *Reproductive Anthropology.* New York: John Wiley & Sons, 1981.

Gibb, Elias J. W. *A History of Ottoman Poetry,* vol I. London: Luzac and Co., 1958.

Gibran, Kahlil. *Sand and Foam.* New York: Alfred A. Knopf, 2008.

———. *A Third Treasury of Kahlil Gibran.* New York: Carol Publishing, 1975.

Gibson, Arvin S. *Echoes from Eternity.* Bountiful, UT: Horizon Publishers, 1993.

———. *Glimpses of Eternity.* Bountiful, UT: Horizon Publishers, 1992.

Gifford, Edward W. "The Cocopa." *University of California Publications in American Archeology and Ethnology* 31:5 (1933).

Gifford, Edward W., and Robert H. Lowie. "Notes on the Akwa'ala Indians of Lower California." *University of California Publications in American Archeology and Ethnology* 23:7 (1928), 338–52.

Ginzberg, Louis. *Legends of the Jews,* vol. II. Philadelphia: Jewish Publication Society, 1913.

Gomes, Edwin H. *Seventeen Years among the Sea Dyaks of Borneo.* London: Seeley & Co., 1911.

Goodale, Jane C. *Tiwi Wives: A Study of the Women of Melville Island, North Australia.* Seattle: University of Washington Press, 1971.

Goodwin, William W. *Plutarch's Morals,* vol. V. Boston: Little, Brown & Co., 1870.

Govinda, Lama Anagarika. *The Way of the White Clouds.* Berkeley, CA: Shambhala, 1970.

Guerry, Vincent. *Life with the Baoulé.* Washington, DC: Three Continents Press, 1975.

Guthrie, Kenneth Sylvan. *The Philosophy of Plotinos,* vol. II. Philadelphia: Dunlap, 1896.

Halevi, Z'ev ben Shimon. *A Kabbalistic Universe.* Boston: Red Wheel, 1977.

Hallett, Elisabeth. *Soul Trek: Meeting Our Children on the Way to Birth.* Hamilton, MT: Light Hearts Publishing, 1995.

———. *Stories of the Unborn Soul.* San Jose, CA: Writers Club Press, 2002.

Hallowell, A. Irving. "Spirits of the Dead in Saulteaux Life and Thought." *Journal of the Royal Anthropological Institute of Great Britain and Ireland* 70 (1940), 29–51.

Harrington, John Peabody. "A Yuma Account of Origins." *Journal of American Folklore* 21 (1908).

Hartland, Edwin Sidney. *Primitive Paternity,* vol. I London: David Nutt, 1909.

Hartmann, Franz. *The Life of Philippus Theophrastus Bombast of Hohenheim, Known by the Name of Paracelsus, and the Substance of His Teachings.* London: Kegan Paul, Trench, Trubner, & Co., 1896.

Hastings, James. *Encyclopedia of Religion and Ethics,* vol. VII. Edinburgh: T. & T. Clark, 1914.

Head, Joseph, and Cranston, Sylvia L. *Reincarnation in World Thought.* New York: Julian Press, 1967.

———. *Reincarnation: The Phoenix Fire Mystery.* New York: Julian Press, 1977.

Heckewelder, John. *History, Manners, and Customs of the Indian Nations Who Once Inhabited Pennsylvania and the Neighboring States.* Memoirs of the Historical Society of Pennsylvania, vol. XII. Historical Society of Pennsylvania, 1881.

Hernandez, T. "Social Organization of the Drysdale River Tribes." *Oceania* 11:3 (1941).

Hicks, Roger and Chögyam Ngakpa. *Great Ocean, An Authorized Biography of the Buddhist Monk Tenzin Gyatso, His Holiness the Fourteenth Dalai Lama,* London, England: Penguin Books, 1984.

Hilger, M. Inez. "Chippewa Child Life." *Smithsonian Bureau of American Ethnology* Bulletin 146 (1952).

Hinze, Sarah. *Coming from the Light: Spiritual Accounts of Life before Life.* New York: Pocket Books, 1997.

Hixon, Lex. *Great Swan: Meetings with Ramakrishna.* Boston: Shambhala Publications, 1992.

Hodson, Geoffrey. *The Miracle of Birth: A Clairvoyant Study of Prenatal Life.* Wheaton, Illinois: Theosophical Publishing, 1981.

———. *Occult Powers in Nature and in Man.* Adyar, India: Theosophical Publishing House, 1955.

Holmberg, Uno. *The Mythology of All Races,* vol. IV. Finno-Ugric, Siberian. Boston: Marshall Jones Co., Archaeological Institute of America, 1927.

The Holy Bible, English Standard Version. Wheaton, IL: Crossway Bibles, 2001.

Hudson, J. W. "Indian Myth of San Joaquin Basin." *Journal of American Folklore* 15 (1902), 104–6.

Hultkrantz, Åke. *Conceptions of the Soul among North American Indians.* Stockholm: Caslon Press, 1953.

Imerti, Arthur D. *Expulsion of the Triumphant Beast, Giordano Bruno,* New Brunswick, NJ: Rutgers University Press, 1964.

Inayat Khan, Hazrat. *The Sufi Message of Hazrat Inayat,* vol. I. London: Barrie and Rockliff, 1968.

———. *Sufi Teachings.* London: Barrie and Rockliff, 1961.

Inge, William Ralph. *Christian Mysticism: Considered in Eight Lectures Delivered Before the University of Oxford.* London: Methuen, 1899.

———. *The Philosophy of Plotinus,* vol. I. London: Longmans, Green and Co., 1918.

James, William. *Psychology.* American Science Series, Briefer Course. New York: Henry Holt, 1892.

Jiyu-Kennett, Roshi, and Mac Phillamy. *Daizui: The Book of Life.* Mount Shasta, CA: Shasta Abbey Press, 1979.

Jochelson, W. "Jesup North Pacific Expedition." *Memoirs of the American Museum of Natural History* 1905.

———. "Yukaghir." *Memoirs of the American Museum of Natural History* 11 (1926).

Johnson, Julian P. M. *The Path of the Masters: The Science of Surat Shabd Yoga.* Punjab, India: Radha Soami Satsang Beas, 1939.
Johnson, Thomas Moore. *The Platonist: An Exponent of the Philosophic Truth* 4 (1888): 1–6. Cambridge, MA: Harvard University Press.
Jonas, Hans. *The Gnostic Religion.* Boston: Beacon Press, 1963.
Jones, William."Ethnology of Fox Indians." *Smithsonian Bureau of American Ethnology* Bulletin 123 (1939).
Jowett, Benjamin. *The Dialogues of Plato.* New York: Random House, 1937.
———. *Republic of Plato.* Oxford, UK: Clarendon Press, 1888.
Kaberry, Phyllis M. *Aboriginal Woman.* Philadelphia: Blakiston Co., 1939.
———. "Spirit Children and Spirit-Centres." *Oceania* 6 (1935–1936), 394–400.
Kak, Subhash, trans. Garbha Upanishad. www.omtemple.com/kak.html.
Kamala. *Priceless Precepts.* Oakland, CA: Kamala, 1979.
Kapleau, Philip. *The Wheel of Life and Death.* New York: Doubleday, 1989.
Keshavadas, Sadguru Sant. *Liberation from Karma and Rebirth.* Virginia Beach, VA: Colonial, 1976.
Kroeber, A. "Mohave." *Handbook of Indians of California.* Bulletin of American Ethnology 78 (1925).
Lambdin, Thomas O., trans. The Gospel of Thomas. http://gnosis.org/naghamm/gthlamb.html.
Lambert, George C. *Treasures in Heaven: Designed for the Instruction and Encouragement of Young Latter-day Saints.* Salt Lake City: Church of Jesus Christ of Latter-day Saints, 1914.
Larson, Raymond. *Plato: The Republic.* Arlington Heights, IL: AHM Publishing, 1979.
Lawlor, Robert. *Voices of the First Day.* Rochester, VT: Inner Traditions, 1991.
Leadbeater, Charles Webster. *A Textbook of Theosophy.* 1912. Repr. New York: Cosimo Classics, 2007.

Leininger, Bruce, and Andrea Leininger. *Soul Survivor: The Reincarnation of a World War II Fighter Pilot.* New York: Grand Central Publishing, 2010.

Lincoln, Jackson Steward. *The Dream in Primitive Cultures.* Baltimore: William Wilkins, 1935.

Lockwood, Douglas. *I, the Aboriginal.* New York: Meridian Books, 1970.

Lommel, Andreas. "Modern Culture Influences on the Aborigines." *Oceania* 21 (1950).

———. "Notes on Sexual Behavior and Initiation." *Oceania* 20 (1949).

Lundahl, Craig. *Eternal Journey.* New York: Warner Books, 1997.

Lundwall, N. B. *The Vision, or the Degrees of Glory.* Salt Lake City: Bookcraft Publishing, 1942.

MacFarlane, Aidan. *The Psychology of Childbirth.* Cambridge, MA: Harvard University Press, 1977.

Madhusudandasji, Dhyanyogi Shri. *Death, Dying and Beyond.* Antioch, CA: Dhyanyoga Centers, 1979.

Maeterlinck, Maurice. *The Blue Bird: A Fairy Play in Five Acts.* 1906. Repr. New York: Dodd, Mead and Co., 1961.

Malik, Inder L. *Dalai Lamas of Tibet: Succession of Births.* New Delhi: [no publisher], 1984.

Malinowski, Bronislaw. "Baloma." *Journal of the Royal Anthropological Institute of Great Britain and Ireland* 46 (1916).

Manrique, Beatriz, M. Contasti, M. A. Alvarado, Monica Zypman, N. Palma, M. T. Ierrobino, I. Ramirez, and D. Carini. "A Controlled Experiment in Prenatal Enrichment with 684 Families in Caracas, Venezuela: Results to Age Six." *Journal of Prenatal and Perinatal Psychology and Health* 12:3–4 (1998), 209–34.

McCarty, Wendy Anne. *Welcoming Consciousness: Supporting Babies Wholeness from the Beginning of Life—an Integrated Model of Early Development.* Santa Barbara, CA: Wondrous Beginnings Publishing, 2009.

McConnel, U. "A Moon Legend from Bloomfield River." *Oceania* 2 (1931).

McCurdy, Edward. *Leonardo da Vinci's Note-books: Arranged and Rendered into English with Introductions.* London: Duckworth & Co., 1907.

McGarey, Gladys Taylor. *Born to Live: A Holistic Approach to Childbirth.* Phoenix: Gabriel Press, 1980.

McGarey, Gladys Taylor, and Jess Stearn. *The Physician within You: Discovering the Power of Inner Healing.* Deerfield Beach, FL: Health Communications, 1997.

Mead, George Robert Stow. *Doctrine of the Subtle Body in Western Tradition.* Wheaton, IL: Theosophical Publishing House, 1967.

———. *Echoes from the Gnosis,* vol. X: *The Hymn of the Robe of Glory.* Wheaton, IL: Theosophical Publishing House, 1908.

———. *Fragments of a Faith Forgotten.* London: Theosophical Publishing Society, 1906.

———. *Plotinus: Select Works.* trans. Thomas Taylor. London: G. Bell & Sons, 1914.

Michelson, Truman. "Notes on Fox Mortuary Customs and Beliefs." *Annual Reports of the Bureau American Ethnology* 40 (1925).

Montagu, Ashley. *Coming into Being among the Australian Aborigines: A Study of the Procreative Beliefs of the Native Tribes of Australia.* London: Routledge & Kegan Paul, 1974.

Moody, Raymond. *Life after Life: The Investigation of a Phenomenon—Survival of Bodily Death.* Harrisburg, PA: Stackpole Books, 1976.

Moore, Edward. "Origen of Alexandria." http://www.iep.utm.edu/origen-of-alexandria, 2005.

Mountford, Charles P. *Ayers Rock: Its People.* Honolulu: East-West Center Press, 1965.

———. *Brown Men and Red Sand: Wanderings in Wild Australia.* Melbourne: Robertson and Mullens, 1948.

———. *The Tiwi: Their Art, Myth and Ceremony.* London: Phoenix House, 1958.

Mountford, Charles P., and A. Harvey. "Women of the Adnjamatana Tribe." *Oceania* 5:12 (1941), 155–63.

Mullin, Glenn H. *Mystical Verses of a Mad Dalai Lama.* Wheaton, IL: Theosophical Publishing House, 1994.

Myer, Isaac. *Qabbalah: The Philosophical Writings of Solomon Ben Yehudah Ibn Gebirol or Avicebron.* Philadelphia: MacCalla & Co., 1888.

Nachman, Moses ben. "From the Beginning, Before the World Ever Was (from Before the World Ever Was)." Trans. Peter Cole. http://www .poetry-chaikhana.com/N/NachmanidesN/Frombeginnin.htm.

Nerburn, Kent. *The Soul of an Indian.* San Rafael, CA: New World Library, 1993.

Nicholson, Reynold A. *The Mystics of Islam.* London: Routledge, Kegan, Paul, 1914.

O'Bryan, Aileen. "The Dine." *Smithsonian Bureau of American Ethnology* Bulletin 163 (1956).

Osgood, C. "Great Bear Lake Indians." National Museum of Canada. *Canadian Department of Mines* 70 (1932).

Page, Thomas Etherbert. *The Aeneid of Virgil,* vol. I. Cambridge, MA: Loeb Classical Library, 1938.

Parker, K. L. *Euahlayi Tribe.* London: Archibald Constable and Co., 1905.

Patchen, Nancy. *The Journey of a Master: Swami Chinmayananda—the Man, the Path, the Teaching.* Berkeley, CA: Asian Humanities Press, 1989.

Percival, Harold W. *Thinking and Destiny.* Dallas: Word Foundation, 1974.

Pickthall, Mohammed Marmaduke. *The Glorious Koran.* New York: New American Library, 1959.

Pond, Gideon H. *Dakota Superstitions.* St. Paul, MN: Minnesota Historical Society, 1889.

Powers, Marla N. *Oglala Women: Myth, Ritual, and Reality.* Chicago: University of Chicago Press, 1986.

Prabhupada, A. C. Bhaktivedanta Swami. *Coming Back.* Los Angeles: Bhaktivedanta Book Trust, 1986.

Pratt, Parley P. *Spirituality: The Key to the Science of Theology.* Project Gutenberg Ebook, #35470, Mormon Texts Project, http://bencrowder.net/books/mtp., March 3, 2011.

Radin, Paul. "Personal Reminiscences of a Winnebago Indian." *Journal of American Folklore* 26 (1913).

———. "Religion of the North American Indians." *Journal of American Folklore* 27 (1914).

———. *The Road of Life and Death.* New York: Pantheon Books, 1945.

———. "Winnebago Tribe." *Annual Reports of Bureau of American Ethnology* 37 (1923).

Ramabadran, R. S. "Sri Ramakrishna as Siva." *Koshur Samachar* (March 1994). http://www.koausa.org/KoshSam/Ramakrishna.html.

Ray, Verne F. *Lower Chinook Ethnographic Notes.* Publications in Anthropology, vol. 7. Seattle: University of Washington Press, 1938.

Rhys, Ernest, ed. *Five Dialogues of Plato.* London: J. M. Dent & Sons, 1931.

Robinson, James M., ed. *The Nag Hammadi Library in English.* New York: Harper & Row, 1988.

Roheim, G. "Women and their Life in Central Australia." *Journal of the Royal Anthropological Institute* 63 (1933).

Saraydarian, Torkom. *Woman, Torch of the Future.* Cave Creek, AZ: T.S.G. Publishing, 1999.

Sarkar, Rabindra Nath. *Latest Revelation in the East.* Calcutta: Sanskrit Pustak Bhandar, 1987.

Satchidananda, Sri Swami. *Golden Present.* Yogaville, VA: Integral Yoga Publications, 1987.

Satguru Sivaya Subramuniyaswami. *Dancing with Siva: Hinduism's Contemporary Catechism.* Kapaa, HI: Himalayan Academy, 2003.

Schoolcraft, Henry Rowe. *Historical and Statistical Information Respecting the History, Condition, and Prospects of the Indian Tribes of the United States.* Philadelphia: Lippincott, Grambo, 1851.

Schultz, K. A. *Theosophical Guide for Parents.* Ojai, CA: Parents Theosophical Research Group, 1984.

Schuré, Edouard. *Pythagoras and the Delphic Mysteries.* London: Wm. Rider & Son, 1906.

Schwarcz, Vera. *Bridge Across Broken Time, Chinese and Jewish Cultural Memory.* New Haven, CT: Yale University Press, 1998.

Schwartz, Howard. *Tree of Souls: The Mythology of Judaism.* Oxford, UK: Oxford University Press, 2004.

Seligson, Fred Jeremy. *Oriental Birth Dreams.* Elizabeth, NJ: Holly, 1990.

Shai, Cherry. *Torah through Time: Understanding Bible Commentary from the Rabbinic Period from the Rabbinic Period to Modern Times.* Philadelphia: Jewish Publication Society, 2007.

Shear, Jonathan. *The Inner Dimension: Philosophy and the Experience of Consciousness.* New York: Peter Lang Publishing, 1990.

Singer, Isodore, ed. *The Jewish Encyclopedia,* vol. X–XI. New York: Funk & Wagnalls, 1905.

Singh, Maharaj Charan. *The Master Answers.* Punjab, India: Radha Aoami Satsang Beas, 1966.

Skinner, Alanson. "Social Life and Ceremonial Bundles." *Anthropological Papers of the American Museum of Natural History* 13:1 (1913).

——. "Songs of the Menomini Medicine Ceremony." *American Anthropologist* 27 (1925).

——. "Traditions of the Iowa Indians." *Journal of American Folklore* 38:150 (1925).

Somé, Sobonfu. *Welcoming Spirit Home: Ancient African Teachings.* Novato, CA: New World Library, 1999.

Speck, F. G. "Penobscot Tales and Religious Beliefs." *Journal of American Folklore* 50 (1935).

Spencer, S. B., and F.J. Gillen. *Arunta.* Oosterhout, Netherlands: Anthropological Publications, 1966.

Spier, Leslie. *Yuman Tribes of the Gila River.* Chicago: University of Chicago Press, 1933.

Stanner, William Edward Hanley. "Murrinh-Patha Kinship and Totemism." *Oceania* 7 (1936), 186–216.

——. *White Man Got No Dreaming: Essays, 1938–1973.* Canberra: Australian National University Press, 1979.

Stern, Bernhard J. *The Lummi Indians of Northwest Washington: The Cycle of Life, Tribal Culture, Legend and Lore.* New York: Columbia University Press, 1934.

Stevenson, Ian. *Cases of the Reincarnation Type,* vol. IV. Charlottesville, VA: University Press of Virginia, 1983.

——. *Children Who Remember Previous Lives.* Charlottesville, VA: University Press of Virginia, 1987.

Stewart, John Alexander. *The Myths of Plato.* Carbondale, IL: Southern Illinois University Press, 1960.

Storm, Howard. *My Descent into Death: A Second Chance at Life.* New York: Doubleday, 2005.

Sugrue, Thomas. *There Is a River: The Story of Edgar Cayce.* New York: Henry Holt, 1945.

Sullivan, Lawrence E., ed. *Death, Afterlife, and the Soul.* New York: Macmillan, 1989.

Swanton, John R. *Indian Tribes of the Lower Mississippi Valley and Adjacent Coast of the Gulf of Mexico.* 1911. Repr. Mineola, NY: Dover Publications, 1998.

Talbot, P. Amaury. *Peoples of Southern Nigeria.* London: Oxford University Press, 1926.

———. *Tribes of the Niger Delta.* New York: Barnes & Noble, 1967.

Taplin, G. *Folklore of South Australian Aborigines.* Adelaide: Johnson Reprint Corp., 1879.

Taylor, Thomas. *Eleusinian and Bacchic Mysteries.* New York: J. W. Bouton, 1891.

Taylor, Thomas, and G. R. S. Mead. *Plotinus and the Theosophy of the Greeks.* Whitefish, MT: Kessinger Publishing, 2005.

———. *Select Works of Plotinus.* New York: G. Bell, 1895.

Thoreau, Henry David. *Walden* or *Life in the Woods,* Princeton, NJ: Princeton University Press, 2004.

Tishby, Isaiah. *The Wisdom of the Zohar,* vol. II. New York: Oxford University Press, 1989.

Tucker, Jim B. *Life before Life: Children's Memories of Previous Lives.* New York: St. Martin's Press, 2005.

Turnbull, Grace H. *The Essence of Plotinus.* New York: Oxford University Press, 1948.

Uchendu, Victor C. *Igbo of Southeast Nigeria.* New York: Holt, Rinehart and Winston, 1965.

Underhill, Ruth. *Indians of the Pacific Northwest.* Washington, DC: Bureau of Indian Affairs, 1945.

Vaughan, Henry. "The Retreat." In Henry Charles Beeching, ed. *Lyra Sacra: A Book of Religious Verse.* London: Methuen, 1903.

Verny, Thomas, and John Kelly. *The Secret Life of the Unborn Child: How You Can Prepare Your Baby for a Happy, Healthy Life.* New York: Dell, 1981.

Viereck, George Sylvester. "What Life Means to Einstein: An Interview." *The Saturday Evening Post,* October 26, 1929.

Waite, Arthur Edward. *The Works of Thomas Vaughan.* Whitefish, MT: Kessinger Publishing, 1992.

Wallis, Wilson D. "Canadian Dakota." *Anthropological Papers of the American Museum of Natural History* 41:1 (1947).

Walker, Edward Dwight. *Reincarnation: A Study of Forgotten Truth.* New York: John W. Lovell Co., 1888.

Ward, John A., "The Universe as Theatre," nisaragatta-advaita-vedanta .blogspot.com.

Warner, Lloyd. *A Black Civilization: A Social Study of an Australian Tribe.* New York: Harper & Brothers, 1937.

Watson, Burton. *Chuang Tzu.* New York: Columbia University Press, 1964.

Webster, John. *The Duchess of Malfi.* New York: P. F. Collier, 1909.

Wheelwright, Philip Ellis. *Heraclitus.* Princeton, NJ: Princeton University Press, 1959.

Whinfield, E. H. *Masnavi of Rumi.* London: Kegan Paul, 1898.

Widdison, Harold. *Trailing Clouds of Glory.* Springville, UT: CFI, 2004.

Wiener, Leo. *The Complete Works of Count Tolstoy,* vol. 19. New York: Colonial Press, 1904.

Wordsworth, William. *Poems in Two Volumes.* London: Longman, Hurst & Co., 1807.

Wright, M. R. *Empedocles: The Extant Fragments.* New Haven, CT: Yale University Press, 1981.

Yatiswarananda, Swami. *The Divine Life, Its Practice and Realisation.* Madras: Sri Ramakrishna Math Mylapore, 1939.

Yogananda, Paramahansa. *Autobiography of a Yogi.* Los Angeles: Self Realization Fellowship, 1992.

——. *Man's Eternal Quest.* Los Angeles: Self Realization Fellowship, 1972.

——. *Whispers of Eternity.* Los Angeles: Self Realization Fellowship, 1929.

Index

Australia, indigenous peoples of,
xxii, 163, 225–237
  effects of acculturation,
    234–237
  pre-birth worlds of, 231–234
  reincarnation, 229–230

B

Benedict, Mellen-Thomas
(NDE), 108
Big Bang (spiritual), memory of,
142–144
birth
  bonding (parent/child bond
    at birth), xxviii, 84, 127
  breech, 43
  C–Section, 17, 43, 212
  circumcision, 40–42, 49
  memories of, 21, 30, 43–50,
    75, 83–84, 95–96, 102, 104,
    106, 127, 142, 212, 249
  Soul's entry to body at birth,
    25–26
  Soul's entry after birth, 193
  trauma, 30, 102, 127
bliss
  as a spiritual experience, xxvi,
    117, 151, 159
  as a state of consciousness,
    xvii, 24
  in the conception of a child,
    152, 153, 165, 186–187
  pre-birth memories of, xxvi,
    11–12, 43, 102, 120
  pre-existence as, 303
  NDE as, 72, 107

Blue Bird, 22, 93, 252
Bowman, Carol, 4–5, 204–205
brain, xvii
Bruno, Giordano, 298, 301
Buddhism. *See also* Tibetan
  Buddhism and Zen Buddhism.
  xxii, 111, 130, 163, 303
  bodhisattva, 288
  four ways of descent into
    fetus, 288
bumblebee, 200

C

Cayce, Edgar, xxviii, 263
Chamberlain, David, xxvii–xxvii,
3, 4, 44, 206
children,
  a child's communications
    with future children, 21,
    161
  and after-death
    communications, 6
  and past-life memories, 6, 17
  early infancy memories, 46,
    104
  elements of children's pre-
    birth memories, xxx, 9, 47
  indicator signs of real pre-
    birth memories, 4
  pre-birth memories of, xvii,
    3–21
  validation of memories, 6,
    46–47, 84, 86, 106, 107,
    113–114, 193, 208–209
China, xxii, 167, 294
  Chuang Tzu, xxxiii

Acknowledgements

WE ARE GRATEFUL TO THE hundreds of Souls who inspired our research in the exploration of the pre-birth process and higher states of consciousness. This book is a revised version of 1999's *Cosmic Cradle* with new stories and information.

Our personal and scientific explorations in the field of consciousness began in 1969. We have learned from masters, guides, angels, and teachers who laid the consciousness foundation for us to evolve. The wisdom of dozens of sages and scholars, Western and Eastern philosophers and mystics, has been helpful.

Our heartfelt thanks goes to all the parents and their children who were willing to share their pre-birth experiences with us: Beverly A., Taylor A., Teresa A., Kirsten A., Lorrie A., Susan A., Janice B., Rennie B., Mark B., Matthew B., Nancy B., Stacy B., Mat B., Inelia B., Lezlie B., Vincent B., Diane C., Deyon D., Judy D., Lania D., Drew, Vimala D., David D., Frankie F., Stephanie F., Kathy F., Mary Jane G., Stacy G., Catcher G., Rani H., Susan H., Henry H., Francine I., Jordan H., Daniela J., Sharon J., Stephana J., Springley J., Kiki, Angie K., Judy K., Caitlin K., Roger K., Kyle L., Ritamarie L., Suzanne L., Elizabeth M., Linda M., Cheryl M., Chancey M., Neel M., Joanie N., Vanessa R., Vimala R., Deborah S., Derek S., Elron S., Floyd S., Gerry S., Jan S., Linda S., Skye, Megan S., Tim S., Kaylene S., George S., Prashant S., Raghavan S., Anna S., Len S., Ty S., Karla T., Henny V., Linda W., and Signe W. We extend our deepest gratitude to interviewees who have passed into the Light: Rennie B., Lorenzo C., Ellen M., Jan W., and Nan M.

Special appreciation goes to publisher Richard Grossinger at North Atlantic Books who inspired us to revise our original *Cosmic Cradle*. We express thanks to pre-birth and NDE researchers Elisabeth Hallett, Michael Maguire, Titus Rivas, John Sloat, Dr. Jeffrey and Jody Long. We thank Jan Bocskay, our sister Dr. Bonnie Carman Harvey, Jeanine Sih Christensen, and Margaret Weston for taking time to read our rough drafts and to make comments. We also thank spiritual artist Paul Heussenstamm, whose beautiful mandala, *Light of Heaven,* graces our cover.

To our loving parents—George and Martha Ulrickson, William and Lena Carman—we owe the deepest love and gratitude, for without their devotion this book would have been impossible.

About the Authors

⌒

ELIZABETH CARMAN, a philosopher-psychologist and pre-birth researcher, has pursued a life-long interest in self-actualization and people's full potential. Elizabeth received a BA in psychology from Michigan State University and an MA in interdisciplinary studies from Maharishi International University. She served as a social worker in Chicago. In 2002 Elizabeth received an honorary PhD from the International Institute of Integral Studies in Montreal for her pre-birth research published in *Cosmic Cradle: Souls Waiting in the Wings for Birth.* Elizabeth has spent more than forty years researching consciousness, including long-term inner development courses in North America, Europe, and Asia. She has taught meditation workshops and served on university faculty. Elizabeth is a native of the Upper Peninsula of Michigan on Lake Superior and lives in Austin, Texas, where she enjoys Sanskrit chanting on the harmonium with her husband, Neil.

NEIL CARMAN has a life-long love for nature and metaphysics, receiving botany degrees from the University of Iowa and a PhD in phytochemistry from the University of Texas at Austin, and also teaching biology and the science of consciousness. Environmental interests inspired his more than thirty-year career in Texas, currently with the Sierra Club. Neil serves as a resource for citizens in industrial communities and has received awards for his service. He has spent over forty years investigating consciousness through meditation. He is a native of Iowa City, Iowa, and lives in Austin, Texas, with his wife, Elizabeth.